MENTAL ILLNESS IN PRIMARY CARE SETTINGS

Conference held at the
Institute of Psychiatry, London
17–18 July 1984

MENTAL ILLNESS
IN PRIMARY CARE
SETTINGS

Edited by
Michael Shepherd,
Greg Wilkinson,
and Paul Williams

Tavistock Publications
London and New York

First published in 1986 by
Tavistock Publications Ltd
11 New Fetter Lane, London EC4P 4EE

Published in the USA by
Tavistock Publications
in association with Methuen, Inc.
29 West 35th Street, New York, NY 10001

Typeset by Keyset Composition,
Colchester
Printed in Great Britain
at the University Press, Cambridge

British Library Cataloguing in Publication Data
Mental illness in primary care settings.
1. Mental health services
I. Shepherd, Michael, 1923–
II. Wilkinson, Greg III. Williams, Paul
IV. University of London. *Institute of Psychiatry*
362.2   RA790.5
ISBN 0-422-80360-X

Library of Congress Cataloging-in-Publication Data
Main entry under title:
Mental illness in primary care settings.
Proceedings of the Conference on Mental
Illness in Primary Care Settings.
Bibliography: p.
Includes index.
1. Mental health services – Congresses.
2. Family medicine – Congresses.
3. Health care teams – Congresses.
4. Social psychiatry – Congresses.
I. Shepherd, Michael, 1923–
II. Wilkinson, Greg, 1951–
III. Williams, Paul, D.P.M.
IV. Conference on Mental Illness in
Primary Care Settings (1984: London,
England)
RA790.A2M46 1986   616.89   85-27741
ISBN 0-422-80360-X

Contents

E. D. Acheson

Introduction

The objectives of this Conference on Mental Illness in Primary Care Settings are threefold. First, to foster and deepen exchanges between researchers and policy-makers; second, to review the present lessons from research in this field; and, third, to help construct a future research strategy which will assist policy decisions. I can also assure you that the Department of Health will be looking attentively at planning and policy issues which emerge from the Conference.

Perhaps I can devote a few words to the historical background. The post-war movement towards an approach to psychiatry with diminished use of inpatient care followed on the recognition that long periods of hospitalization of the mentally ill could actually be harmful. The need for early discharge and continuing care thereafter was important. The 1959 Mental Health Act provided the necessary legislative framework to facilitate the transition of services to a community base, which started in the 1930s. The subsequent changes in the care of the mentally ill outside institutions had been monitored to some extent by departmental research and development funding; for example, the development of psychiatric case registers and the evaluation of the Worcester Development Project and a number of smaller projects. The concentration on mental hospitals, however, tended to identify the notion of community psychiatry with the after-care of discharged hospital patients. Meanwhile, a wholly new dimension had begun to emerge with the realization that the great majority of emotionally disturbed patients make no contact at all with the mental health services and, of course, have never been in hospital.

Within the structure of the National Health Service, the medical responsibility for the care of these patients falls principally on the general practitioner. Much of what we know about the nature and extent of their disorders derives from the work of Michael Shepherd and his colleagues in the distinguished General Practice Research Unit set up in the late 1950s.

The pioneering studies were primarily epidemiological, but as Sir Aubrey Lewis pointed out in the foreword to Michael Shepherd's book, *Psychiatric Illness in General Practice* (1966), results of these inquiries have considerable implications for the future organization of medical services in this country as well as for medical education, and, indeed, that book has had a profound effect.

The relationship between the placement of the mentally ill outside institutions and the wider role of primary care poses questions for which answers have to be supplied if executive actions, particularly on staffing aspects, are to be effective for planning and service provision.

Primary health care is increasingly being seen as a team activity involving not just the GP and his/her own employed staff, but also nursing and other staff employed by health authorities. Although government has made efforts to foster and to encourage the development of a team approach to primary health care and considerable progress has been made, it would be misleading to imply that there is not still a long way to go.

The Harding Report on the Primary Health Care Team identified some of the obstacles to effective teamwork, and highlighted inner cities as areas where these obstacles were greatest. The study group which I chaired on primary health care in Inner London also looked at the situation in some detail. While one can find excellent examples of teamwork in primary health care even in Inner London, these are far from universal. Even where the core primary health care team identified by Harding – that is, GP, district nurse, health visitor, and midwife – exists, it rarely yet extends to include a community psychiatric nurse or social worker. My study group recommended that community psychiatric nurses should work with GPs and other members of the primary health care team both for caring for patients who are already mentally ill and their families, and attempting to prevent the onset of mental illness. I think it is important that we continue to press for this kind of development to enhance the capacity of the primary health team to provide effective services.

The development of effective anti-depressant drugs and less effective anti-psychotic drugs has provided GPs with better treatment for a wide range of mental disorders, but these compounds also pose their own problems in relation to their proper use.

The relevance of the nation's demographic changes is also of immense importance in this field; an ageing society with populations of pensionable age now ranging from 10 to 30 per cent depending on the part of the country, will remain with us for several decades, and the proportion of the elderly will increase. The dramatic rise of senile psychiatric disorders and the burdens they pose for society as a whole obviously are a major aspect of this development. Similarly, we must not forget the problems of the mentally handicapped and those suffering from addiction.

This Conference on mental illness in primary care settings can be seen to follow naturally the autumn 1981 Conference on psychiatry and general practice at Magdalen College, Oxford, which was generously supported by the Mental Health Foundation. This Conference is linked very closely to the three major policy issues that the Department pursued: first, to give mental health greater priority, not as a separate, but as an integral part of health and social provision; second, to emphasize prevention and draw attention to the links between this and mental health care and general practice; and, third, to provide increased co-operation between primary care teams and specialists of voluntary organizations. The purpose of this Conference is once again to focus on the advances made in these issues.

© *1986 E. D. Acheson*

PART 1

CLASSIFICATION

Anthony W. Clare and Russell Blacker

Some problems affecting the diagnosis and classification of depressive disorders in primary care

INTRODUCTION

The problems which surround the classification and diagnosis of affective disorder in psychiatry lose none of their complexity when the focus of discussion shifts from psychiatry to general practice and primary care. Much of the extraordinary variation in reported prevalence in the latter setting is due in part at least to problems of classification and diagnosis. Studies which have drawn their data from a retrospective examination of general practice (GP) case records generally report low prevalence rates for affective disorder in primary care because of the low detection rate. From such studies it appears that general practitioners record having detected depressive disorder in approximately 0.6 per cent of consulting patients seen in one year (range = 0.2 per cent–1.5 per cent, both sexes) (Bebbington 1978; Mazer 1967; Watts 1958; Wing, Wing, and Hailey 1967).

On the other hand, other studies which have drawn their data from the results of diagnostic interviews report higher prevalence rates: for *major depressive disorder* in primary care, Casey, Dillon, and Tyrer (1984), Hoeper *et al.* (1979) and Nielsen and Williams (1980), report rates of between 3.5 per cent and 5.6 per cent of consulting patients (one-year prevalence, both sexes; diagnoses based on the ninth revision of the International Classification of Diseases and the third edition of the Diagnostic and Statistical Manual of the American Psychiatric Association).

There are relatively few studies which have looked at the prevalence of *minor depressive disorder* probably because of the difficulty in establishing appropriate criteria for 'caseness'. Weissman, Myers, and Thompson (1981) using the Schedule for Affective Disorders and Schizophrenia/Research Diagnostic Criteria (SADS/RDC) achieved a point prevalence rate for minor depressive disorder in primary care of 2.5 per cent of consulting patients (both sexes). Crombie (1974) reporting on the 1970 National Morbidity Survey (data from GP case records) showed a prevalence rate for *neurotic depression* of 3.1 per cent consulting patients at risk.

Some of the more pressing problems which have a bearing on the question of affective disorder classification are considered below in more detail. While these are by no means the sum total of difficulties – space does not permit a detailed discussion of the importance of personality, for example – they do reflect the complexity of identifying and managing depression outside the specialized psychiatric setting.

THE PROBLEM OF SYMPTOM RELIABILITY

Several authors have looked at the prevalence of depressive *symptoms* in primary care but have emerged with an enormous degree of variation in their reported rates, variation which cannot be simply explained as due to differences in practice population. For example, Salkind (1969), basing his data upon the Beck Depression Inventory, achieved a prevalence rate for consecutive consulting patients of 48 per cent at cut-off score = 11, and 25 per cent at cut-off score = 25. Nielsen and Williams (1980), again using the Beck Inventory, reported varying rates according to cut-off score:

Rate	Cut-off score
52.7%	5
19.8%	10
12.2%	13
8.4%	15
5.5%	17
3.0%	20
0.4%	30

Shepherd *et al.* (1966), basing their data on the Cornell Medical Index (a self-report instrument), achieved the following breakdowns for primary care patients:

7% males and 13% females = 'usually felt unhappy'
2% males and   6% females = 'felt so unhappy that they wished they were dead'
1.8% males and 2.5% females = 'always felt miserable and blue'
2.7% males and 4.4% females = 'felt that life was entirely hopeless'

More recently, rates of depression varying from 13.2 per cent (Zung *et al.* 1983) to 42 per cent (Linn and Yager 1980) have been reported in various samples. One of the factors which doubtless contributes to this variation is that a patient may choose to disclose or withhold depressive symptoms. Whether he does so appears to be dependent upon a number of factors the first of which is the 'level of expectation', i.e. what the patient expects from the consultation. The patients referred to a psychiatrist have (usually) agreed to this move, have been identified as having a psychiatric problem, and are expecting to have to talk about themselves, their problems or their feelings. Not so the distressed patient visiting the general practitioner who may not yet have formulated his or her problems in personal or psychological terms. In support of this, recent studies in primary care (Goldberg and Blackwell 1970) have reported high rates of 'hidden psychiatric morbidity' in primary care even when psychiatrically trained and vigilant investigators are employed. Patients who are relatively unsophisticated in psychological terms, such as the elderly or those who, having physical illnesses, perceive all their experiences as originating from their particular complaint, are less likely to volunteer psychological symptoms and so less likely to be 'picked up' by their doctor.

Other reasons for patients' non-disclosure of psychiatric symptoms include the 'somatizers' who have a tendency to translate and express psychological symptoms in somatic terms. Such people are believed to account for a large proportion of this 'hidden' morbidity in primary care (Goldberg and Blackwell 1970). In other patients, non-disclosure may result from an unwillingness to 'bother the doctor' with complaints which they believe are neither of interest to the doctor nor his or her job to deal with. However, such patients will often volunteer their symptoms if directly asked and this has prompted several authors to suggest the use of screening-questionnaires. In other patients, the 'deniers', the 'highly defended' and the less psychologically articulate, screening-questionnaires may be comparatively ineffective. Weissman *et al.* (1981) have shown that such patients are responsible for a substantial number of false negative cases not picked up on self-report depression questionnaires.

At the other extreme there are the 'yea-sayers' who too readily admit to symptoms which they do not have. These patients typically use terms such as 'depression' in a liberal and non-specific way possibly in an attempt to communicate distress. In our experience, many patients in primary care who consult for physical or social reasons, admit to being depressed as though this were expected in the circumstances! Such patients account for a substantial proportion of the false positive cases obtained by screening instruments such as the General Health Questionnaire (GHQ). The disclosing or withholding of depressive symptoms appears, too, to be strongly influenced by other factors such as age, class, sex, civil status, degree of current stress, and the presence or absence of physical disorder (Blumenthal 1975; Brown and Harris 1978; Craig and Van Natta 1979, 1983; Ilfield 1977, 1978; Uhlenhuth *et al.* 1974; Warheit 1979; Wright *et al.* 1980).

THE PROBLEM OF SYMPTOM DEFINITION

Once it has been established that the patient *is* complaining of symptoms of depression and that these *do* refer to some underlying psychological malaise the problem becomes one of *symptom definition*. The term 'depression' has now entered common parlance and patients in primary care use it loosely to refer to a wide variety of psychological experiences. Recognizing this problem, several authors have called for more reliable operative definitions of depressed mood, but this could be difficult. Each person's feelings are subjective and the unique product of an interaction between the present stress, personality, constitution, past life-experiences, genetic loading, and belief system. It is to be expected, therefore, that the depression experience will vary from person to person particularly when the disorder is mild (in more severe depressive disorder patients, experiences are less heterogeneous). In support of this it is interesting to note that, without exception, all epidemiological studies of affective disorder have shown an increasing heterogeneity and variation of illness-form as one descends towards the bottom of the severity spectrum. Applying strict criteria of definition for depressed affect might therefore be diagnostically inappropriate. One possible solution is to look for depression experiences which are equivalent to, or approximate to, those which are recognized in patients with more severe disorders, that is, patients whose experiences are not so subject to variation. The problem here is that many of these depressive experiences and 'specific' symptoms which are seen in the more severe disorders only appear once a threshold of severity is crossed. As yet we do not know whether 'characteristic' experiences such as loss of interest, sadness, or hopelessness are distributed on some kind of sliding scale, that is, whether mildly or moderately depressed patients have a *degree* of sadness, or a *touch* of hopelessness equivalent to their overall degree of severity.

Another solution to this problem might be to invoke the use of metaphor, especially since it is frequently resorted to in clinical practice both by patients and doctors. Thus the anxious patients could be asked whether they could identify their feelings with those experienced when going to see the dentist, or the mildly depressed subject might be asked whether they could identify with other experiences involving loss or failure. Presumably a repertoire of examples could be constructed using everyday experiences and which could then be 'typed' or even arranged in some form of hierarchy so as to allow for some objective measure of severity.

A further problem is that the individual symptoms which go to make up the syndromal diagnoses such as major depressive disorder are also to be found in a wide variety of non-mood-disordered situations. Many more patients complain of feeling depressed, lacking in energy, and sleeping poorly than have formal depressive disorder. These problems can be considered under several headings:

1. Depressive symptoms are common in a normal sample of the general population.
2. Depressive symptoms are also very common in people who have a variety of physical illnesses either because of the illness itself or because of the secondary limitations it imposes upon them.
3. Depressive symptoms are also common in patients who have other, non-depressive psychiatric disorders.

First, there is the problem that occasional symptoms of depression, regarded as a 'normal' part of life experiences, are very common in the general population. Weissman, recalculating reported estimates from several studies, cites point prevalence rates of depressive symptoms in the community of 11 per cent for men and 20 per cent for women. Compared with this the point prevalence of formal depressive illness in the community is only about 3 per cent for men and 6 per cent for women (Barrett, Hurst, and Discala 1978; Bebbington 1978; Blazer and Williams 1980; Blumenthal 1975; Brown and Harris 1978; Byrne 1980; Comstock and Helsing 1976; Craig and Van Natta 1979; Eastwood 1981; Radloff 1977; Roberts and Vernon 1983; Weissman and Myers 1978; Weissman *et al.* 1981; Wing *et al.* 1978). Clearly not all 'depressed' people have diagnosable depressive illness.

Psychiatrists appear to have little difficulty in distinguishing genuinely depressed (ill) patients from normal subjects who have depressive symptoms (Gastpar, Gilsdorf, and Gastpar 1981), probably because they take into account other variables such as duration and severity of symptoms. The bias among general practitioners in the diagnosis of psychiatric disorder is not towards the allocation of diagnoses where they do not exist but in the failure to detect cases which are already established. The reasons for this have been discussed in detail by Goldberg and Huxley (1980) and will not be discussed further here. However, one factor that may well make a significant contribution to this failure is the problem of coexisting physical illness.

THE RELATIONSHIP BETWEEN DEPRESSION AND PHYSICAL ILLNESS

It is almost a platitude to say that the majority of persons who consult their GP are suffering from physical illnesses of one form or another. The physically sick are especially at risk of developing depression and up to 20 per cent of patients with chronic cardiovascular, collagen, gastroenteric, cerebrovascular or neurological disorders suffer also from depressive reactions (Sartorius 1979). In addition, certain illnesses such as some endocrine, neurological, and metabolic disorders, are potent precipitators of depressive illness in their own right. A proportion of illness-related depressions are also iatrogenic: a significant number of currently prescribed drugs are associated with depressive side-effects and the increased use of medicaments and alcohol over the past few decades has been suggested as a further cause for the apparent increase in depressive morbidity in the general population (Craig and Van Natta 1978; Mellinger *et al.* 1978).

Conversely, persons suffering from psychiatric disorders appear to have a greater physical-illness expectancy than the non-psychiatrically ill (Eastwood and Trevelyan 1972; Shepherd *et al.* 1966; Sklaroff 1963; Widmer and Cadoret 1978). It is surprising that so little work on this strong and interesting association between physical and psychiatric morbidity should have been done since the mid-1960s, especially since only two studies (Kessel 1960; Kreitman, Pearce, and Ryle 1966) failed to find a positive correlation between physical and psychiatric disorder.

Between these two poles lie a range of conditions which can loosely be described as 'psychosomatic', some of which (for example, chronic facial pain) have acquired a particular association with underlying depressive illness. This is not the place to discuss the true status of such conditions except to say that they find no satisfactory place in the major systems of classification even though in one form or another they appear to account for some two-thirds of the total psychiatric morbidity in general practice in the studies referred to above.

Thus wherever the illness experience is touched upon, sooner or later depression is encountered. Thus general practitioners, because of their dual role as healers and counsellors, can expect to see in the course of their work a remarkable amount of depression which is associated one way or another with physical symptoms and physical morbidity. One confounding problem for the diagnostician is that somatic symptoms are responsible for a considerable slice of the presentation of many depressive illnesses.

The majority of patients consulting their general practitioners present with somatic/physical symptoms, but not all such patients are suffering from diagnosable physical illnesses; a proportion are in fact suffering from psychiatric disorders. The reasons why emotionally disturbed patients choose to present with physical symptoms is not fully understood but include a tendency for certain sociodemographic sub-groups to 'somatize' emotional experiences.

Goldberg and Blackwell (1976) demonstrated that although almost a quarter of the patients were thought to be psychiatrically ill only 7.8 per cent presented with symptoms that were entirely psychological in nature, the remainder having a combination of psychological and somatic symptoms. They found that although the patients were aware of their psychological symptoms (i.e. owned to having them on direct questioning) they tended to interpret them in terms of 'non-specific illnesses' rather than believing themselves to be psychiatrically ill; such patients apparently sought advice from their GPs for *somatic* symptoms!

In a similar study in the USA, Goldberg *et al.* (1970) demonstrated that although 31.3 per cent of primary care patients were believed to have, or demonstrated having, significant psychiatric disorder only 3 per cent presented with symptoms that were purely psychological in nature. In this study, the twelve most commonly presented symptoms were:

82% anxiety and worry
71% despondency, sadness and fatigue
52% backache, headache, pains elsewhere, dizzy spells
50% sleep disturbance
38% irritability
27% excessive concern with bodily functions
21% depressive thoughts and inability to concentrate
19% obsessions and compulsions
11% phobias
6% depersonalization

In a study by Widmer and Cadoret (1978) the presenting complaints in 154 depressed primary care patients could be broken down into three categories:

1. ill-defined 'functional' complaints;
2. pain of undetermined aetiology in a wide variety of sites;
3. 'nervous complaints' including mainly tension and feelings of anxiety.

In 9 per cent physical complaints were the *sole* presenting symptoms; for 26 per cent, somatic symptoms ranked high in the list of presenting complaints.

Gastpar, Gilsdorf, and Gastpar (1981) in a World Health Organisation primary care study, found that their depressed primary care patients presented predominantly with somatic complaints. In addition they claimed that five symptoms were characteristic of depressed patients: feelings of worthlessness, loss of energy, sleep disturbance, anxiety, and depressed mood. However, the last two symptoms were shared with other patients suffering from neurotic disorders while anergia and sleep disturbance were shared by many patients with physical illnesses or conditions such as pregnancy.

The relationship between the physical and psychological components of any illness is complex and at present poorly understood. There is a need for descriptive epidemiological studies of disorders in which both physical and psychological components are conspicuous, but the success of such studies will depend to a greater extent upon the ability to develop first some adequate and reliable system for typing, measuring and classifying such disorders. At present no such system exists. In the ICD–8 there were facilities for rating 'combined categories' of physical and psychological disorders but they were removed in the ninth revision. The Clinical Interview Schedule, however (Goldberg *et al.* 1970), contains a skeleton for rating combined psychological and physical components and presumably this could be fleshed out for use in this field.

DEPRESSIVE SYMPTOMS AND DEPRESSIVE ILLNESS

Of course, depressive symptoms are not unrelated to depressive illness although recent research suggests that it is not so much the symptoms themselves as their overall number, statistical relation, duration and persistence over time which assume equal or greater importance from the point of view of diagnostic reliability. This means that the mere presence of depressive symptoms may be of relatively little value in the identification of depressive disorder unless other factors are taken into account. Which factors are important from this point of view continues to be discussed.

Symptom number

There is some evidence that that overall *number* of symptoms does correlate with the degree of 'caseness' (Wing 1978) and it has been shown that Present State Examination and Clinical Interview Schedule summed-severity scores correlate highly with overall scores on the General Health Questionnaire (Goldberg and Huxley 1980). Craig and Van Natta, comparing inpatient depressives, non-depressed psychiatric inpatients and normal general population controls, reported high prevalence rates of depressive symptoms in all three groups; however, one of the distinguishing factors between the groups was the presence of significantly *more* depressive symptoms in the depressed group (Craig and Van Natta 1976).

Not all authors agree that the number of symptoms is a reliable index of psychiatric disorder; using the GHQ, Tarnopolsky found that the correlation between GHQ score and severity of condition as measured on psychiatric interview was too low to be reliable (Tarnopolsky *et al.* 1979). Boyd *et al.* (1982), and Blazer and Williams (1980) have also found only a modest correlation between high scores on self-report depressive symptom inventories and independent diagnosis of depressive syndrome made by pairs of psychiatrists.

Symptom type

Traditionally, this is of importance in establishing whether a depressive disorder is present: the appearance of certain 'specific' symptoms of a vegetative/physiological and melancholic nature are an important part of the psychotic depression syndrome. There is considerable evidence that these symptoms *do* cluster in the more severe depressive illnesses but individually they may be less reliable than was previously believed; some of these 'specific' symptoms such as early-morning waking, diurnal variation with morning worsening, impaired concentration, subjective anergia, etc., can be found in other psychiatric disorders and also in subjects who have various physical illnesses. Their presence, therefore, should not be taken as absolute indicators of underlying depressive illness (Akiskal *et al.* 1979; Endicott and Spitzer 1979; Ní Bhrolcháin, Brown, and Harris 1979). The SADS/RDC stresses the importance of the symptom of anhedonia or 'loss of interest' which must be present as well as depressed mood in order to make a diagnosis of depressive disorder. In addition, a minimum number of 'associated' symptoms must be present, but do all symptoms carry equal weight from a diagnostic point of view? The symptom of retardation is held by many clinicians to be fairly specific to depression, but can it really be of equal diagnostic weight as 'impairment of concentration' which, as a symptom, is ubiquitous? A number of these associated symptoms may also be mimicked by other things such as physical illness; for example, retardation may be present or even mimicked by illnesses in which fatigue is a leading feature. A 'typical' primary care presentation is that of depressive symptoms which arise out of 'flu-like illnesses where symptoms of subjective anergia, sleep disturbance, loss of interest, depression, and even retardation or something very akin to it often occur. This is recognized by the RDC which disqualifies such patients from receiving a diagnosis of depressive disorder.

Clearly some form of compromise has to be reached. On the one hand, one cannot decide that all physically ill patients who have associated depressive symptoms are not suffering from major depressive disorder given the fact that they are a group at risk of developing depressive disorder. On the other hand, it would be foolish to suggest that all these physically ill persons who also have some depressive symptoms have depressive disorder.

Symptom duration

It is becoming increasingly clear from the results of more recent studies that a factor which is more important than symptom type, number or severity, when differentiating a possible depressive illness from another form of psychiatric disorder in which depressive symptoms are also present, or from depressive symptoms in the context of a transient reaction to stress, is the *duration* of the key symptoms (Craig and Van Natta 1976; Dohrenwend and Crandell 1970). Patients with depressive illness appear to have their symptoms for longer than those whose depressive symptoms may be only the prodromal form of some other psychiatric disorder. Hankin and Locke (1982), who administered the Center for Epidemiologic Studies Depression Scale to 309 primary care patients complaining of depressive symptoms (and again one year later), concluded that duration of symptoms at the outset was a reliable differential guide between those who did and those who did not still have symptoms at the end of one year. Retrospectively, many more of the 'chronic' sample had originally reported cognitive symptoms such as feelings of helplessness and hopelessness and affective feelings of sadness and lack of interest/enjoyment (anhedonia). Interestingly, these patients were also found to have a greater prevalence of physical illness than those whose complaints were short-lived suggestive of a further complicating factor – the prolongation of symptoms by physical illness or other handicap such as cerebrovascular accident (Robinson, Starr, and Price 1984).

For a diagnosis of definite major depressive disorder, the RDC specifies that the depressed mood and associated depressive symptoms should have been present for at least *two weeks*. For this, the instrument has received criticism from a number of authors (e.g. Winokur, Tsuang, and Crose 1982) who feel that this duration criterion is too short. Coryell, Winokur, and Andreasen (1981) found that 28 per cent of the *relatives* of patients with affective disorder were, on the basis of the Research Diagnostic Criteria's two-week duration, 'likely to show an affective disorder themselves'; once the duration was extended to one month the prevalence among relatives fell to 21 per cent. For this reason many epidemiologists who formerly applied RDC criteria now follow Feighner's criterion of one-month duration of symptoms (Feighner, Robins, and Guze 1972). On a purely anecdotal basis it is interesting to note that many general practitioners prefer to suspend the making of a diagnosis of psychiatric disorder until the patient has presented with the symptoms on several occasions: a strategy probably evolved from their experience with large numbers of patients with transient disorders but which may also reflect the value of duration in the making of a sure diagnosis of depressive disorder.

Symptom persistence

Closely allied to duration is the *persistence* of symptoms. It appears that persons who have depressive disorders are more likely to exhibit their symptoms on a consistent daily basis and this is recognized by the RDC which insists that key symptoms should have been present daily for at least two weeks. Although persistence of symptoms is recognized as an important consideration, surprisingly little work has been done to test this by following individual symptoms throughout the course of an illness (e.g. Russell and De Silva 1983). Craig and Van Natta (1976) in the study referred to above found that their three groups (depressed inpatients, non-depressed psychiatric inpatients, and normal community subjects scoring 'positive' on the Center for Epidemiologic Studies Depression Scale) could also be differentiated on the basis of the persistence of depressive symptoms over time. A symptom-by-symptom comparison showed that the values for non-depressed psychiatric inpatients in this respect were almost identical with those for the community sample. They concluded that depressive symptoms *per se* are more indicative of overall distress and not specific to depressive disorder but that persistence of these symptoms over a defined period (one week in this case) is significantly more closely related to depressive illness. Roberts and Vernon (1983) found that using a screening criterion of two weeks persistence of depressive symptoms yielded a false negative diagnostic rate, when compared with the RDC, of only 10 per cent. However, Weissman and Myers (1978) do not agree that persistence of symptoms is a particularly reliable indicator of depressive illness. They found that their sample of depressed patients sorted according to the criterion of persistence of symptoms, when compared with RDC criteria, yielded a false positive rate of 16 per cent for major depressive disorder and an unacceptably high false negative rate of 32 per cent.

SYNDROMAL VALIDITY: THE DIFFERENTIATION
OF DISORDER TYPES

The arguments over classification thus far reviewed have taken place between psychiatrists, yet it is now recognized that the vast majority of individuals in this country who suffer from affective disturbances never see a psychiatrist and are treated by their general practitioner. It is argued that the bulk of these suffer from conditions which are difficult to classify according to the accepted diagnostic types and categories applied within specialized psychiatry. Most cases in the community are characterized by 'such features as depression, anxiety, preoccupation with health, irritability, and insomnia' (Williams and Clare 1979). In order to try to type these disorders, various new categories have been suggested such as 'subclinical neurosis' (Taylor and Chave 1964), 'dysthymia' (Foulds and Bedford 1975) and 'nervous tension' (Wing 1976). However, current concepts of classification are weak on the specification of these milder affective disorders, and the validity of many of the current concepts, such as neurotic depression, may seriously be doubted. From the point of view of depression in primary care there are two areas which merit special attention:

1. differentiation of depression from anxiety, and
2. the problem of neurotic depression and mixed neurotic disorders.

The problem of anxiety

Symptoms of anxiety are ubiquitous and can be found in many different psychiatric disorders. This is especially true of depressive illness in which anxiety is complained of in up to 95 per cent of cases and associated autonomic symptoms in up to 85 per cent of cases (Gersh and Fowles 1979; Hamilton 1983). Conversely, complaints of depressed mood have been reported in 89 per cent of anxiety states (Hamilton 1983).

Making a diagnostic distinction between anxiety and depressive disorders when both are quite severe is not especially difficult. However, in primary care where the conditions encountered are of a milder or mixed nature, this distinction is harder to make. Prusoff and Klerman (1974) working with female outpatients with neurotic affective symptoms were 'consistently able' to separate them into depressed and anxious groups although there was a significant 25–40 per cent 'overlap' and 30–40 per cent of cases were mis-classified. Downing and Rickels (1974) have shown how psychiatrists and general practitioners tend to prescribe and diagnose in situations of mixed symptomatology, according to the predominance of anxiety or depressive symptoms. Despite these difficulties, general practitioners often find them-selves under criticism for failing to differentiate anxiety from depression and for using anxiolytics in a rather inappropriate and cavalier manner (Craig and Van Natta 1978; Nielsen and Nielsen 1979; Tyrer 1978; Weissman, Myers, and Thompson 1981). No doubt some of them do but the reasons for this may be more complex than their critics would imply. In situations of mixed symptomatology or diagnostic confusion the usual practice is to examine other non-symptomatic variables the most useful of which from the point of view of discriminating between the two appear to be:

1. a history of previous psychiatric disorder (depressive illness or anxiety neurosis);
2. age of onset;
3. family history.

For example, Lader and Marks (1971) show that whereas most anxiety neuroses begin in the early teenage years, depressive disorder tends to present during the third and fourth decades. Pollitt and Young (1971) claimed that the later the onset of the symptoms of anxiety the more likely it is that the patient is suffering from underlying depression. In favour of depression was (once again) a relatively persistent mood change which was stable over time, the depth and quality of this depressed mood, and the presence of retarda-tion. This is supported by Roth *et al.* (1972) who found severe and persistent depression in 65 per cent of their depressives but only 21 per cent of their patients with anxiety neurosis.

Traditionally the presence of prominent anxiety symptoms in cases of depressive illness has tended to favour the application of labels such as 'neurotic depression' or 'anxious depression' rather than that of major depressive disorder, particularly where, in addition, some clearly identified precipitant can be demonstrated. Partially because of a belief that depressive illnesses are more severe than anxiety neuroses, it has been traditional to give greater status to depressive symptoms in the hierarchy of diagnosis and classification than to those of anxiety. This strategy reflects the underlying assumption that depressive illnesses are essentially biological, biochemical or constitutional in nature whereas anxiety neuroses are believed to be largely psychogenic in origin. For this reason classification systems tend to be heavily biased towards depressive illness, whereas anxiety-type disorders which are not 'pure' in their presentation are obliged to seek lodgings under a variety of different and perhaps unsuitable categories which include depressive neurosis, stress reaction, adjustment disorder, and atypical depression. In most systems of classification the opportunity for the specification of affective disorder in which anxiety and depressive symptoms have equal prominence, is non-existent.

Recently there has been considerable discussion over whether anxiety neurosis and depression are distinct conditions (Fleiss, Gurland, and Cooper 1971; Hamilton 1983; Roth et al. 1972) or members of a continuum (Johnstone et al. 1980; Mendels, Weinstein, and Cochrane 1972; Pichot, Guelfi, and Pull 1980; Russell and De Silva 1983). To date it has not been possible to show conclusively whether the dichotomous or the continuum view of anxiety and depression is correct and it is hard to put Feighner's conclusion that 'we are still at a loss as to how to label mixed anxious-depressives more accurately and how to divide them' (Feighner 1983) into context.

It is probable that the traditional depressive illness/anxiety neurosis dichotomy is an artefact of the psychiatric specialty population and referral bias: patients with neurotic disorders are not often referred by GPs to psychiatric departments unless the disorders are either very severe or have other conspicuous and troublesome components such as personality disorder. This means that psychiatric-specialty neurotic patients are even less representative of their population of origin than patients suffering from depressive disorders. Studies which base their findings upon samples of patients drawn from psychiatric hospital settings are therefore suspect.

Some general practitioners argue that the anxiety/depression question should be decided on the basis of treatment response since their prime concern is not with the niceties of psychiatric theorizing but with delivering care to the enormous numbers of psychiatrically ill patients in their surgeries. Appealing as this is, to design a pragmatic classification upon a foundation such as treatment response is neither a sound tactic, nor one which at the end of the day would prove much help in making the management decisions these GPs would wish. Although it is clear that 'pure' depressive illnesses respond best to tricyclic anti-depressants and electroconvulsive therapy, and 'pure' anxiety neurosis to minor tranquillizers and behavioural methods, it is also evident that some patients with anxiety neurosis respond very well to tricyclic anti-depressants or Monoamine oxidase inhibitors and some non-retarded depressives may respond well to benzodiazepines (Widlocher, Lecrubier, and Le Goc 1983). Also, milder forms of depression appear to respond differently to treatments which are appropriate and successful in more severe cases. In mixed groups many patients respond well to benzodiazepines and to tricyclic antidepressants and to combinations of both (Rickels, Downing, and Howard 1971). Rickels found, using a classificatory system based upon relative degrees of depression and anxiety (high depression + low anxiety, low depression + high anxiety) that in 'mixed' cases of anxiety/depression, where anxiety dominated, chlordiazepoxide was superior to amitriptyline and where depression dominated, amitriptyline was superior. Recent reviews (Paykel

1979) suggest, therefore, that the relationship between anxiety and depression cannot be resolved on the basis of treatment response. As regards primary care there is a greater priority which is first to examine and study the efficacy of *standard* treatments on *standard* psychiatric conditions presenting in this setting; only then can issues of difference in treatment responsiveness be sorted out.

THE PROBLEM OF NEUROTIC DEPRESSION

The neurotic/psychotic depression dichotomy is probably the classificatory distinction most widely employed in this country and yet one which continues to be a source of considerable controversy. Parallel to this controversy has been the increasing conspicuousness of neurotic depressions in clinical practice. According to current usage 'neurotic depression' is a term applied to milder depressive illnesses which are believed to be stress-related, less severe, relatively unresponsive to formal anti-depressant treatment, having a poorer long-term prognosis, associated with an abnormality of pre-morbid personality, and which lack the traditional vegetative and melancholic symptoms of 'psychotic' depression.

Another reason for the importance of neurotic depression to primary care is that of the difficulty in differentiating psychotic from neurotic forms together with the treatment implications (perhaps mistaken) that this carries. The majority of the depressions encountered in primary care lie in the mild to moderate range of severity where formal distinction between 'neurotic' and 'psychotic' forms may be difficult to demonstrate. Although 'pure' or classical presentations of both forms certainly do exist in primary care, many, perhaps up to a third, of general practice depressions defy satisfactory allocation to either category because they share features of both (Watts 1966). To an extent this may be because of factors connected with the evolution of a particular episode. As Kraepelin noted in 1921, 'it is scarcely possible from the psychic state alone to come to a reliable decision whether a first episode of mild depression represents a self-limiting situational affective disturbance, the prodromal phase of a non-affective disorder, or the first episode of a manic-depressive disorder'.

Differentiation between neurotic and psychotic forms of depression is easier in psychiatric-specialty populations because of the referral bias which ensures that hospital-based psychiatrists only tend to see the more conspicuous stereotypes of each form. Psychiatric-specialty depressives have, as a rule, already evolved thereby making the distinction between neurotic and psychotic depression more apparent that real. An alternative explanation is that these 'unclassifiable' depressions represent depressive interforms which lie between neurotic and psychotic illness-types or even a third category of depressive illness altogether. The battle between the dichotomists on the one hand and the continuum school on the other has been fought mainly over this issue of whether boundaries, points of rarity, or interforms can or cannot be demonstrated in a population of depressed patients. Increasingly sophisticated statistical techniques have been employed in an attempt to resolve these questions but many studies, particularly those of the dichotomist party, have begun with unrepresentative populations on which to base their findings. Those who belong to the continuum camp have generally based their opinions upon experience with community populations. Dichotomists such as Roth and his colleagues in the so-called Newcastle school argue that interforms are rare and that psychotic and neurotic depression are distinct but overlapping conditions. Other authors such as Kendell and Van Praag, who have worked with better chosen samples, have been unable to demonstrate valid boundaries between neurotic and psychotic forms; they have argued that depressive disorders lie on a continuum whose poles correspond to more 'pure' manifestations of neurotic and psychotic disorder. A third position is taken by those such as Ní Bhrolcháin who, unable to demonstrate any symptoms peculiar to either 'neurotic' or 'psychotic' patterns of depression, argue that depressive illness is essentially one condition whose various manifestations differ only in terms of severity. Foulds postulates a hierarchical model in which disorders are arranged in a stack along an axis which simultaneously expresses both quantitative and qualitative change.

Some American epidemiologists adopt an interim strategy, putting aside debate over the sub-classification of depression, and include all non-bipolar depressive disorders under the single rubric of 'non-bipolar depression'. This position has its attractions but can only be seen as an interim measure since neurotic depression is too conspicuous an entity to be simply subsumed into a single illness called unipolar depression. The American-based instruments, such as the Research Diagnostic Criteria of Spitzer, Endicott, and Robins (1978) and the DSM III, do not enforce the traditional neurotic/psychotic distinction, being more concerned with distinctions based upon overall severity. Not surprisingly, these instruments produce groups of depressed patients which are criticized for being 'mixed' and therefore 'unreliable' (Feinberg *et al*. 1979; Nelson *et al*. 1978).

CONCLUSIONS

Some conclusions can be drawn as to the nature of depressive disorder in the community although further epidemiological research of the right kind is needed before they can be fully accepted. The success of such research will depend upon the ability to develop instruments of diagnosis and classification which are tailored for use in this setting and which are open to modification as new concepts emerge. Dimensional, multi-axial systems would appear to be the models for classification in the future although which axes are likely to prove to be most reliable and useful and how they are to be measured is uncertain. Biological markers may have a substantial contribution to make towards the diagnosis and classification of depressive disorder in the future although they have so far proved too capricious to be reliable. From the point of view of the general practitioner who finds himself responsible for the management of a considerable amount of psychiatric morbidity in the general population, any new system of classification which is developed will have to be reliable, quick to use and relevant to that population as a whole. It will be no good having a tortuous, bulky, and complex system useful only for those involved in the higher flights of psychiatric research. Perhaps it may be possible to design a system compatible with both needs by having a complex parent system to which is attached a simplified and yet still effective daughter schedule?

There is a pressing need for a complete re-examination and re-thinking of the concept of neurotic depression including the provision of positive diagnostic criteria and a rationalization of its supposed aetiological basis. Other issues needing clarification include the relationship of forms of depressive illness such as 'neurotic' and 'psychotic', and how diagnostic reliability might be affected or improved by giving increased weighting to variables such as symptom duration, persistence and number. The relationship between depression and physical illness is a particularly under-researched area in which crucial questions remain to be answered, in particular whether the depression is independent or purely 'reactive' in nature. A further examination of the nosological status of mixed anxiety-depression disorders, whether they merit a separate category of their own or should continue to be subsumed, as at present, under depressive disorder, is yet another area of worthwhile research to which the primary care team and setting could make a substantial and useful contribution.

REFERENCES

Akiskal, H., Pizantiam, V., Rosenthal, T., Parks, W., and Walker, W. (1978) The nosological status of neurotic depression. *Archives of General Psychiatry* 35: 756–66.

Akiskal, H. S., Rosenthal, R. H., Rosenthal, T., Kashgarian, M., Khani, M. K., and Puzantian, V. R. (1979) Differentiation of primary affective illness from situational, symptomatic, and secondary depressions. *Archives of General Psychiatry* 36: 635–43.

Barrett, J., Hurst, M. W., and DiScala, C. (1978) Prevalence of depression over a 12-month period in a non-patient population. *Archives of General Psychiatry* 35: 741–44.

Bebbington, P. E. (1978) The epidemiology of depressive disorders. In A. M. Kleinman (ed.) *Culture, Medicine and Psychiatry*. Dordrecht, The Netherlands: D. Reidel Publishing Co., pp. 297–341.

Blazer, D. and Williams, C. D. (1980). Epidemiology of dysphoria and depression in an elderly population. *American Journal of Psychiatry* 137: 439–44.

Blumenthal, M. D. (1975) Measuring depressive symptomatology in a general population. *Archives of General Psychiatry* 32: 971–78.

Boyd, J. H., Weissman, M., Thompson, W. D., and Myers, J. K. (1982) Screening for depression in a community sample: Understanding the discrepancies between depression symptom and diagnostic scales. *Archives of General Psychiatry* 39: 1195–200.

Brown, G. and Harris, T. (1978) *Social Origins of Depression*. London: Tavistock Publications.

Byrne, D. G. (1980) The prevalence of symptoms of depression in an Australian general population. *Australia and New Zealand Journal of Psychiatry*, 14: 65–71.

Casey, P. R., Dillon, S., and Tyrer, P. J. (1984) The diagnostic status of patients with conspicuous psychiatric morbidity in primary care. *Psychological Medicine*, 14: 673–82.

Comstock, G. W. and Helsing, K. J. (1976) Symptoms of depression in two communities. *Psychological Medicine*, 6: 551–63.

Coryell, W., Winokur, G., and Andreasen, N. (1981) Affective case definition on affective disorder rates. *American Journal of Psychiatry* 138: 1106–109.

Craig, T. J. and Van Natta, P. (1976) Presence and persistence of depressive symptoms in patient and community populations. *American Journal of Psychiatry* 133: 1426–429.

—— (1978) Current medication use and symptoms of depression in a general population. *American Journal of Psychiatry* 135: 1036–039.

—— (1979) Influence of demographic characteristics on two measures of depressive symptoms. *Archives of General Psychiatry* 36: 149–54.

—— (1983) Disability and depressive symptoms in two communities. *American Journal of Psychiatry* 140: 5, 598–600.

Crombie, D. L. (1974) Changes in patterns of recorded morbidity. In D. Taylor (ed.) *Benefits and Risks of Medical Care*. London: Office of Health Economics, pp. 17–41.

Dohrenwend, B. P. and Crandell, D. L. (1970). Psychiatric symptoms in community, clinic, and mental hospital groups. *American Journal of Psychiatry* 126: 1611–621.

Downing, R. W. and Rickels, K. (1974) Mixed anxiety and depression: Fact or myth? *Archives of General Psychiatry* 30: 312–17.

Eastwood, M. R. (1981) Epidemiology and depression. (Review article.) *Psychological Medicine* 11: 229–34.

Eastwood, M. R. and Trevelyan, M. H. (1972) Relationship between physical and psychiatric disorder. *Psychological Medicine* 2: 363–72.

Endicott, J. and Spitzer, R. L. (1979) Use of the Research Diagnostic Criteria and the Schedule for Affective Disorders and Schizophrenia to study Affective Disorders. *American Journal of Psychiatry* 136: 1, 52–6.

Feighner, J., Robins, E., and Guze, S. (1972) Diagnostic criteria for use in psychiatric research. *Archives of General Psychiatry* 26: 57–63.

Feighner, J. (1983) Discussion article. *British Journal of Pharmacology* 15: 178S–79S.

Feinberg, M. *et al.* (1979) Misdiagnosis of endogenous depression with RDC. (Letter.) *Lancet*, 3 February, p. 267.

Fleiss, J. L., Gurland, B. J., and Cooper, J. E. (1971) Some contributions to the measurement of psychopathology. *British Journal of Psychiatry* 119: 647–56.

Foulds, G. A. and Bedford, F. (1975) Hierarchy of classes of personal illness. *Psychological Medicine* 5: 181–92.

Gastpar, M., Gilsdorf, U., and Gastpar, G. (1981) Diagnosis of depression in general practice. In T. A. Ban, R. Gonzalez, A. S. Jablensky, W. Sartorius, and F. E. Vartanian (eds) *Prevention and Treatment of Depression*. Baltimore, MD: University Park Press.

Gersh, F. S. and Fowles, D. C. (1979) Neurotic Depression: The concept of anxious depression. In R. A. Depue (ed.) *Psychobiology of Depressive Disorders*, pp. 81–104.

Goldberg, D., Cooper, B., Eastwood, M. R., Kedward, H. B., and Shepherd, M. (1970) A psychiatric interview suitable for using in community services. *British Journal of Preventive and Social Medicine* 24: 18–26.

Goldberg, D. and Blackwell, B. (1970) Psychiatric illness in general practice: A detailed study using a new method of case identification. *British Medical Journal* 2: 439.

Goldberg, D. and Huxley, P. (1980) *Mental Illness in the Community*. London: Tavistock Publications.

Goldberg, D., Rickels, K., Downing, R., and Hesbacher, P. (1976) A comparison of two psychiatric screening tests. *British Journal of Psychiatry* 129: 61–7.

Hamilton, M. (1983) The clinical distinction between anxiety and depression. *British Journal of Clinical Pharmacology* 15: 165S–69S.

Hankin, J. and Locke, B. (1982) The persistence of depressive symptomatology among prepaid group practice enrollees: An exploratory study. *American Journal of Public Health* 72: 1000–007.

Hoeper, E. W., Nycz, G. R., Cleary, P. D., Regier, D. A., and Goldberg, I. D. (1979) Estimated prevalence of RDC mental disorder in primary medical care. *International Journal of Mental Health*, 8, 6–15.

Ilfield, F. W. (1977) Current social stressors and symptoms of depression. *American Journal of Psychiatry* 134: 161–66.

Ilfield, F. W. (1978) Psychological status of community residents and major demographic dimensions. *Archives of General Psychiatry* 35: 716–24.

Johnstone, E., Cunningham-Owens, D. G., Frith, C. D., McPherson, K., Dowie, C., Riley, G., and Gold, A. (1980) Neurotic illness and its response to anxiolytic and antidepressant treatment. *Psychological Medicine* 10: 321–8.

Kessel, N. (1960) Psychiatric morbidity in a London general practice. *British Journal of Preventive and Social Medicine* 14: 16–22.

Kraepelin, E. (1921) *Manic-Depression Insanity and Paranoia*. Edinburgh: Livingstone.

Kreitman, N., Pearce, K. I., and Ryle, A. (1966) The relationship of psychiatric, psychosomatic and organic illness in a general practice. *British Journal of Psychiatry* 112: 569–79.

Lader, M. H. and Marks, I. M. (1971) *Clinical Anxiety*. London: Heinemann.

Linn, L. S. and Yager, H. (1980) The effect of screening, sensitisation and feedback on notation of depression. *Journal of Medical Education* 55: 942–49.

Mazer, M. (1967) Psychiatric disorders in general practice: The experience of an island community. *American Journal of Psychiatry* 124: 609–15.

Mellinger, G. D. *et al.* (1978) Psychic distress, life crisis and use of psychotherapeutic medications. *Archives of General Psychiatry* 35: 1045.

Mendels, J., Weinstein, N., and Cochrane, C. (1972) The relationship between depression and anxiety. *Archives of General Psychiatry* 27: 649–53.

Nelson, J. C., Charney, D. S., and Vingiano, A. W. (1978) False positive diagnosis with Primary Affective Disorder Criteria. (Letter.) *Lancet*, 9 December, 1252–3.

Ní Bhrolcháin, M., Brown, G., and Harris, T. O. (1979) Psychotic and neurotic depression. 2. Clinical characteristics. *British Journal of Psychiatry* 134: 94–107.

Nielsen, J. and Nielsen, J. A. (1979) Treatment prevalence in a community mental health service with special regard to depressive disorders. *Comprehensive Psychiatry* 20: 1, 67–77.

Nielsen, A. C. and Williams, T. A. (1980) Depression in ambulatory medical patients. *Archives of General Psychiatry* 37: 999–1004.

Paykel, E. S. (1979) Predictors of treatment response. In E. S. Paykel and A. Coppen (eds) *Psychopharmacology of Affective Disorders*. London: Oxford University Press, pp. 193–220.

Pichot, P., Guelfi, J. D., and Pull, C. B. (1980) Semiologie de la depression. *Encycl. Med. Chir. Paris, Psychiatr.* 37110 A 10, 12.

Pollitt, J. and Young, J. (1971) Anxiety state of masked depression? A study based on the action of Monoamine Oxidase Inhibitors. *British Journal of Psychiatry* 119: 143–49.

Prusoff, B. and Klerman, G. L. (1974) Differentiating depressed from anxious neurotic outpatients. *Archives of General Psychiatry* 30: 302–09.

Radloff, L. S. (1977) The CES-D scale: A self-report depression scale for research in the general population. *Applied Psychological Measurement* 1: 385–401.

Rickels, K., Downing, R., and Howard, K. (1971) Predictors of Chlordiazepoxide response in anxiety. *Clinical Pharmacology and Therapeutics*, 12: 262–73.

Roberts, R. E. and Vernon, S. W. (1983) The Center for Epidemiological Studies Depression Scale: Its use in a community sample. *American Journal of Psychiatry* 140: 41–6.

Robinson, R. G., Starr, L. B., and Price, T. R. (1984) A two year longitudinal study of mood disorders following stroke: Prevalence and duration at six months follow-up. *British Journal of Psychiatry* 144: 256–62.

Roth, M., Gurney, C., Garside, R. F., and Kerr, T. A. (1972) Studies in the Classification of Affective Disorders: The relationship between anxiety states and depressive illness. *British Journal of Psychiatry* 121: 147–66.

Russell, G. F. M. and De Silva, P. (1983) Observations on the relationship between anxiety and depressive symptoms during the course of depressive illness. *British Journal of Clinical Pharmacology* 15: 147S–53S.

Salkind, M. R. (1969) Beck Depression Inventory in General Practice. *Journal of the Royal College of General Practitioners* 18: 267.

Sartorius, N. (1979) Research on affective psychoses within the framework of the WHO programme. In M. Schou and E. Stromgren *Origin, Prevention and Treatment of Affective Disorders*. London: Academic Press.

Shepherd, M., Cooper, B., Brown, A. C., and Kalton, G. (1966) *Psychiatric Illness in General Practice*. Oxford: Oxford University Press.

Sklaroff, S. A. (1963) Use of the National Health Service general practice records in epidemiological inquiries. *British Journal of Preventive Medicine* 17: 177.

Spitzer, R. L., Endicott, J., and Robins, E. (1978) Research Diagnostic Criteria. *Archives of General Psychiatry* 35: 773–82.

Tarnopolsky, A., Hand, D. J., McLean, E. K., Roberts, H., and Wiggins, R. D. (1979) Validity and uses of a screening questionnaire in the community. *British*

Journal of Psychiatry 134: 508–15.

Taylor, S. and Chave, S. (1964) *Mental Health and Environment*. London.

Tyrer, P. (1978) Drug treatment of psychiatric patients in general practice. *British Medical Journal* ii, 1008.

Uhlenhuth, E. H., Lipman, R. S., and Balter, M. B. (1974) Symptom intensity and life stress in the city. *Archives of General Psychiatry* 31: 759–64.

Warheit, G. J. (1979) Life events, coping, stress, and depressive symptomatology. *American Journal of Psychiatry* 136: 502–07.

Watts, C. A. H. (1958) Morbidity statistics from general practice. Vol 3. *Studies on Medical and Population Subjects*. No. 14. London: HMSO.

Watts, C. A. H. (1966) *Depressive disorders in the community*. Bristol: John Wright and Son.

Weissman, M. and Myers, J. K. (1978) Rates and risks of depressive symptoms in a US urban community. *Acta Psychiatrica Scandinavica* 57: 219–31.

Weissman, M., Myers, J. K., and Thompson, W. D. (1981) Depression and its treatment in a US urban community. *Archives of General Psychiatry* 38: 417–21.

Widlocher, D., Lecrubier, Y., and Le Goc, Y. (1983) The place of anxiety in depressive symptomatology. *British Journal of Clinical Pharmacology* 15: 171S–79S.

Widmer, R. and Cadoret, R. (1978) Depression in primary care: Changes in the pattern of patient visits and complaints during a developing depression. *Journal of Family Practice* 7: 293–302.

Williams, P. and Clare, A. W. (1979) *Psychosocial disorders in general practice*. London: Academic Press.

Wing, L., Wing, K. J., and Hailey, A. (1967) The use of psychiatric services in three urban areas. An international case register study. *Social Psychiatry* 2: 158–67.

Wing, J. K. (1976) A technique for studying psychiatric morbidity in in-patient and out-patient series and a general population sample. *Psychological Medicine* 6: 665–71.

Wing, J. K. (1978) *Reasoning About Madness*. London: Oxford University Press.

Wing, J. K., Mann, S. A., Leff, J. P., and Nixon, J. M. (1978) The concept of a 'case' in psychiatric population surveys. *Psychological Medicine* 8: 203–17.

Winokur, G., Tsuang, M., and Crose, R. (1982) The Iowa 500: Affective disorder in the relatives of manic and depressed patients. *American Journal of Psychiatry* 139: 209–12.

Wright, J. H., Bell, R. A., Kuhn, C. C., Rush, E. A., Patel, N., and Redmon, J. E. (1980) Depression in family practice patients. *Southern Medical Journal* 73: 1031–4.

Zung, W. W. K., Magill, M., Moore, J. and George, D. T. (1983) Recognition and treatment of depression in a family medicine practice. *Journal of Clinical Psychiatry* 44: 1.

D. L. Crombie

Classification of mental illness for primary care

The primary purposes of a set of rubrics for classifying the problems that patients bring to their general practitioners in primary care are, first, that there should be a suitable rubric for all such clinical problems and, second, that each rubric should be used consistently by all users. It goes without saying that these criteria are not met by any present classifications of morbidity used in primary care. However, before examining diagnostic labels we must look at the diagnostic process itself.

The final goal, aim, outcome or solution of all clinical problem-solving is the action taken to achieve amelioration, resolution, prevention or antici-pation of clinical problems. The word 'clinical' covers all problems our patients bring to us in the belief or hope that we can help them. It therefore includes all the elements of organic and psycho-emotional pathology as well as socioeconomic and secondary personality and communication factors, problems that patients have but are unaware of, and problems which can be prevented or anticipated with benefit.

The purpose of all clinical problem-solving is the reduction of uncertainty in the choice of appropriate action taken to ameliorate, frustrate, anticipate or resolve our patients' problems. The diagnostic process is an element in this reduction of uncertainty, but only in so far as 'diagnoses are provisional formulae designed for action'.[1]

There are three main sources of uncertainty:

1. the way in which problems are identified by doctors interacting with patients;
2. the way in which doctors then apply diagnostic or descriptive labels to these problems as a necessary step to action and;
3. uncertainty arising from deficiencies in the labels themselves.

Let us now examine in detail these potential sources of uncertainty, working backwards in our original list.

THE LABELS

These were studied some twenty years ago by the Birmingham Research Unit.[2] The work was concerned with an estimate on a three point scale of the then current knowledge (1963) of the aetiology, pathology, and morphology implied by the disease labels in the current College Classification of Disease. For only 4.2 per cent of the diagnostic labels was there a maximum rating for knowledge of pathology. All but one of these were communicable diseases, accidents, poisoning or violence. For knowledge of aetiology, only 4.8 per cent of the labels received a maximum score from at least 75 per cent of the assessors. These labels were also confined to communicable diseases, accidents, poisoning, and violence. Organic psychoses and senility were among the 19 categories from a total of over 300 with the lowest ratings for aetiology.

Neoplasms classified on pathological grounds in the International Classification of Diseases had high average accuracy ratings for implied pathology. The ratings of accuracy for aetiology and pathology for diseases of the blood and blood-forming organs were moderately high. The average ratings for all other main sections of the ICD indicated no great confidence in the accuracy with which the labels imply aetiology or pathology. The lowest ratings of all were for mental and psychoneurotic personality disorders, followed closely by diseases of the nervous system. The disease groupings with the highest or lowest values for implied accuracy were also those with maximum agreement of assessment.

The disease labels given the highest ratings for implied accuracy of morphology included once again communicable diseases, neoplasms, accidents, poisoning, and violence. We have to remember that these are the basic bricks from which we have to create our problem-solving models. The categories with low ratings, and much disagreement between observers, include psychoses and psychoneuroses.

THE WAY IN WHICH DOCTORS APPLY THEIR LABELS

Strictly speaking, an assessment of the accuracy of application of labels should take into account any inaccuracy inherent in the labels themselves.

The study which we carried out in 1958[3] was marred by non-recognition of this source of confusion and, so far as I can see, all subsequent studies have fallen into the same trap. Our study was a survey of between observer differences (so-called errors) of the interpretation of clinical problems, in which diagnostic accuracy was measured at first consultation according to the following four degrees of precision: no diagnosis; tentative diagnosis; exclusion of serious alternatives; and firm diagnosis.

The variation between the practitioners with the highest figure (72.4 per cent) and the lowest (25.2 per cent) for the proportions of 'firm' diagnoses represent differences both in the interpreation of the clinical picture and in the value of the diagnostic label attached to it. The former rate reflects the accuracy with which the label, with all its defects and deficiencies in information content, was applied to the clinical condition, while the lower rate reflects the compounded effects of both these influences.

The conditions with the lowest ratings for firmness or accuracy of diagnosis used in this study are similar to those identified by Sheldon *et al.* in their more recent study.[4] The conditions with ratings of less than 40 per cent are sciatica, disc, lesions, lumbago (12.2 per cent), unspecified neuralgia and neuritis (21.1 per cent), influenza (21.4 per cent), peptic ulcer (40.0 per cent), diseases of liver and biliary system and pancreas (42.4 per cent), abdominal pain and other abdominal disorders (31.3 per cent), acute urinary tract infections (28.6 per cent), arthritis unspecified (33.3 per cent), rheumatism unspecified, fibrositis (26.9 per cent), cough (36.4 per cent), diarrhoea and/or vomiting (17.1 per cent), PUO (4.7 per cent), and dyspepsia (3.6 per cent). Notwithstanding the poor information content of psychiatric labels, the ratings for firmness of diagnosis for psychoses, psychoneurotic disorders and other psychoneurotic illnesses were, 57.1, 60.9, and 69.0 respectively, all above the average value of 55.1.

High values were evident for otitis media, varicose veins, obstetric delivery, boils and carbuncles, cellulitis of finger and toe, lacerations.

ACCURACY OF PROBLEM IDENTIFICATION

This has been considered in the previous sections in so far as it has been possible to do so at all. The findings of the 1958 study suggested that a maximum of 72.4 per cent (average of 55.1 per cent) of clinical problems could be identified firmly by an appropriate label, however poor the information content of that label. The practitioner with this highest score, for example, classified all his diagnoses of 'cough' as firm. On the other hand, the lowest rate of 25.6 per cent for the proportion of firm diagnoses represents the use of the classification system by a recorder who compounded the inaccuracies inherent in the label with the inaccuracies of his own problem-solving processes.

PERCEPTION OF CLINICAL PROBLEMS

Inter-practice variability

These difficulties, arising from the confusion of inaccuracies in the use of diagnostic labels and the inherent deficiencies of the labels themselves, are evident in the results from the National Morbidity Surveys (NMS).[5-7] We can take the data in *Table 1* as an example. In the first (1970–1971) and second (1971–1972) years of the second NMS, 60 and 43 practices took part respectively. Among these practices were 25 single-handed practitioners who

Table 1   *Diagnostic accuracy (range and mean) in a one month study of all clinical problems by 11 general practitioners*

	range	mean
0 no diagnosis	(2.2–15.2)	7.9%
1 tentative diagnosis	(14.6–60.6)	29.6%
2 exclusion of serious alternatives	(0–15.6)	5.9%
3 firm diagnosis	(25.6–72.4)	55.1%

Taken from Royal College of General Practitioners (Research Committee of Council) (1958) Continuing Observations and Recording of Morbidity. *Journal of the Royal College of General Practitioners* 1: 107–28.

participated in both years. The consultation rates per 1,000 population at risk are given for these 25 practices. The rates are expressed as the means and their standard deviations though, strictly speaking, the standard deviations should be calculated on total consultations for each practice. Four groups of mental illnesses are presented: psychoses; anxiety neurosis; depressive neurosis; and psychogenic problems presenting with physical problems. There are differences in the rates from one year to another, partly because of changes in the participating practices and partly because of secular changes from one year to the next. The most important point about these consultation rates is the huge standard deviation. Another way of presenting this is to show the fifth and ninth percentile rates in each year for each of these four categories and for all mental illness combined (*Table 3*). The standard deviations for psychoses are so large that it is clear that the individual practice rates cannot be normally distributed and therefore in theory should not be analysed by parametric statistical techniques.

It is not surprising, therefore, that there is a factor difference between the fifth and ninety-fifth centiles of five for depressive-neuroses in males (1971–1972), the category with the smallest factorial difference. These results make

Table 2   *National Morbidity Survey (NMS) II consultation rates per 1,000 population at risk for the 25 participating single-handed practices in year 1 and year 2 of second NMS*

	1970–1971 mean (SD)	1971–1972 mean (SD)	correlation coefficient
psychoses	36.09 (34.13)	32.57 (39.22)	0.86
anxiety neuroses	79.64 (71.57)	91.15 (67.72)	0.93
depressive neuroses	102.97 (63.91)	110.14 (65.68)	0.83
psychogenic physical disorders	44.34 (35.45)	31.16 (30.80)	0.80

Table 3   *National Morbidity Survey II, 5th and 95th percentiles standardized morbidity ratios based on consultation rates (1970–1971 and 1971–1972)*

	1970–1971				1971–1972			
	5th		95th		5th		95th	
	m	f	m	f	m	f	m	f
anxiety neuroses	12	18	192	183	24	26	185	150
depressive neuroses	27	26	212	205	37	28	186	181
psychogenic physical disorders	0	3	298	313	4	0	272	265
all mental disorders	52	58	175	161	52	58	159	146

it certain that the practitioners concerned could not possibly have been perceiving and interpreting the clinical problems of their patients in any kind of standardized way or using consistent criteria with any *a priori* agreement.

Consistency of perception

Notwithstanding this enormous variability between individual practitioners, there is evidence of consistency in the way in which each recorder continues to use his/her own idiosyncratic perceptions and definitions of mental illness. This emerges from the correlation coefficients of the scores in one year for any one practitioner with the score in the second year (*Table 2*). All these correlation coefficients are above 0.8, and for anxiety neuroses are as high as 0.93. For all mental illness combined, the correlation coefficient is 0.96. These large correlation coefficients indicate consistency of a very high order from one year to another.

Variability in management ('action')

These ranges of variation are evident for all other practice activities which have been measured in general practice. A selection of these is given in *Tables 4* and *5*. Equally, there is equivalent consistency and perseverance in performance from one time period to another, as demonstrated by the correlation coefficients for these other activities (*Tables 4* and *5*). The correlation coefficients are highest for those categories of the classification system with the lowest information content in their rubrics. Highest of all ($r = 0.96$) is the consistency of performance in perceiving and labelling mental illness. Lowest of all ($r = 0.48$) is 'infectious and communicable' diseases.

Psychotropic drug prescribing

This inter-doctor variability is also evident in psychotropic drug prescribing. *Table 6* shows the range of rates from 100 British and 40 Belgian practitioners. There was a fourfold difference between the highest and the lowest practice rates for patients consulting with mental illness in the Second National Morbidity Survey. The equivalent range for the prescription of psychotropic

Table 4   *Comparison of workload measures in all practices in the second National Morbidity Survey, 1970–1971 and 1971–1972*

workload measure	1970–1971 mean	(SD)	1971–1972 mean	(SD)	correlation coefficient
patients consulting per 1,000 population at risk	660	(74)	678	66	0.90
episode rate per person at risk	1.80	(0.41)	1.87	0.41	0.92
consultation per person at risk	3.17	(0.74)	3.28	0.73	0.93
inpatient and outpatient referrals per 1,000 population at risk	111	(42)	111	49	0.87

Taken from Royal College of General Practitioners (1984) Occasional Paper No. 25. Social Class and Health Status Inequalities or Difference. April. Table 9, p. 6.

Table 5 *Consultation and correlation of individual practice consultation rates*.
Second National Morbidity Survey 1970–1971 (rates per 1,000 patients at risk)*

	1970–1971 mean (SD)	1971–1972 mean (SD)	correlation coefficient
ineffective and parasitic disorders	127 (61)	135 (51)	0.48
mental disorder	367 (180)	360 (189)	0.96
disease of nervous system	230 (59)	226 (61)	0.84
cardiovascular disease	294 (101)	288 (115)	0.89
respiratory disease	642 (195)	613 (192)	0.93
genito-urinary disorders	173 (57)	168 (48)	0.90
all consultations	3458 (741)	3320 (792)	0.94

*Rates derived from 25 single-handed recorders chosen where there had been no change in principal from one year to another.
Taken from Royal College of General Practitioners (1984) Occasional Paper No. 25. Social Class and Health Status – Inequality or Difference, April. Table 10, p. 6.

Table 6 *A comparison of median values and range of results for psychotropic drugs prescribing (rates per 1,000 consultations) from the United Kingdom (100 practitioners) and Belgium (40 practitioners)*

	min.	20th centile	40th centile	median	60th centile	80th centile	max.
UK (100 GPs)	40	110	160	187	218	267	415
Belgium (40 GPs)	39	97	120	134	144	196	358

Results taken from Practice Activity Analysis returns to Birmingham Research Unit (RCGP).

drugs is tenfold. Incidentally, the whole of the excess of psychotropic drug prescribing is related to repeat prescribing, and approximately 60 per cent of this excess to repeat prescriptions given without a face-to-face consultation with the patient (*Figure 1*).

These huge ranges of variation between the rates in different practices can be shown to have very little to do with characteristics of the patients or of the environment. At the same time, it has also been shown that almost none of the variance can be attributed to conventional characteristics of either the practices or the general practitioners normally considered in such comparative situations.[8] How, then, does this paradox affect our conventional view of clinical problem solving?

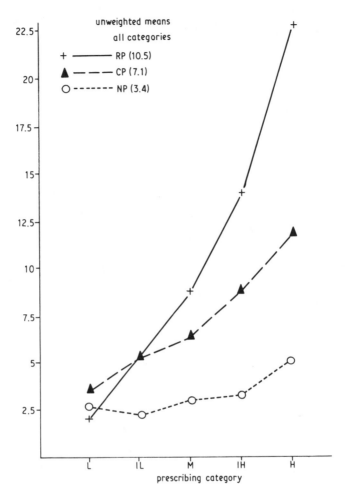

Figure 1 Psychotropic drug prescription rates per 1,000 list by prescribing category and mode

Source: Fleming, D. M. and Cross, K. W. (1984) Practice activity analysis – psychotropic drug prescribing. *Journal of the Royal College of General Practitioners*, April, 216–20.

Implications of this consistent variability

Logically we should devise a primary set of direct links between appropriate problem labels and actions. Howie[9] has already indicated the outline of such an approach for problems involving respiratory infections. The essence of such an approach, as implied in the word *appropriate*, is that all possible alternative actions which are open must determine the classification and identification of the problems. Such a taxonomy will not necessarily be identical with norological system of problems which is based on and organized by the organic and psychiatric aetiology and pathology underlying these problems. This 'direct' type of clinical problem solving (*Figure 2*) was evident in the effective treatment of malaria and cinchona bark, the prevention of smallpox by vaccination and the treatment and prevention of scurvy by lemon and lime juice long before any scientific 'cause and effect' models existed.

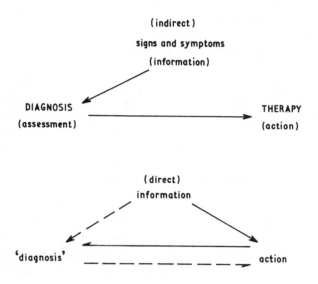

Figure 2   Clinical problem solving

Source: Crombie, D. L. (1975) The rationale of clinical problem solving. In J. P. Nicholson (ed.) *Scientific Aids in Hospital Diagnosis*. New York: Plenum Press, p. 251.

A calculus of probabilities based on therapeutic action for example rather than on formal diagnoses requires only the frequency distributions of all possible actions with the frequency distributions of all possible problems associated with those actions for the Bayesian approach to be appropriate. The frequencies will, of course, depend on scientific appraisal by controlled trial of actual clinical situtations. A suitable set of problem labels will be *dictated* by the initial and primary set of all possible actions.

In parallel to this direct problem/action model, runs the indirect conventional illness/formal diagnosis model (*Figure 2*).

A rational problem-solving strategy, however, employs the opportunities presented by both systems running in parallel. There are various *ad hoc* tactical rules which enable these two strategies to be integrated. The direct problem/action model has the following virtues or benefits:

1. it is more economical of time and other resources than the indirect model;
2. it has a better chance of indicating appropriate action in the simpler problems where patients are not seriously ill and where actual knowledge of the indirect links to aetiology and pathology are not known;
3. it is entirely reproducible within the limits of the explicit criteria and definitions used for labels;
4. it often indicates relevant action when the more complex system is unable to do so; and
5. in cases of doubt, the indirect system can be invoked as a fail-safe.

However, the direct system is not an alternative to the indirect system. Ideal clinical problem solving involves the dynamic integration of both systems. For example, with the patient who presents initially with a cough, problem solving would switch from the direct system to the indirect system if the clinician regards him/her as being seriously ill; or, at a later stage, whether seriously ill or not, abnormal chest signs are disclosed; or there should come to light any other information which might suggest that the patient could be seriously ill, e.g. the continuation of symptoms a week after taking antibiotics.

WHAT IS A SCIENTIFIC 'APPROACH' TO PROBLEM SOLVING?

There are many ways of defining a scientific approach, but basically they all aim at consistently achieving appropriate answers to consistently perceived problems. All the elements in this chain must be understood and therefore be describable in terms which are explicitly shared by the problem solvers. There must be a shared model of the process in which the elements will be consistently identified with the same aspect of real problems by all users. This shared consistency of perception and subsequent action is only achieved by a common symbol system with shared consistent criteria and definitions for all the terms. Finally, the elements of this model should be linked as a 'cause and effect' sequence to model the events as they occur in reality.

The *minimum* element of such a scientific model must therefore be symbols for all possible problems in the context of the problem-solving area, linked to symbols for all possible appropriate actions as a response to those problems. This consistency in the use of the symbols demands sufficient specification of both problems and actions for real problem situations to be perceived consistently by different observers. This is the essence of all consistent communications using natural language.

The set of definitions and criteria for the different problem situations needs only to be detailed enough to consistently identify each possible problem from all the other possible problems that may be met by the problem solver. This is analogous to the way in which economy is possible with natural language by restricting the universal to the local context, which can actually be perceived by the communicants. For example, it is only necessary for one parent to say 'the baby is crying' for the other parent to know for certain that 'the' baby from the millions of all possible babies must be their only child for that child is the only one within the perceived or relevant context.

Our example of the patient with a cough can only be as simple as it is because the problem-solving context is so restricted. 'Cough' restricts us to the context of the 'respiratory' system, and 'yellow' sputum makes it highly likely that it is the 'infectious' sub-context from all others. Absence of bronchospasm as an abnormal physical sign, or on questioning, probably excludes the allergic respiratory context.

There are certain paradoxical implications of this argument. The most important is the variability of meaning of words as symbols according to context or sub-context. For example, 'cough' in the infectious respiratory sub-context is simply the entry point and further discrimination of a problem immediately moves on to other criteria – sputum, wheeze, etc. However, in a patient with a past history of carcinoma of the ovary, the onset of cough has other implications based on the different frequencies of occurrence of cough with other characteristics, such as pulmonary secondaries which are associated with neoplasm compared with the simple respiratory infectious contexts. This problem of differences in meaning with different contexts is at its most obvious in the dichotomy or organic and psychogenic pathologies.

The scientific approach is one which puts a premium on external model making and therefore also on symbols with unequivocal meaning. The art of clinical problem solving is to know when the direct problem–action model (*Figure 2*) can safely be used. On the whole, this is in circumstances where the problem solver is certain that the condition is not 'serious', or, if 'serious', that there is no specific action which, if not invoked, would be to the patient's detriment. The first is the pathway via the causal links from the problem to its aetiology or cause on the one hand and to the detailed pathological changes which have taken place in the patient's psyche and soma on the other. This detailed additional knowledge provides the basis for the conventional choice of a logically appropriate management plan.

All these processes are implicit in the labels used to symbolize them. The model will have weaknesses and deficiencies to the extent that the labels, and/or the perceptive and other cognitive processes of the problem solver, are defective.

The examples given here have not been for mental illness. This is mainly because there is even less of a consensus about clinical actions in this area than there would be for minor respiratory complaints. For example, it could be that the only actions that are relevant to the management of mental illness are subsumed by effective anti-depressant drugs; manipulation of interpersonal relationships; sympathetic understanding by the professional problem-solver and/or others involved in the patients' problems; phenothiazine and other drugs appropriate to 'psychotic' conditions; manipulation of physical environment and work situation; involvement in appropriate group activities; and anxiolytic drugs.

In this caricature of the real life situation, 'depression' would be defined as a mental illness which is helped by 'anti-depressant' drugs. Perhaps the most important general point to be made by this roundabout examination of the problem of classification of mental illness is that such an examination is almost meaningless unless carried out in the larger context of the whole diagnostic, assessment and management process.

There is one other important souce of inaccuracy in labelling. Many clinical problems have an organic and psycho-emotional component, but the conventional classification system demands a label which is one or the other. For example,[10] where general practitioners use a conventional classification system, 5 per cent of males and 10 per cent of females will be diagnosed as suffering from psycho-emotional problems. However, a very different picture emerges if the practitioners are asked to allocate the problem to one of five categories:

1. an illness all or nearly all organic;
2. an illness, mainly organic, but with some abnormal emotional context;
3. an illness with emotional and organic components in equal proportion;
4. a mainly emotional illness but with some organic content;
5. an illness all, or nearly all, emotional.

This classification renders it possible to make a realistic assessment even though the subjective element must vary from practitioner to practitioner. The results in one study involving twelve practitioners[10] were reasonably consistent. On average, the emotional element was at least as important as the organic in 27 per cent of all illnesses encountered by those practitioners, and was appreciable in a further 21 per cent. The discrepancy between these figures and the usually accepted figure of 5–10 per cent is a measure of the distortion introduced by current medical nomenclature.

IMPLICATIONS FOR RESEARCH

These anomalies, superficially, might seem to preclude any scientific inquiry involving classification of clinical and administrative activity in any general practice, mental illness apart. However, all is not lost in this strange situation of enormous inter-doctor variability and counter-balancing doctor consistency in performance over time. Where the patient or the population is the area of interest, then rates can still be meaningful provided that the sample of patients is drawn in such a way as to include patients from a sufficient number of individual general practitioners. For example, from the National Morbidity Survey we find that, provided the sample is from a mimimum of about twenty practitioners or practices, the mean and standard deviations stabilize.

For this reason the data from the National Morbidity Survey can be dis-aggregated to three regional areas of Great Britain, north, middle and south, but not to the thirteen standard regions. There is only one standard region with more than four practices.

In any study where the effects of some external factor like a drug are being examined, the results will still be satisfactory, provided that the study is confined to the same group of doctors for any before and after or alternative A and alternative B situations. So long as (a) each control group and index case is drawn from the same populations, and (b) the same general practitioner assumes clinical responsibility over the whole time of the study, then com-parative data will give sound results. However idiosyncratic the practitioner may be in perceiving and recording morbidity or any other characteristic of the patient, this idiosyncrasy will be equally evident in controls and index cases both in any one period and any subsequent period of time. Without some agreed nomenclature, however unsatisfactory in other respects, there is babel.

Finally, there is the new Classification of The Royal College of General Practitioners. We may look briefly at its section on mental illness.

This classification system was designed primarily for micro-computer usage. The number of rubrics has been increased, and categories additional to those found in the ICD have been added (*Table 7*). The limitation on numbers of rubrics is set primarily by the number of sheets that can be comfortably held in a manual indexing system (approximately 500 at the most) and, second, by the problems of looking up indexes when the alternatives exceed this number. Both these limitations are by-passed by the computer-based system which will accept any label and find its own way to the appropriate classifying rubric within the system. However, for the rubrics in the mental illness chapter, the compatibility with the ninth revision of the International Classification of Diseases is complete, except for the categories of smoking which are included here. There are, in addition, eight extra sections (*Table 8*) which supplement the morbidity classification based on ICD–9. Some of these are obviously relevant to the classification of clinical problems involving mental illness. This principle of multi-dimensional classification systems could be extended to include axes for disability, impairment, and handicap presenting symptoms and/or reasons for encounter and dependency.

CRITERIA AND DEFINITIONS

It could be maintained that a first step must be the establishment of agreed definitions and criteria for all the terms used in any classification system. Within our own working systems, we have taken the line that practitioners should use the accepted textbook criteria where a scientific consensus exists. For the more serious conditions and for conditions like the exanthemata, with characteristic and consistent stigmata, this works reasonably well. For the

Table 7   *Mental disorders*

1000   290
        dementia
        pre-senile dementia
        pre-senile dementia (giving psychiatric symptoms)

1005   291
        alcoholic psychosis
        delirium tremens
        Korsakoff's psychosis

1010   292
        drug induced psychosis

1015   293, 294
        other transient organic psychosis
        other chronic organic psychosis
        puerperal psychosis

1020   295
        paranoid schizophrenia
        schizophrenia

1025   296
        endogenous depression
        hypomania
        manic depressive psychosis
        mania
        psychotic depression

1030   297
        paranoid state
        paraphrenia

1035   298, 299
        other non-organic psychoses
        childhood autism

1040   300
        anxiety state (except causing specific somatic complaint)
        neurotic personality
        anxious personality

1045   300.1
        hysteria
        panic attacks

1050   300.2
        phobia state
        agoraphobia
        claustrophobia
        phobic anxiety

1055   300.3
        obsessional neurosis

1060 300.4
neurotic depression (excluding brief situation depression reaction)
reactive depression (excluding brief situation depression reaction)
anxiety/depression
agitated depression

1065 300.5
neurasthenia

1070 300.7
hypochondriasis

1076 300.6, .8, .9
other neuroses

1080 301
hysterical personality
psychopathic personality
depressive personality
personality disorder (deeply ingrained maladaptive behaviour)
explosive personality
asthenic personality
inadequate personality
cyclothymic personality
schizoid personality

1085 302.0
homosexuality (male and female)
lesbianism

1090 302.1, .2, .3, .4, .5, .6, .8, .9
sexual deviation (except homosexuality)

1095 302.7
dyspareunia (psychogenic)
frigidity
impotence
lack of libido
psychosexual problems
premature ejaculation

1100 303
alcoholism (excluding psychosis)
alcoholic, sober
alcohol problem

1110 304
glue sniffing
addiction to drugs (excluding drug psychosis)

1115 305.0
drunkenness
hangover, alcoholic
alcohol abuse, non-dependent

1120 non-smoker

1125 smoker, pipe
smoker, cigar (does not inhale)

1130 smoker <5 cigarettes/day)

1135 305.1
smoker 5–15 cigarettes/day

1140 smoker >15 cigarettes/day

1145 ex-smoker (to record date when stopped)

1150 306.1
hyperventilation
psychogenic aphonia
air hunger

1155 306.2
cardiac neurosis

1160 306.4
aerophagy
air swallowing
nervous stomach

1165 306.5
vaginismus (psychogenic)

1170 307.1
anorexia nervosa

1175 307.4
sleep disorder (of non-organic origin)
insomnia (of non-organic origin)

1180 307.5
feeding problem (due to behaviour problem in childhood)
pica
psychogenic vomiting
bulimia nervosa

1185 307.6
enuresis (of emotional origin, excluding incontinence of urine nos)
nocturnal enuresis

1190 307.8
tension headache (excluding migraine)
psychogenic backache
psychogenic back pain (excluding lumbago)

1200 308, 309
examination phobia
bereavement reaction
grief reaction
transient situational disturbance
adjustment reaction
brief situational reaction
acute stress reaction
stress (due to acute transient situational disturbance)

1205 310
      mental disorder following organic brain damage
1210 310–314
      behaviour disorder (any age excluding personality disorders)
      delinquency
      kleptomania
      overactive child
1215 315
      dyslexia
      specific learning delay (excluding mental retardation)
1220 317, 319
      mental retardation
1225 306.0, .3, .5, .6, .8, .9, 307.0, .2, .7, 316, 505.2–.9
      other mental, psychological, or psychophysiological disorder
      stammer and stutter
      tic

Taken from Occasional Paper Royal College of General Practitioners (1984) No. 26. Classification of Diseases, Problems and Procedures, 1984. May, p. 16.

Table 8 *Additional group F categories – new College classification*

contact and carriers of disease
patients on high risk medication
history of drug allergy
family history of illness
administrative procedures
general medical examinations and screening
screening procedures
surgical operations
medically relevant life events

Taken from Royal College of General Practitioners (1984) Occasional Paper No. 26. Classification of Diseases, Problems and Procedures, 1984. May.

infectious and communicable diseases routinely surveyed by our Weekly Returns system we go further and have a supplementary, arbitrary definition for certain categories, for example, 'influenza-like' illness. We also hold inquiries to establish what criteria may have been used for diagnoses when retrospective studies are carried out, using the National Morbidity Survey files as the baseline. Such studies have been carried out, for example, in malignant hypertension, cerebro-vascular accidents, Parkinson's Disease, hay fever and gout.

The World Organisation of National Colleges, Academies, and Academic Associations of General Practitioners/Family Physicians (WONCA) is about to produce a set of arbitrary definitions for the 300+ rubrics in their short-list of the ICD–9 for primary care usage. This will be available soon. However, two problems remain. The first, and most important, is that the information necessary for these definitions does not exist for many categories, and this is particularly so for mental illness. Arbitrary definitions in this situation can simply stultify and frustrate any further scientific examination of the disorders. Second, the poor understanding of the conditions means that there will be many clinical situations where one or more of the criteria may not be met and the problem must be allocated to some residual or grouped category. This problem can be partially solved by having two categories for every rubric: (a) conditions fulfilling all criteria; and (b) conditions not fulfilling all criteria but where the rubric is still believed to be appropriate.

CONCLUSIONS

I have concentrated in this presentation on the problems that relate to classification systems. At the moment there is no complete answer to these difficulties. We believe that the sort of classification devised for the National Morbidity Surveys and the more recent extended classification system for use in the micro-computer age are reasonable compromises and must suffice until we have more knowledge and information about the clinical situations which the rubrics purport to describe.

Classification systems must be relevant to their purpose. Those for research purposes will be different from those for clinical purposes, and for primary care, with its emphasis on primary assessment of clinical problems, and will be different from those for specialized clinical areas. Any general purpose classification system will need to be multi-dimensional.

REFERENCES

1. Cohen, H. (1943) The nature, methods and purpose of diagnosis. *Lancet* i: 23.
2. Royal College of General Practitioners (Research Committee of Council) (1963) Disease Labels. *Journal of the Royal College of General Practitioners* 7: 29, 197–204.
3. —— (Research Committee of Council) (1958) Continuing Observations and Recording of Morbidity. *Journal of the Royal College of General Practitioners* 1: 107–28.
4. Department of Community Medicine, University of Nottingham (1984) Proceedings of the Nottingham Decision Making Workshop (in preparation).
5. Office of Population Censuses and Surveys, RCGP, DHSS (1974) Studies on Medical and Population Subjects No. 26. Second National Study, 1970–1971. *Morbidity Statistics from General Practice*. London: HMSO.

6. —— (1979) Studies on Medical Population Subjects No. 36. Second National Study 1971–1972. *Morbidity Statistics from General Practice*. London: HMSO.
7. —— (1982) Studies on Medical Population Subjects No. 46. Socio-economic analyses. *Morbidity Statistics from General Practice*. 1970–1971. London: HMSO. London: HMSO.
8. Crombie, D. L. (1984) Social Class and Health Status Inequality or Difference. McConaghy Memorial Lecture. Occasional paper 25. *Journal of the Royal College of General Practitioners* April.
9. Howie, J. (1972) Diagnosis – the Achilles heel. *Journal of the Royal College of General Practitioners* 22: 310–15.
10. Crombie, D. L. (1963). The Procrustean Bed of Medical Nomenclature. *Lancet*, June: 1205–206.

Rachel Jenkins

Discussant

Dr Crombie has discussed the main sources of uncertainty in clinical problem-solving, namely the variation in the way in which problems are identified and diagnosed by doctors, and the lack of aetiological and pathological knowledge at present about our diagnostic entities. He has shown us most interesting data from the National Morbidity Survey which demonstrate the enormous inter-practice variation in consultation rates for the different mental disorders, indicating that the GPs cannot possibly be diagnosing clinical problems in any standardized way. Dr Graham Dunn, from the General Practice Research Unit, has also highlighted this issue by his own work on the second National Morbidity Survey, where he found that in one practice almost 10 per cent of the registered patients were diagnosed as suffering from affective psychosis at least once during the six years of the survey, whereas in most practices there were no records at all. As Dr Dunn has pointed out, considerable emphasis needs to be placed on evolving standard diagnostic criteria before such surveys can provide valid data on national morbidity.

Professor Clare and Dr Blacker have given us a careful review of modern classificatory systems of affective disorder in primary care, demonstrating their major shortcomings, particularly when psychological illness occurs in the context of physical disease with its own weight loss, appetite loss, malaise and irritability. It is clear that until we can improve our classification systems so that doctors can apply them in a valid and reliable manner, both clinical work and research are grossly handicapped. The importance of this need cannot be stated too strongly.

Classification is one of the devices for bringing order out of chaos both in the universe and in our own thinking. It divides a given set of things into sub-classes. Each of the sub-classes is defined by specifying the necessary and sufficient conditions of membership in it; that is, by stating the characteristics which all and only the members of this sub-class must possess.

The specification of a classificatory system therefore requires a corresponding set of classificatory concepts, and each class in the system is based on one of those concepts. This means that the establishment of a suitable system of classification in a given domain of investigation may be considered as a special kind of scientific concept formation which endeavours to describe, explain, and predict.

Thus, not only do we need clear and objective criteria of application but also, to be scientifically useful, a concept must lend itself to the formulation of general laws or theoretical principles which reflect uniformities in the subject matter under study, and which thus provide a basis for explanation, prediction and in general, scientific understanding. For example, the periodic table has been shown to reflect atomic structure, taxonomy in biology, and evolutional phylogeny. Similarly, for mental disorders, I would argue that our ultimate aim must be to develop a classificatory system whose conceptual basis is clear and systematic.

Dr Crombie has carefully argued the case for the view that the purpose of all clinical problem solving is the reduction of uncertainty in the choice of appropriate action taken to ameliorate, frustrate, anticipate, or resolve our patients' problems. This is the treatment-oriented approach. However, if classification is limited to this purpose it can only be as complex as our range of treatment options, and can only be refined alongside treatment developments. Important descriptive information may then be ignored or lost, and opportunities for refining our classification system may not be taken.

Professor Clare and Dr Blacker do not doubt that classification is an essential activity, independent of treatment options, and point out that for the present, psychiatric labels are essentially descriptive. Our range of treatments at present are few, and while our knowledge of aetiology is increasing, it is frequently very difficult to distinguish aetiological factors from consequential factors in a clinical setting. It is clear that the single label, naming a syndrome, is grossly inadequate for psychiatric purposes, and none of the International Classification of Diseases (ICD) or Diagnostic and Statistical Manual (DSM) series of classifications systems has achieved mutually exclusive categories. Within primary care, most psychological disorders could be termed depressive neurosis or anxiety neurosis. While this may be of some value to Dr Crombie, in that it might indicate the use of an anti-depressant or an anxiolytic, it has major shortcomings, in that no account is taken of more precise phenomenological features, any concurrent physical disorders in which the

psychological illness may be influential or consequential, the social environment, the social consequences, or the constitution and temperament of the
patient. An overall formulation is obviously a better tool for the clinician than
a single label, and it is this realization which underlines current attempts to
develop a multi-axial system of classification.

Attention must, of course, be paid to the particular features of illness at the
primary care level which will influence the value of any particular system of
classification. In primary care there is a high incidence of transient morbidity,
and illness is often seen early in its inception before the full clinical picture has
developed. The presenting conditions, furthermore, are often a complex
mixture of physical, emotional, and social elements, and the GP has a continuous relationship with his patients which transcends individual episodes of
illness.

Professor Shepherd, Dr Marinker and I have been showing videotaped
consultations in general practice to highly experienced GPs and have found
that, while it is possible to obtain agreement on what may be called multiaxial
observations (that is, important psychological, social, and physical and
personality features), there is relatively low agreement on the assignment of
either ICD or International Classification of Health Problems in Primary
Care *diagnoses*, or indeed, on the GPs own formulation. One example is a
tape of a middle-aged man with a history of cardiac surgery, who presents in
the surgery with pain in his arm, shows agitation at the then recent assassina-
tion of Lord Mountbatten and actually breaks down and cries in the interview.
The labels applied by the GPs who watched the tape ranged from 'miseries –
going through a bad patch', through 'a man who is sensitive to external
happenings and has difficulty coping', through 'mild anxiety state', 'anxiety
depressive state', 'depression with residue of agitation', 'depression' to
'affective psychosis – depressed type'. It was, therefore, to be expected that
agreement on management was only moderate. Such results highlight the
present inadequacies of ICD and ICHPPC for primary care, and underline
the potential value of developing a multi-axial method of classifying patients
in this context.

General Discussion

Dr. G. Dunn: I should like to underline the lack of validity in GPs' diagnosis of psychiatric disorders and to ask Dr Crombie, in face of this deficiency (1) how one assesses treatment effectiveness which involves some sort of formal service evaluation or a controlled clinical trial, and (2) how does one carry out effective epidemiological studies? The problems arise strikingly from the interpretation of the second National Morbidity Survey from which I have studied the psychiatric records.

Dr Crombie has emphasized the fact that the variability between GPs on any psychiatric diagnosis is considerable. By far the most common disorder recognized by GPs seems to be anxiety, although as soon as a psychiatrist goes into a practice the most common disorder appears to be depression. The data in the National Morbidity Survey appear to be records of GP opinion, and they lack validity. How can published national statistics such as the second National Morbidity Survey tell one anything about true levels of morbidity? What I should like to see is far more effort put into validating these methods rather than repeating the same sort of surveys over and over again.

Dr. D. L. Crombie: Let me start with the point on the evaluation of outcome and treatment. The one great saving grace about this situation, and presumably why controlled trials have produced valid results from general practice, is that in any kind of controlled trial the control includes the same practitioner as the person perceiving and recording whatever is to be perceived and recorded about index and control cases, so that all his/her prejudices and aberrations are distributed equally between the two groups. Equally with treatment, if he/she has some idiosyncratic way of treating, then that idiosyncrasy is equally and even-handedly distributed across the practice.

Coming back to the validity of what is going on and what we are measuring, I do not accept Dr Dunn's criticisms except in respect of his comment that there is no point in repeating the same procedures that we have been carrying out. I should be very surprised if there is another National Morbidity Survey exactly the same as the last one. However, there is a very good reason for carrying out the third one which has just been completed: a large minority of the participating practices also took part in the second survey and we have here a method of studying one group of doctors self-controlled over a ten year period. On this basis I think we can start to sort out secular changes with some prospect of success.

Dr J. C. Ingham: One of the problems in this field is that by and large general practitioners and psychiatrists are dealing with different populations. The methods of classification and diagnostic instruments which have been developed have on the whole been developed within the context of mental hospitals and psychiatric clinics, and therefore they are appropriate for classifying patients at a fairly severe level of psychiatric disorder. I do not have any precise figures, but most of the psychiatric patients in primary care, the depressives for example, are most likely to be suffering from minor depression in Research Diagnostic Criteria (RDC) terms; a relatively small proportion come into the major depressive category; and most primary care patients present minor depression or anxiety states. It seems to me, therefore, that in primary care there is great overlap between normal reactions to problems of living and psychiatric illness.

I am a strong advocate of the continuum concept of illness at this level of disorder. Even if one accepts a clear distinction between illness and normal emotional reactions, these can be very hard to distinguish and the general practitioner may be placed in a difficult situation. I would prefer to say that the whole area, certainly up to the level of affective psychoses, is one that is best regarded in terms of a continuum. It then becomes better to talk in terms of the classification of emotion states rather than of classifications of illness.

Professor D. P. Goldberg: While agreeing with Dr Ingham's comments on the continuum model, I have to dispute his assertion that most of the affective diagnoses in primary care are of minor depressions. In fact, the commonest diagnosis in DSM III terms is that of major depressive disorder. Minor depressive illness no longer exists in DSM III, but we have used the concept and have discovered that it is not the commonest form of depressive disorder. Major depression comes first, followed by general anxiety and panic disorder. I would add that both the Present State Examination and the Diagnostic Interview Schedule are gadgets devised by hospital-based psychiatrists for imposing the views of hospital-based psychiatry on the community. What is needed is a multi-dimensional research interview which is geared to the kinds of disorder that occur in the community.

Dr R. Blacker: On the basis of a fairly large number of people seen in general practice I too would regard major depressive disorder as the commonest psychiatric disorder. It is far more prevalent than minor depressive disorder, however defined.

Professor A. W. Clare: I think this is an interesting example of where the discussion about classification ceases to be academic and bears on Graham Dunn's point about validity. It is often assumed that the question is irrelevant because the disorders cannot be differentiated, and that it does not matter very much because our treatments are not particularly effective or, if they are, then many of the patients recover spontaneously. In fact, when a more careful approach is made to primary care, admittedly with the rather crude instruments of classification that we have, it begins to seem as if the nosological confusion is actually contributing to poor patient management.

Dr G. Dunn: As a statistician I am often asked to estimate the numbers required for a clinical trial of some sort of therapy. Take as an example a trial in which some form of placebo leads to 30 per cent recovery, which is fairly common in psychiatric or general practice; further, let us say that you want to test a new form of therapy which is highly specific for one form of disorder and achieves 60 per cent recovery. Using a level of significance of, say, 0.05 and a significance test to assess that therapy and a power of 0.9 – which means that if that effect is there, then your chances of discovering it are 90 per cent – approximately 53 or 55 patients in the controlled and the therapy groups are needed to demonstrate that therapy. If you then take a situation where you have misdiagnosed the patients, and have diluted both control and therapy groups equally by including subjects who are un-responsive to therapy, then the trial size required is about 214, i.e. four times as many people are required to show that the treatment is effective. You can easily work out that the difference you are trying to demonstrate is between 30 and 45 per cent rather than 30 and 60 per cent.

Most clinical trials of psychiatric treatments are very small in size, badly conducted, and dependent on poorly diagnosed patients. The smaller the trial, the more important the need for accurate diagnosis. If you cannot diagnose accurately, you need much larger numbers but you then en-counter the ethical problem of giving patients the incorrect treatment because you have misclassified them.

N. Smeeton: It is most important to agree on the relevant symptoms for each illness, on the understanding that not all symptoms need be present in every case identified. It is, however, also of importance to agree on the levels of severity at which symptoms become medically significant. Some time ago I was involved in a study involving five histopathologists in the grading of fifty biopsy and fifty tumour specimens of rectal cancer. All specimens had been classified as positive cases and they merely had to be graded as being well, moderately, or poorly differentiated. Despite there being only three categories, pairwise agreement was only in the region of 48 per cent to 78 per cent and kappa values ranged from only 0.115 to 0.532. A great deal of the disagreement could be explained in terms of the differing thresholds, at which observers applied the various grades; some were more 'optimistic' than others and some clung to the moderate rating except in extreme cases. Not only in histopathology but in many branches of medicine including psychiatry, the perceived level of severity must influence the chosen remedy. The classification problem should therefore include considerations of this nature.

Professor I. Marks: I should like to play devil's advocate and suggest to our speakers and the discussant that perhaps a lot of the vast amount of energy spent in differentiating depression from anxiety might be misplaced, and that perhaps they could be part of one and the same condition. To say that in several studies anxiety has turned out to be more persistent might simply mean it is a more persistent feature of one and the same condition in which depression, comparable to acute inflammation, remits more readily. In aetiological terms we have as yet no data showing that the phenomena represent two conditions and as far as treatment is concerned, several studies suggest that anti-depressant drugs are effective in some of the anxiety disorders.

Professor J. R. M. Copeland: To take up Professor Marks' point, I would refer to our community studies of the elderly, in which the highest levels of all neurotic symptoms, including anxiety, were to be found in major affective disorder. These decline gradually down the scale to the minor depressive disorders. General practice may be providing a biased sample, whereas in the community one sees a much wider, less concentrated range of conditions, and here there is certainly a continuum of mental disorders, clearly evident among depressive conditions. I would also confirm that the major affective disorders form the largest group, although we find too that minor affective disorders are about as common, though often not recognized by general practitioners. Usually most of these conditions have improved within twelve months, so that the duration of illness is crucial.

Ultimately we may be splitting hairs in trying to refine symptomatic diagnosis in this field. Large numbers of symptoms in various combinations are exhibited by normal people in the community, and they only begin to differentiate as severity increases. The important question is why we are trying to identify these cases. The answer is surely for some kind of intervention or treatment, and we do not know at present which conditions need such intervention. This is perhaps the biggest area on which research should be concentrated.

Finally, I should like to add dementia to the list of conditions in the community for which diagnosis is important. In the early stages it is just as difficult to diagnose as affective disorder.

Dr H. Katschnig: The health care system in Austria is very different from the British NHS. None the less, we have carried out a study of depression in general practice and have found a relatively low diagnostic agreement between research psychiatrists and general practitioners in respect of depression. We have also studied some possible reasons for these differences and have found that the GPs' diagnoses were not based on symptomatology. There is a very close similarity between the profiles of psychologically healthy people and depressed patients in general practice. The research psychiatrist, of course, found a much larger difference between these two groups. The conclusion we have reached, and there is some evidence from other data, is that GPs rely much more on life's stress and life events reported by patients in this setting when they make a diagnosis. This may be another reason for introducing multi-axial systems and attempting to disentangle these axes. As long as psychiatrists fail to do so and continue to use the pragmatic approach to diagnosis we cannot expect GPs to employ a multi-axial system.

Dr I. Falloon: I would like to suggest that we may be tackling this question in the wrong way by assuming that we know more about these disorders than the GPs whom we are trying to teach. Perhaps we ought to go to the grass roots and look at general practice and at general practitioners to try and see that they are actually doing. It seems that they use a very effective and functional problem-orientated approach, something that has been used quite widely in psychiatry, particularly in the United States. It leads away from medical diagnosis to practical management issues. I would suggest that some of us start looking at what the GPs actually do and try to build up a classification system from that level rather than from a theoretical ivory tower.

Dr D. L. Crombie: The multi-dimensional approach applies as much to treatment as to diagnosis in this field. There is no uni-modal treatment in general practice, where no patient is treated by one drug or by a placebo. For this reason therapeutic trials in primary care pose special problems to which the answers must come from an increase in the structure of knowledge. Mental illness appears to differ from our model for organic illness which is the one used commonly.

Professor Adelstein: Having had to use these international and national classifications for my work for many years, I should point out that it is not only in psychiatry that these problems occur but in almost every branch of medicine. My introduction to the difficulties was in a study which involved ten leading London physicians who were asked to diagnose a chest condition. After much trouble in trying to standardize their methods, they ended up in great confusion because of the differences in their concepts of the disorder. The attitude of concentrating too much on the particular areas and on the difficulties may be non-productive. At a certain stage of development of the art you cannot do better than the practising doctors who know that no classifications will change their activities until new knowledge has been established. What one should ask is how to obtain some signals besides all this noise emanating from the current classifications.

In my opinion the National Morbidity Surveys are probably the best sources of information in general about community health in the world. Despite its weaknesses there is a good deal of information to be found in it. For example, there is a clear message that doctors diagnose anxiety and depression differently according to social classes. They diagnose patients in social class V as being depressed and social class I as being anxious. So clearly there are messages besides the noise, and it is important for us to grasp the significance of the messages and not concentrate only on the noise.

PART 2

SCREENING

Paul Williams

Mental illness and primary care: screening

In 1975, the *Lancet* carried a series of articles on various aspects of screening for disease: these provoked an extensive and at times vigorous correspondence. Sackett and Holland (1975), in an assessment of the series and the correspondence, came to the conclusion that one of the major sources of controversy was the failure to distinguish between three related but crucially different procedures: epidemiological surveys, screening, and case-finding.

As Sackett and Holland (1975) observed, *epidemiological surveys* involve the measurement of a variety of health-related and other characteristics in carefully selected representative samples. They noted further that 'because the objective of the survey is new knowledge, no health benefit to the participant is implied' (p. 357).

By contrast, *screening* is a procedure whereby a test is applied to apparently healthy volunteers from the general population, in order to identify those individuals who are at high risk of having otherwise unrecognized disease. Sackett and Holland (1975) point out that although this procedure has in common with the epidemiological survey the characteristic that 'the encounter is initiated by those who do the tests', there is a crucial difference. In prescriptive screening of this kind (McKeown 1968), 'there is an implicit promise that those who volunteer to be screened will benefit, i.e. that they will be followed up to exact diagnosis and long-term care, and will receive treatments of proven efficacy' (Sackett and Holland 1975, p. 357).

In contrast to screening, *case-finding*, according to the definition of Sackett and Holland, is a process whereby patients who have sought health care (e.g. from their general practitioner) are tested, with their consent, for disorders which may be unrelated to their presenting complaint. Crucial differences between this procedure and screening are that here

'the encounter is initiated by the patient, and the purpose is a (more) comprehensive assessment of health. While the results of the manoeuvre (i.e. case-finding) may require long-term arrangements for clinical services case-finding does not carry any implied guarantee that patients will benefit.'

(Sackett and Holland 1975)

With these definitions in mind, we can now consider screening and case-finding for psychiatric disorder. The discussion will largely be concerned with these varieties of morbidity that might be expected to occur most commonly in community and general practice samples, rather than with severe forms of psychiatric disorder. Furthermore, such morbidity will be considered as a whole – 'minor psychiatric morbidity' – rather than in separate diagnostic groups.

SCREENING FOR PSYCHIATRIC DISORDER

According to the definition proposed by Sackett and Holland (1975), a screening programme for psychiatric disorder would be arranged as follows. Members of the public would be contacted, either by letter (e.g. as in the South-East London Screening Study, D'Souza 1979) or by advertisement, and invited to attend for screening. Individuals attending would be given a screening instrument – a questionnaire – the function of which is to classify them into two groups. These are the 'probable cases' and the 'probable normals', those with a low probability of so being. (The issue of how, in such a context, a psychiatric case is defined has been dealt with at length elsewhere; see, for example Blum 1962; Williams, Tarnopolsky, and Hand 1980; Wing 1980; Wing, Bebbington, and Robins 1981. For the present purposes a 'case' can be regarded simply as an individual who would be thought to have clinically significantly psychiatric disturbance if interviewed by a psychiatrist (Goldberg 1972)). Probable cases would then be referred to their general practitioners for confirmatory diagnosis and treatment.

A number of authors have put forward what they consider to be the criteria that need to be met, or the questions that need to be answered, in the evaluation of screening procedures. For example, Wilson and Jungner (1968) outlined ten principles for the evaluation of screening (*Table 1*), while McKeown (1968) listed six areas that should be assessed when a screening programme is being evaluated (*Table 2*). More recently, Grant (1982) has suggested three 'conditions that need to be satisfied' for screening to be medically, socially, and economically justified (*Table 3*), while Simpson,

Table 1   *Criteria for screening: Wilson and Jungner's (1968) ten principles*

1. the condition should be an important health problem;
2. the disease should have an accepted treatment;
3. there should be diagnosis and treatment facilities;
4. there should be a recognizable latent or early symptomatic stage;
5. there should be a suitable test or examination;
6. the screening should be acceptable to the population being surveyed;
7. the natural history of the condition should be understood;
8. there should be agreement on the groups for treatment;
9. the cost effectiveness of screening should be compared with the cost of pre-existing services;
10. case-finding should be a continuous process.

Table 2   *Criteria for screening: McKeown's (1968) six 'areas for assessment'*

1. definition of the problem;
2. the position before screening;
3. evidence concerning the screening procedure;
4. evidence concerning the total problem;
5. proposals for the acquisition of further evidence;
6. proposals for the initial application of the procedure.

Table 3   *Criteria for screening: Grant's (1982) three conditions*

1. the methods must be reliable;
2. the number of positive findings must be commensurate with the cost;
3. evidence is needed that diagnosing the disease before symptoms appear will improve the prognosis.

Chamberlain, and Gravelle (1978) and Drummond (1980) have summarized the economic assessment of screening programmes.

Some years ago, Eastwood (1971) evaluated, on the basis of the then available evidence, screening for psychiatric disorder according to the criteria of Wilson and Jungner (1968). His assessment will be presented and compared with the present state of affairs.

With regard to *criterion 1* (see *Table 1*), Eastwood observed that 'it can be accepted that the condition is an important health problem'. This is of course still true: indeed, there is evidence to suggest that some forms of psychiatric morbidity are becoming increasingly common (Hagnell *et al*. 1982).

For *criterion 2*, Eastwood noted that 'treatment is far from specific in psychiatric disorder . . . the approach to treatment is idiosyncratic'. There is evidence that this is still true today, certainly with regard to the management of psychiatric disorder in general practice (where the bulk of morbidity continues to be managed, Williams and Clare 1981). For example, there is wide variation between GPs in the extent to which they prescribe psychotropic drugs (Royal College of General Practitioners 1978), refer to psychiatrists (Robertson 1979) and there are marked differences in general practitioners' evaluations of patients for social work referral (Williams and Clare 1979). Eastwood also observed that 'evaluation of treatment programmes and their prescribing is required', a remark which is still relevant today.

The continued availability of diagnostic and treatment facilities means that *criterion 3* can still be met. With regard to *criterion 4* ('there should be a recognisable latent or early symptomatic stage'), Eastwood (1971) observed that 'it is not known whether there is a presymptomatic stage', i.e. of psychiatric disorder in the community. Indeed, it is difficult to see how the concept of a 'latent stage' can apply to minor psychiatric disorder at all. This form of morbidity consists almost exclusively of symptoms and problems, so the notion that such a disorder can be said to exist in a latent form, i.e. in the absence of symptoms, seems illogical. Certainly, all the relevant screening instruments consist in symptom questionnaires, so that even if a presymptomatic or latent stage could be said to exist, it could not be identified.

Eastwood (1971) observed that Taylor and Chave (1964) had described 'subclinical neurosis': however, neither this nor the 'threshold level' of Wing *et al.* (1978) can be regarded as presymptomatic conditions, since they are merely levels of symptomatology not high enough to meet the criterion for caseness.

For *criterion 5* ('there should be a suitable test or examination'), Eastwood observed that 'screening instruments have become available during the past few years . . . they have not been used widely'. During the years since these comments were written there has been an explosion of research concerned with the development of screening questionnaires. Most workers (with some exceptions, e.g. Benjamin, Decalmer, and Haran 1982) would probably agree that sufficient knowledge and experience of one or other screening questionnaire has now accumulated to enable these instruments to be used with some degree of confidence.

It must be said, however, that a significant proportion of the work concerned with the evaluation of psychiatric screening questionnaires is methodologically and statistically unsophisticated, and compares unfavourably with instrument evaluation studies conducted within 'mainstream' epidemiology. Common problems include the use of a (second stage) criterion instrument unsuited to the nature of the morbidity under investigation; the testing of a screening instrument on a population different in relevant ways from that on which it is to be used or to which it is said to apply; the failure to adjust indices of agreement for the bias in the 'case mix' of the validation sample, and a failure to appreciate the crucial importance of predictive values in the evaluation of the screening potential of a questionnaire.

With regard to *criterion 6*, Eastwood (1971) observed that screening questionnaires appeared to be acceptable to respondents: no subsequent evidence has emerged to contradict this view.

Criterion 7 requires that 'the natural history of the condition should be understood'. Eastwood observed that in 1972, information on this topic was 'limited'. Since then, a number of longitudinal studies of minor psychiatric morbidity in general practice and in the community (e.g. Mann, Jenkins, and Belsey 1981; Dunn and Skuse 1981; Dunn 1983) have been conducted.

Eastwood (1971) made no comment on *criterion 8* ('there should be agreement on the groups for treatment'), but inherent in the variations in the prescription of treatments referred to in the context of criterion 2 is the notion of considerable current *disagreement* as to who should be treated.

Criterion 9 ('the cost effectiveness of screening should be compared with the cost of pre-existing medical services') calls for a cost-benefit approach (Kollin 1972; Simpson, Chamberlain, and Gravelle 1978; Drummond 1980). Eastwood observed that in 1971 nothing was known about this aspect of psychiatric screening, and this remains the case.

Criterion 10 ('case-finding should be a continuous process') is not really a criterion, but rather a statement about how screening should be carried out. It is possible, like Eastwood, to concur with that view (i.e. that if screening were to be carried out at all, it should be a continuous process).

Eastwood's (1971) assessment caused him to conclude that 'there are many uncertainties . . . for the present, screening for psychiatric disorder must remain at the experimental phase and is not ready for inclusion in the health services'. The implication from his conclusion is that there might come a time when screening for psychiatric disorder *would* become 'ready for inclusion in the health services'. While this may or may not be the case, this time has clearly not yet arrived. This is at least in part the case because of the dearth of pragmatically-based (Schwartz and Lelouch 1967) information about the outcome of treatment, and the absence of information about the relevant cost-benefit relationships (Goldberg 1984a).

It should be pointed out that this conclusion, arrived at largely because of the absence of evidence, is the same as that appertaining to multiphasic screening, obtained on the basis of a large clinical trial (South East London Screening Study Group 1977; D'Souza 1979).

CASE-FINDING FOR PSYCHIATRIC DISORDER

According to the definition proposed by Sackett and Holland (1975) (see p. 58) a case-finding programme for psychiatric disorder would be arranged as follows. All attenders at general practice surgeries would be invited to complete a psychiatric screening questionnaire before seeing the doctor. The information obtained by the questionnaire – essentially the classification of the patient as either a probable case or a probable normal (see p. 58) – would then be available to the general practitioner when he/she sees the patient.

As Sackett and Holland (1975) point out, no promise of benefit is implied, only that the patient will receive the best care available in that situation (i.e. with their general practitioner). Thus, not all of Wilson and Jungner's criteria for screening will apply to case-finding.

For case-finding, just as for screening, the disorder in question should be an important health problem (*criterion 1* – see *Table 1*), and there should be a suitable test (*criterion 5*) which should be acceptable to respondents (*criterion 6*). If the procedure is to be implemented at all, it should probably be on a more or less continuous basis (*criterion 10*).

Case-finding does not require that there be a latent stage to the disorder (*criterion 4*), only that there exists a situation in which the disorder remains unrecognized in the absence of the case-finding procedure. This is clearly the case with regard to psychiatric disorder in general practice. There is by now abundant evidence that the extent of the 'hidden psychiatric morbidity', that is, the psychiatric morbidity presented to general practitioners but not recognized by them as such, can be substantial (e.g. Goldberg and Blackwell 1970; Marks, Goldberg, and Hillier 1979; Goldberg and Huxley 1980; Skuse and Williams 1984).

Because of the absence of an implied guarantee of benefit, it cannot be regarded as mandatory for case-finding that the 'disease should have an accepted treatment' (Wilson and Jungner 1968, *criterion 2*), or that there should be agreement as to who should be treated (*criterion 8*) or that the natural history should be *fully* understood (*criterion 7*). Clearly, these characteristics are desirable, but so they are for medical treatment in general, whether or not special case-finding procedures are used.

Wilson and Jungner's *criterion 9* was that the 'cost effectiveness of screening should be compared with the cost of pre-existing medical services'. Whether or not the benefits exceed the costs (both benefit and cost being used in a broad, rather than exclusively monetary sense) should be a mandatory consideration for any procedure that is recommended for use in a service (rather than a research) setting: this aspect of case-finding for psychiatric disorder in general practice will now be considered in some detail.

CASE-FINDING FOR PSYCHIATRIC DISORDER IN GENERAL PRACTICE – COST-BENEFIT ASPECTS

Consider a consecutive series of patients attending a practitioner. A proportion of them will be suffering from psychiatric disorder that is not recognized as such (i.e. the hidden psychiatric morbidity, or false negatives). The number of such patients will be designated F_{n_1}. Further patients will wrongly be identified by the general practitioner as suffering from psychiatric disorder – the false positives – and their number will be designated F_{p_1}.

A cost (C) is incurred by the false positives. This consists in the costs incurred by visiting the GP (costs incurred by all patients[1]), plus the cost, in terms of distress, of being falsely labelled a psychiatric case, plus possibly the costs (e.g. pain, suffering, time off work) due to the real nature of illness or complaint being undetected.

A cost is also incurred by the false negatives (the hidden psychiatric morbidity): this is equal in value (but different in sign) to the *net benefit* derived from accurate identification of the disorder (i.e. the cost of having one's psychiatric disorder missed is not receiving the benefit that would accrue if the disorder were correctly identified and treated).

The net benefit which accrues from the accurate identification of existing psychiatric disorder is all the benefit (direct and indirect) of accurate diagnosis and treatment, *minus* the cost of attending the doctor and the cost of the treatment (e.g. prescription charges, cost of further attendance). Since this net benefit (B) does not accrue to those whose psychiatric disorder is missed, the cost incurred by them is $-B$.

Consider now the introduction of a case-finding procedure into the practice. In general, case-finding is in itself not costly (Sackett and Holland 1975), and case-finding for psychiatric disorder is no exception. Questionnaires are cheap, and the 'time price' (the time taken to complete and score the questionnaire) is low. Furthermore, the questionnaire itself is unlikely to have a major impact on the course and treatment of psychiatric disorder *after* identification, so it can be assumed that the introduction of a case-finding procedure does not of itself alter the values of B and C.

However, the case-finding procedure will change (hopefully improve) the extent of misidentification, i.e. F_{p_1} and F_{n_1} will change (to F_{p_2} and F_{n_2} respectively). Thus, the unit marginal benefit which accrues as a result of introducing the case-finding procedure is

$$B(F_{n_1} - F_{n_2}) \qquad [1]$$

and the unit marginal cost incurred as a result of introducing the procedure is

$$C(F_{p_2} - F_{p_1}). \qquad [2]$$

Note that $B(F_{n_1} - F_{n_2})$ and $C(F_{p_2} - F_{p_1})$ may each be negative, positive or zero.

The *net* unit marginal benefit of the case-finding procedure is therefore $[1] - [2]$, so that the overall effect of introducing the case-finding procedure is beneficial if the benefit [1] is greater than the cost [2], i.e. if

$$B(F_{n_1} - F_{n_2}) > C(F_{p_2} - F_{p_1}), \text{ or}$$

$$\frac{B}{C} > \frac{F_{n_1} - F_{n_2}}{F_{p_2} - F_{p_1}} \qquad [3]$$

Equation [3] shows that there are two factors which determine whether the introduction of a case-finding procedure for psychiatric disorder into general practice will be beneficial. These are (a) the change in misclassification and (b) the benefit-to-cost ratio.

The change in misclassification which occurs as a consequence of the introduction of a case-finding procedure depends on three factors. First, the 'baseline' accuracy of the general practitioner(s) involved. A general practitioner may, for example, be so accurate that no improvement is possible. There is wide variation in the extent to which individual general practitioners identify psychiatric disorder (Marks, Goldberg, and Hillier 1979; Goldberg and Huxley 1980), so that the extent to which a case-finding procedure can change misclassification may vary accordingly.

Second, psychiatric screening questionnaires vary in their performance. Thus, the change in misclassification consequent on their use may vary, and, in theory at least, could be negative (i.e. the misclassification may be rendered worse).

Third, the change in misclassification will depend on the way in which the result of the screening questionnaire (i.e. the classification of patients into probable cases or probable normals) is taken into account along with the clinical judgement of the general practitioner in coming to a 'caseness decision'. Skuse and Williams (1984) show that there are four such strategies for case finding: *Strategy I* is the baseline, i.e. no case-finding procedure other than the GP's judgement. *Strategy II* is one in which *only* the result of the questionnaire is taken into account – the GP either makes no assessment or ignores it. In *Strategies III and IV*, both GP assessment and questionnaire result contribute information to the caseness decision: in *Strategy III*, a patient is considered to be a psychiatric case if and only if he/she is so classified by *both* questionnaire and GP (acting independently), while in *Strategy IV* a patient is considered to be a case if he/she is so classified by either the questionnaire or the general practitioner.

Skuse and Williams (1984), using Bayesian decision analytic methods (see Weinstein and Fineberg 1980), have derived a set of equations which relate GP performance (i.e. at case identification) and questionnaire performance with the benefit-to-cost ratio (B/C) for the different case-finding strategies outlined above (B/C in equation [3] above is identical to w in Skuse and Williams (1984), and it can be shown that equations [1] to [4] in Skuse and Williams (1984) are each equivalent to Equation [3] above). They show (Skuse and Williams 1984, Equations [7a]–[7d], [8a]–[8d], *Table 9* and *Figure 1*) that it is possible to specify whether any, and if so which, strategy yields a positive marginal net benefit. Furthermore, they show that for a general practitioner whose ability to detect psychiatric disorder is equivalent to the average of the large sample of GPs studied by Marks, Goldberg, and Hillier (1979) and Goldberg and Huxley (1980), using the General Health Questionnaire (GHQ) (Goldberg 1972, 1978) as the case-finding instrument, the introduction of a case-finding procedure using Strategy IV is beneficial if the benefit-to-cost ratio is more than about two.

While the notion that the benefit-to-cost ratio of case-finding for psychiatric disorder in general practice is two or more (i.e. that the net benefit of identifying hidden psychiatric morbidity is more than twice the cost of false labelling) seems reasonable, there are few outcome data available.

Only two studies have attempted to assess the outcome of screening for psychiatric disorder in general practice. Johnstone and Goldberg (1976) compared, using an ingenious experimental design, in one general practice, the one-year outcome of a group of patients whose hidden psychiatric morbidity was revealed by the researchers to the GP (a procedure equivalent to case-finding) with that of a control group whose morbidity remained hidden. Both groups were compared with patients whose psychiatric morbidity was conspicuous.

They found that revealing the hidden morbidity had no effect on the outcome of patients whose morbidity at entry into the study was judged to be 'mild'. However, for patients whose morbidity was judged to be 'severe', exposing the hidden morbidity had a profound and significant effect. For example, there was an average drop in the GHQ score of 6.3 for those whose psychiatric morbidity remained concealed, compared with an average drop of 16.5 for those whose morbidity was revealed to the GP.

Hoeper *et al.* (1984) conducted a study using a somewhat similar design, to investigate the effect of a screening questionnaire (the GHQ) on the *identification* of psychiatric morbidity. They found that there was no effect, indicating, as Goldberg (1984b) pointed out, that the general practitioners who participated in the study appeared not to make use of the additional information provided by the questionnaire. Why this was so remains unclear.

CONCLUSIONS

The conclusions to be drawn from this review are as follows. First, screening for psychiatric disorder in the community (screening being defined according to Sackett and Holland 1975) should not become health policy. Second, case-finding for psychiatric disorder in general practice (case-finding being defined according to Sackett and Holland 1975) should probably be adopted as policy. There exists a method (Skuse and Williams 1984) for estimating, with precision, the likely outcome of introducing a case-finding procedure into general practice. There is, however, a relative shortage of data from which to derive values for cost and benefit to enter into the Skuse and Williams model. These data are urgently needed.

NOTE

1. The cost to the patient of visiting a general practitioner includes: a *direct* cost, i.e. the cost of getting to the surgery; an *opportunity* cost, i.e. the satisfaction foregone

of the activities that would have been carried out if the individual had not been visiting the doctor; and the *cost of treatment*, both direct (e.g. prescription charges) and indirect (via the National Health Service). As used here, the terms *B* and *C* subsume *valuation* as well as pricing of cost and benefit.

REFERENCES

Benjamin, S., Decalmer, P., and Haran, D. (1982) Community screening for mental illness: a validity study of the General Health Questionnaire. *British Journal of Psychiatry* 140: 174–80.

Blum, R. H. (1962) Case identification in psychiatric epidemiology: methods and problems. *Millbank Memorial Fund Quarterly* 40: 253–88.

Drummond, M. (1980) *Principles of Economic Appraisal in Health Care*. Oxford: Oxford University Press.

D'Souza, M. F. (1979) The use of the controlled trial to measure new health care systems: multiphasic screening as an adjunct to the United Kingdom National Health Service. In W. W. Holland, J. Ipsen, and J. Kostrzewski (eds) *Measurement of Levels of Health*, pp. 225–33. World Health Organisation Regional Publications for Europe Series. Copenhagen: World Health Organisation. 7.

Dunn, G. (1983) Longitudinal records of anxiety and depression in general practice: the second National Morbidity Survey. *Psychological Medicine* 13: 897–906.

Dunn, G. and Skuse, D. (1981) The natural history of depression in general practice: stochastic models. *Psychological Medicine* 11: 755–64.

Eastwood, M. R. (1971) Screening for psychiatric disorder. *Psychological Medicine* 1: 197–208.

Goldberg, D. (1972) *The Detection of Psychiatric Illness by Questionnaire*. London: Oxford University Press.

—— (1978) *Manual of the General Health Questionnaire*. Windsor: NFER.

—— (1984a) Measurement of the benefits in psychiatry. In G. Teeling-Smith (ed.) *Measuring the Social Benefits of Medicines*. London: Office of Health Economics, pp. 68–74.

—— (1984b) Screening for mental illness. (Correspondence.) *Lancet* i: 224.

Goldberg, D. and Blackwell, B. (1970) Psychiatric illness in general practice: a detailed study using a new method of case identification. *British Medical Journal* ii: 439–43.

Goldberg, D. and Huxley, P. (1980) *Mental illness in the community: the pathway to psychiatric care*. London: Tavistock Publications.

Grant, I. W. B. (1982) Screening for lung cancer. *British Medical Journal* 284: 1209–210.

Hagnall, O., Lanke, J., Rorsman, B., and Ojesjo, L. (1982) Are we entering an age of melancholy? Depressive illness in a prospective epidemiological study over 25 years: the Lundby Study, Sweden. *Psychological Medicine* 12: 279–90.

Hoeper, E. W., Nycz, G. R., Kessler, L. G., Burke, J. D., and Pierce, W. E. (1984) The usefulness of screening for mental health. *Lancet* i: 33–5.

Johnstone, A. and Goldberg, D. (1976) Psychiatric screening in general practice. *Lancet* i: 605–08.

Kollin, D. (1972) A note on the cost-benefit problem in screening for breast cancer. *Methods of Information in Medicine* 2: 242–47.

Lancet (1975) *Screening for Disease*. A series from the *Lancet*.

Mann, A. H., Jenkins, R., and Belsey, E. (1981) The twelve month outcome of patients with neurotic illness in general practice. *Psychological Medicine* 9: 337–53.

Marks, J., Goldberg, D., and Hillier, V. E. (1979) Determinants of the ability of general practitioners to detect psychiatric disease. *Psychological Medicine* 9: 337–53.

McKeown, T. (1968) *Screening for Medical Care*. London: Nuffield Provincial Hospitals Trust, Oxford University Press.

Robertson, N. (1979) Variation in referral patterns to the psychiatric services by general practitioners. *Psychological Medicine* 9: 355–64.

Royal College of General Practitioners (Birmingham Research Group) (1978) Practice activity analysis: psychotropic drugs. *Journal of the Royal College of General Practitioners* 28: 122–24.

Sackett, D. L. and Holland, W. W. (1975) Controversy in the detection of disease. *Lancet* ii: 357–59.

Schwartz, D. and Lelouch, J. (1967) Explanatory and pragmatic attitudes in therapeutic trials. *Journal of Chronic Diseases* 20: 637–48.

Simpson, P. R., Chamberlain, J., and Gravelle, H. S. E. (1978) Choice of screening tests. *Journal of Epidemiology and Community Health* 32: 166–70.

Skuse, D. and Williams, P. (1984) Screening for psychiatric disorder in general practice. *Psychological Medicine* 14: 365–78.

South-East London Screening Study Group (1977) A controlled trial of multiphasic screening: results of the South-East London screening study. *International Journal of Epidemiology* 6: 257–63.

Taylor, Lord, S. and Chave, S. P. W. (1964) *Mental Health and Environment*. London: Longmans.

Weinstein, M. C. and Fineberg, H. V. (1980) *Clinical Decision Analysis*. Philadelphia, PA: W. B. Saunders.

Williams, P. and Clare, A. W. (1979) Social workers in primary health care: the general practitioner's viewpoint. *Journal of the Royal College of Practitioners* 29: 554–58.

—— (1981) Patterns of psychiatric care. *British Medical Journal* 282: 357–77.

Williams, P., Tarnopolsky, A., and Hand, D. (1980) Case definition and case identification in psychiatric epidemiology: review and assessment. *Psychological Medicine* 10: 101–14.

Wilson, J. M. G. and Jungner, G. (1968) *The Principles and Practice of Screening for Disease*. World Health Organisation Public Health Papers, No. 34. Geneva: World Health Organisation.

Wing, J. K. (1980) Methodological issues in psychiatric case-definition. *Psychological Medicine* 10: 5–10.

Wing, J. K., Mann, S. A., Leff, J. T., and Nixon, J. N. (1978) The concept of a case in psychiatric population surveys. *Psychological Medicine* 8: 203–19.

Wing, J. K., Bebbington, P. and Robins, L. N. (1981) *What is a Case? The Problem of Definition in Community Surveys*. London: Grant MacIntyre.

John Fry

Screening

In 1968, Dr J. M. G. Wilson co-authored a seminal book on screening, namely *Screening in Medical Care* which was published by Oxford University Press for the Nuffield Provincial Hospitals Trust. It happens that I was, and still am, a trustee of the Trust and I recall how important were the meetings that preceded the writing of this book. Lord Cohen of Birkenhead, a fellow trustee, noted in the foreword that there was concern at the uncritical haste which had marked the activities of screening.

The group evaluated the case for screening for ten diseases. They found a case for screening in only four out of ten diseases reviewed – phenylketonuria, rhesus disorder of pregnancy, tuberculosis, and deafness in children. Even with these conditions, however, there were qualifications.

SCREENING: CRITERIA FOR VALUE

Although it is many years since the Nuffield report was published, its principles for evaluating the application of screening still apply. A number of questions were raised for each disease under consideration:

1. What abnormality of medical significance is to be detected or predicted?
2. What preventive or therapeutic actions can be offered?
3. Who (which group) are to be screened?

4. At what stage (of the disease) is detection aimed?
5. What investigations and tests are proposed?

SCREENING FOR MENTAL ILLNESS IN PRIMARY CARE

Let us apply these questions to screening for mental illness in general practice in the British National Health Service.

What are we dealing with?

We know very little about the 'mental illnesses' to be screened for the following reasons:

1. We do not know the real *nature* of the disorders, neither their causation nor their psychopathology.
2. We have no reliable, useful or practical *classification* of mental illnesses in general practice. We may have labels recommended by various authorities, but they are of little help to general practitioners in defining any specific types.
3. There are no agreed practical tests or investigations that can assist in making an accurate *diagnosis* that commands uniform agreement.
4. The *natural history* of mental illness in general practice is unclear and unappreciated. My own observations over thirty years have led me to *a rule of three thirds*. One third of the cases are patients who experience a single episode with no recurrence. One third are individuals who suffer occasional recurrent bouts of illness, depending on various factors. One third suffer from chronic illness and will continue to experience symptoms; they require permanent continuing support and attempts at cure may be disastrous. Which group is screening aimed at and to what purpose?

What form of prevention or therapy?

Is the object of screening to pick up undiagnosed cases at an early stage of their mental illness? If so, what can we offer them?

I know of no medical or social actions that I can use to prevent the condition altogether or to prevent it progressing. There are many factors that can lead to mental illness – personal, familial, genetic, environmental, social, and medical. Most cannot be corrected by me, however hard I try. I can attempt to enable the individual to fit his/her circumstances, but with questionable success. The British National Formulary contains many psychotropic drugs for treating mental illnesses, but I am never sure whether they cure or relieve or whether the improvements, when they occur, are part of the natural history of the disease.

Who is to be screened?

Am I to apply screening to the whole of my practice population or to selected groups?

In my practice the prevalence of diagnosed mental illness is 15 per cent of all consultations or 10–12 per cent of all persons who consult me in a year. A recent survey in the USA reported that 58 per cent of US citizens reported 'problems of well being'. These almost certainly represent psychiatric conditions, albeit of minor degrees. It is suggested that my population is to be screened to discover large numbers of persons who do not consult me at present – then I want to know what I am to offer them.

Screening at what stage and how often?

Does screening intend to pick up mental illness at a pre-clinical phase or later? Is the intention to monitor progress with regular screening during the rest of the patients' lives?

What screening methods?

There are a number of widely researched questionnaires and other tests intended for 'screening' for mental illness. Many have been tried out in my practice. I have not found them of practical value in my everyday normal work. They are useful in trying to relate the GP's diagnosis of mental illness to the patients' feelings and symptoms. They are also of help in standardizing diagnoses among professionals in research exercises.

Questionnaires and other screening methods are well liked by the public and with computerization they will become simpler and quick. The question remains: what is their practical value?

APPLIED COMMONSENSE:

My case against screening for mental illness in general practice therefore rests on a number of propositions:

1. We do not know what we are screening for or whom to screen.
2. We do not know whether earlier diagnosis and treatment will improve on the natural history of these conditions.
3. We are not sure how to use the screening tools in practice or how effective they are.
4. We do not know what the effects of screening may be on use of available resources and on the costs to the National Health Service.

Nevertheless, I am not pessimistic about the problems and management of mental illnesses in general practice and the community. There has been a gradual build-up of our knowledge and we can now make and take decisions on better foundations. There is still need for much more research to be done in order to discover more about their nature and course, to determine what management is most effective and to inform and teach practitioners on these matters. When we know more about these issues, screening may become a useful procedure.

David Goldberg

Discussant

It is clear that ambivalence concerning psychiatric screening still lives on, despite the uncontested evidence that there is a large pool of undetected psychiatric morbidity both in primary care and in general medical settings. These are not freak findings by enthusiasts such as Dr Williams and myself: the findings are absolutely constant, and I have been unable to find a single study where psychiatrists have used research interviews on patients in these settings and not found a substantial proportion of undetected cases. (For review, see Goldberg 1984.)

Given the uniformity of the findings, it is peculiar that the subject is still thought to be controversial, and that critics of screening include such unlikely bedfellows as a senior British general practitioner and the National Institute of Mental Health in Washington (Hoeper *et al.* 1984).

Dr Williams is to be congratulated for attempting to break the deadlock by drawing attention to the distinction between screening and case-finding. There are two major differences between them: case-finding does not have to benefit the patient, nor does it have to intervene at an early or presymptomatic stage. I am really only interested in the second of these, since any procedure which could not be shown to benefit patients would be of academic rather than practical interest. Although Dr Williams is clearly right to say that screening questionnaires in their present form cannot possibly give information about presymptomatic illness, it is by no means clear that they cannot give useful information about psychiatric disorders when they are at an early, undifferentiated stage. The General Health Questionnaire, with which I am naturally most familiar, is focused on a common core of psychophysiological symptoms which cut across diagnoses, and which occur in a wide range of cultural settings.

Let us consider the time sequence of symptom development for an individual patient. All diagnostic systems require the patient to have a certain critical number of symptoms in order to achieve a diagnosis: let us call patients who do not quite reach the criterion 'sub-clinical disorders'. We do not really know enough about the natural history of these disorders, although it seems probable that a majority will remit without developing diagnosable psychiatric illness. However, what of those whose conditions where the symptoms will increase? Would there be advantages in detecting illnesses before they became differentiated, and perhaps before patients became established in new patterns of illness behaviour? This seems to me to be an empirical question, to which we do not at present know the answer. If some future investigator ever shows that such illnesses can be detected early and prevented, then we would have to consider it screening rather than case-finding.

My main problem with the model which Dr Williams has proposed for measuring the costs and benefits of screening is that I think it is over-complicated, much as I admire his facility with equations. As someone who has himself been associated with a rather over-complicated model (Glass and Goldberg 1978) I now realize that the disadvantage of such models is that they terrify the innumerate: in short, no one uses them.

Let me propose a very simple model. We will not be concerned with patients who have conspicuous morbidity, since we shall assume that they would get whatever treatment their doctor thought they should have with or without the screening procedure.

If we only consider results of the screening test for those thought to be non-cases by the doctor, then we need give the second stage case-finding interview only to those who have high scores (by definition, they will be unpredicted high scores).

These patients can be divided into non-cases (false positives) and cases (true positives). The false positives will get the treatment that they would have had if the screening procedure had not existed, and the costs of this will not concern us. Everything hinges on the true positives. These must be assigned to an index and a control condition, since it must be appreciated that there are economic and social consequences of failing to detect disorder, and these must be measured. Dr Williams says in his paper that 'the cost of having one's disorder missed is not receiving the benefit that would accrue if the disorder were correctly identified and treated'. This is less than the truth. We must also include the costs of inappropriate visits to consultants, physical investigations and physical treatments which might have been avoided.

We can now set out our table of costs and benefits. The following can be assigned a cash value:

costs	benefits (in the sense of avoided costs)
health costs	
costs of administering first and second stage screening procedures to all high scorers.	costs of physical investigations, consultations and physical treatments to the control group.
costs of providing appropriate treatment to the index group.	
public sector expenditure	
social security costs for index group.	social security costs for control group.
local authority costs for index group.	local authority costs for control group.

The difference between the above expenditures should be set against the 'soft' costs and benefits, which cannot be measured in cash terms:

non-monetary costs	non-monetary benefits
any distress caused to false positives by the second stage interview (probably negligible).	earlier recovery, or greater loss of symptoms, among the true positives in the index group when compared with the control group.
	value of any increase in leisure time.

It can be seen that we have ignored the false negatives, these being patients who would not have been detected without our screening programme, and which our screening test is not sensitive enough to detect. We will, of course, have carried out a separate study to measure the extent of cases lost in this way, but the only relevance that such a study has to our cost-benefit analysis is that it allows us to fix a threshold for our screening test which minimizes false negatives without imperilling the cost-benefit study by lowering the positive predictive value of the test too much. It must be appreciated that each threshold on the screening test will produce a different cost-benefit ratio. The lower we set the threshold, the greater will be the number of false positives, and the greater the costs relative to the benefits. The higher the threshold, the more the cases that are missed, and the more the procedure resembles case-finding rather than screening.

Dr Williams has mentioned the work that I carried out with a general practitioner from Yorkshire, Alan Johnstone, on the effects of what we ignorantly called psychiatric screening (Johnstone and Goldberg 1976). Our study was reviewed at the time by John Fry, whose critical stance towards this kind of work was evident then. He wrote:

'The first startling fact reported is that among 1,093 consecutive attenders, no fewer than 32% had conspicuous psychiatric illness and a further 12% had hidden psychiatric morbidity. This implies that according to the GHQ, almost one-half of Dr Johnstone's population is psychiatrically ill. We know that emotional problems are common, but can we really accept that half of us are "ill" from such conditions? Surely, when data such as these are presented, either the measuring device needs to be re-examined or our definition of "illness" needs to be reviewed.'

Dr Fry went on to describe the GHQ as a 'dangerous instrument' because it identified such a high proportion of subjects as ill, and suggested that they all needed treatment (Fry 1976). In fact we did not suggest that 'almost one half' of the patients were cases, and we did make the point that detection of such illnesses did *not* increase the number of consultations by the patients in the ensuing year.

Dr Fry has recently kindly allowed Dr Skuse to carry out research interviews on 272 attenders at his practice, so that it is now possible to compare the state of affairs in Dr Johnstone's practice with that obtaining in Dr Fry's (Skuse and Williams 1984).

	Dr Johnstone's practice	Dr Fry's practice
conspicuous psychiatric morbidity:	31.9%	24.3%
hidden psychiatric morbidity:	11.0%	16.9%
percentage non-cases:	57.1%	58.8%

It can be seen that so far from the total percentage of psychiatric cases being unduly high in Dr Johnstone's practice, it is in fact almost the same as that in Dr Fry's own practice. The striking point of contrast is that the proportion of patients with hidden psychiatric illnesses is greater in Dr Fry's practice.

All the patients had also completed the GHQ as part of the research design. If Dr Fry were prepared to be less critical about psychiatric screening questionnaires, he would only have missed 22 per cent of the cases detected by Dr Skuse, instead of the 49 per cent he did miss. Elsewhere in the paper Drs Skuse and Williams show that Dr Fry would be well advised to consider results of a screening test together with his own clinical judgements.

I do not think that there are grounds for such global pessimism as that displayed by Dr Fry. We *do* know what we are screening for, and we *do* know how effective these screening tests are. At the time of writing there have been 47 well conducted validity studies in 12 different countries. If we confine ourselves to primary care settings, 1,500 patients have received second stage interviews by psychiatrists in 11 different studies: the mean sensitivity has been found to be 81 per cent (SD = 7.3), and the mean specificity 83.8 per cent (SD = 5.6). (Recent reviews are by Goldberg 1983 and by Vieweg and Hedlund 1983.) Nor is it true that we do not know who to screen: the available evidence suggests we should screen all patients not thought to be psychiatrically ill whose symptoms cannot be fully accounted for by known physical disease.

However, there is common ground between myself and Dr Fry. It is true that we do not know what effects screening would have on National Health Service resources, but I think that it is important for us to find out.

It is also very true that there is no reliable and practical taxonomy for minor psychiatric illnesses, and it is also true that the natural history of neurosis is unappreciated by most doctors. It is true that family doctors cannot, by and large, do much to correct the factors that are likely to continue to produce such illnesses in the future, but this is hardly relevant to the question of whether treatment is effective for such disorders.

The study with Alan Johnstone showing that detection of such disorders produces beneficial results has still to be replicated. A recent study of purported replication in Wisconsin showed no beneficial effects of giving family doctors feedback of their patients' GHQ scores. However, the US doctors did not alter their diagnostic or therapeutic behaviour in any way as a result of the feedback.

If screening is to be effective, it is essential that the doctors respond in some way to the distress which has now been drawn to their attention. In Dr Johnstone's study, we were able to show that the hidden cases detected by the GHQ were treated in exactly the same way as the conspicuous cases. It is not feedback of a GHQ score that does the patient any good; it is what might happen as a result of such knowledge.

If further experiments are done on this subject, it seems important that they are confined to places where staff have received some training in the management of such disorders, and are prepared to respond in a helpful way to the patient's distress.

REFERENCES

Fry, J. (1976) Psychiatric Screening in General Practice. *Update* 13: 931–32.
Glass, N. J. and Goldberg, D. P. (1977) Cost benefit analysis and the evaluation of psychiatric services. *Psychological Medicine* 7: 701–07.

Goldberg, D. P. (1983) *The Use of Screening Questionnaires by Family Doctors: Proceedings of the World Congress of Psychiatry*. New York: Plenum Press.
—— (1984) *Mental Health in General Medical Settings*. In N. Sartorius (ed.) *WHO Monograph*. Geneva: WHO.
Hoeper, E. W., Nycz, G. R., Kessler, L. G., Burke, J. D., and Pierce, W. E. (1984) The usefulness of screening for mental health. *Lancet* i: 33–5.
Johnstone, A. and Goldberg, D. P. (1976) Psychiatric screening in general practice. *Lancet* i: 605–08.
Skuse, D. and Williams, P. (1984) Screening for psychiatric disorder in general practice. *Psychological Medicine* 14: 365–77.
Vieweg, B. and Hedlund, J. (1983) The general health questionnaire: a comprehensive review. *The Journal of Operational Psychiatry* 14: 74–81.

General Discussion

CHAIRMAN: DR J. M. G. WILSON

Dr. I. Marks: In the study conducted by Goldberg and Johnstone it is unclear what Dr Johnstone as a GP did to the patients that he would not have done otherwise, how long it took him and how much training would be needed to emulate him.

Professor D. P. Goldberg: I can tell you how much training I think the GP needs, but not how much Dr Johnstone thinks he needs. Dr Johnstone gave psychotropic drugs to the identified patients in just over 40 per cent of the cases detected by the General Health Questionnaire (GHQ). That is almost exactly to within 1 per cent of his prescription rate for conspicuous cases. He gave supportive therapy and discussed problems with 100 per cent of the patients. He allowed return visits and engaged in some form of continuing therapy with about 60 per cent.

With regard to the training that family doctors need in order to handle these disorders, I think that the present systems of vocational training are defective. The time given for the teaching of counselling skills is inadequate, but I think the situation could be remedied with relatively little regular supervision. I know that there are some vocational training schemes which provide such supervision, though very few of these involve psychiatrists.

In Dr Johnstone's practice the consultation rate in the subsequent twelve months was slightly, but not significantly, less for the index group. There are, of course, the costs incurred in not detecting disorder, including the costs in failing to detect disorder which exist in the form of repeated visits to doctors with repeated physical investigations and repeated physical medication. In the event, the control group attended more often, but not significantly more so, than the index group.

Sir Douglas Black: I should like to express myself as a strong advocate of case-finding in the interests of epidemiology because, as I understand it, good epidemiology starts with defined observations and defined problems within it. Bad epidemiology starts with the problem and then looks for a population. I am also a very strong advocate of limited screening for treatable conditions such as hypertension and diabetes. I am distinctly sceptical about global screening. When I was interested in the quality of health, Peter Townsend thought that the way to save the poor was to institute a screening programme. My evidence against that is Walter Holland's evidence that when this was done with controls in a group of practices, it was found that the hard outcome of death was no more prevalent among those who had not been screened than it was among those who had been screened. So I have a certain scepticism about global screening which does not, of course, extend to global screening for psychiatric disorders.

Dr D. R. Hannay: I think the distinction made between case-finding and screening is important, but it does have certain implications for psychiatric illness in the community. We found in Glasgow that a significant part of psychiatric morbidity in the community which does not reach medical care is major depressive illness. It appears to be a behavioural characteristic of major depressive illness that people suffering from it do not seek medical care, a fact which poses problems.

If one suggests that work on the primary care of psychiatric illness be confined to case-finding, there is the implication that attention is focused on people who attend the doctor. There remains, however, a large number of people in the community who do not seek any help because it is the nature of their illness or part of their illness not to seek help. Perhaps one way forward is to take up this contradiction in terms, that there is no such thing as a pre-symptomatic phase to psychiatric illness. That may be so, but there are identifiable risk factors in psychiatric illness, and perhaps it is these risk factors which general practitioners should be looking at in order to provide anticipatory care for the people who would not otherwise come to see them.

The Chairman: The World Health Organisation criterion about the pre-symptomatic phase did, in fact, include 'or early symptomatic stage'. It might have been better to say 'unreported illness' or something like that.

Dr P. Williams: You are expressing a point of view in favour of screening as opposed to case-finding, or as well as case-finding. The evidence, however, is not yet available for us to be absolutely clear one way or the other.

The Chairman: It seems to me that the difference being postulated by Holland and Sackett between case-finding and screening is artefactual. Ethically, there is nothing to choose between whether you ask a person to come to you or you go to him/her, or whether he/she comes to you of his/her own accord for some other reason. In the latter event you may offer to provide tests for some disorder that you think he/she may have. Are you thereby simply offering a lower quality of test and treatment? Dr Williams said that you do not need an accepted treatment. It seems to me you could be just lowering your standards because there is no need to know for the patient.

Dr P. Williams: Case-finding has to do with the collection of extra information for the use (or otherwise) of the general practitioner. At its crudest, one can say of that extra information, that on balance it is better for the GP to have it or, on balance, that it is worse or neither better nor worse for the GP to have it. If, *a priori*, one holds the view that on balance it is not worse because of insufficient evidence, then one could argue in favour of case-finding. However, when one is in a position of not simply carrying out an additional test on someone who comes to the clinic, but of going out to the population and saying 'We wish to test you', then the criteria really ought to be more stringent. For this reason, I would support the distinction made by Holland and Sackett.

Dr A. C. Brown: The difference between screening and case-finding in practice may depend on the accessibility of the general practitioner, and the patient's perception of the doctor as the appropriate person to whom a particular sort of problem can be presented.

The wider open the door of primary care, the less is the need for screening, and with adequate case-finding there is more effective screening. So perhaps we should concentrate some attention on why people do or do not bring their problems to the GP.

Incidentally, we seem to be talking only about screening for disorders of mood. Should we not be aware of the importance of screening for other conditions such as the misuse of alcohol and other drugs, and the early stages of senile dementia?

Dr J. Fry: I think that Professor Goldberg and I are getting embroiled in something that neither of us understands. Like Professor Cochrane, I am trying to resist having imposed on me methods and procedures which may be time-consuming and expensive, and of whose value I am not convinced.

Professor Goldberg has made play with conspicuous and inconspicuous morbidity. We know very little about conspicuous morbidity, and even less about hidden morbidity in the field of mental disorder. This is a situation which, as Cochrane argues, calls for the application of controlled trials. I think that screening has been used as a method for research, and before we go on to extend research into clinical practice we need to know a lot more about treatment. It is the end results of the disorder which constitute the difficulty.

Dr P. Freeling: I am surprised at the bowdlerization of language which has been used by almost everyone here. Dr Williams has not talked about case-finding. He has talked about improving diagnosis. Case-finding is something different. It is diagnosing a condition that could not be diagnosed otherwise. I cannot talk of the signs of hypertension without putting a blood pressure cuff on a patient until somebody gives me another method of inquiry.

My own comment about Hoeper's findings are simple. You do not use what you cannot use. So when Professor Goldberg asked what has to be done to teach GPs to be better diagnosticians, he quite correctly answered that you teach them to be better at treating disease.

With regard to screening, Sir Douglas Black's point remains true. We know very little about the factors which prevent patients or people in the community from presenting doctors with symptoms which other people regard as passports to the surgery. This difference applies as much outside psychiatry as within it.

I regret that the present discussion has focused upon what I still think is no more than an aid to diagnosis. As to case-finding, I would suggest that we should be examining the ways in which people respond to the attitudes of their GPs in selecting which illnesses they think appropriate for presentation to the doctor.

Dr B. Essex: We are nowadays confronted with teams of people in general practice, not just the general practitioner. We work with the community mental health nurse and with social workers, and we know something about the needs of certain groups of families and certain individuals. We know families in which there is an alcoholic or a drug addict or somebody who has had a psychotic illness. These families need more support and closer follow-up, and I should like to emphasize the study risk factors; the use of observations, simple check lists which would train us and train our trainees to identify which are the families that require a much closer follow-up by the community nurse in conjunction with either the general practitioner, the health visitor or the social worker. For example, in our antenatal clinics we have concentrated on a past history of serious depression or psychosis in pregnant women, which proves to be a good predictor of the need for close attention in the *post partum* period.

Professor D. P. Goldberg: It is true that we do not know much about the efficacy of screening and that we ought to know more. I thought I knew, but now that the American study by Hoeper *et al.* (1984) has produced such a dismal result, it is clearly an open question. The work needs to be repeated.

It is also true that there are families at risk, but in so far as we are talking about psychiatric cases which are not detected by physicians, hospital doctors as well as GPs, I would stress that there is an effective treatment for them. We should be using, simple, self-administered inventories to detect these patients' illnesses. This process can be augmented by the examination of high risk patients or families, but you cannot ever be certain in the individual case who is going to become unwell.

Professor E. S. Paykel: I should like to point out that when we are talking about screening, we are talking about a first stage in the detection of disorder. Professor Goldberg's GHQ positives and the approximately 40 per cent of consulters are not suffering from disorders of a quality of kind that would traditionally be regarded as meriting treatment. In our own studies we find that a high GHQ score is needed to identify major depression. This is, of course, not the only psychiatric disorder, but it gives some indication of the range needed to qualify for 'caseness'. So we must think of an inventory as a first stage, to be followed by some other kind of diagnostic technique.

Professor D. P. Goldberg: No one who has worked on screening has ever asserted that people with high scores on screening tests are more than potential cases. They need a second stage case evaluation, and in research studies this is usually carried out by trained psychiatrists with a standardized instrument. If, however, we were talking about screening as a service procedure, then the second stage would fall to the family doctor using the usual methods he uses to detect conspicuous cases. The function of the screening test would simply be to alert the GP to the fact that there were a critical number of symptoms present. It is quite true that for major depressive disorder the threshold is slightly higher than the threshold for any diagnosis, but you do pick up most of the cases of major depressive disorder with the GHQ in most of the studies with which I am familiar. That was my reason for maintaining that such patients can be identified in this way. Their illnesses do constitute a major health burden.

Professor G. Teeling-Smith: The economic implications of Professor Goldberg's comments should be emphasized. If, by screening and bringing to the surface hidden mental illness in the community, we can reduce the practice workload, the economic benefits provide a powerful argument for so doing.

We have heard something about cases that recur and never get better. I do not think that we necessarily have to regard those cases as representing failures of treatment simply because we make patients feel better who would be going to get better in any case. The quality of life has also to be considered, but we should not forget the economics of the matter.

Dr P. Williams: I agree entirely. The cost effectiveness aspects of what I shall persist in calling 'case-finding' need to be thoroughly investigated.

Dr D. L. Crombie: I am unsure about the significance of cost effectiveness in this context because among the control groups there are a number of people who consult as patients at some later stage. The defect is surely in the ability of the general practitioner to pick up more quickly the fact that there are patients with a depressive illness. Picking them up early enough is the biggest problem in general practice to many of us. This is not the same kind of task as a massive screening procedure designed to uncover such patients. I would also draw attention to the fact that many general practitioners carry out unsystematic clinical trials on their chronic patients by administering amitryptiline or imipramine on a trial-and-error basis.

Professor A. W. Clare: One lesson emerging from the use of the GHQ is to remind GPs that by simply asking a number of relevant questions their ability to detect morbidity is increased. Here there is an analogous situation in the field of alcohol abuse.

A whole army of researchers have developed a large battery of screening tests, but it is still clear that a small number of simple questions asked by a general practitioner raises their detection rate of alcohol abuse. From the standpoint of medical education one step may be to persuade GPs to master the items on the GHQ and build them into their routine clinical assessments in the surgery.

Dr B. J. Burns: I should like to offer an interpretation of what has happened in the sphere of screening. The Hoeper *et al.* (1984) study was designed to test the impact of screening information on random patients and not random physicians. What I think happened was that the primary care physicians were sensitized as a result of their experience with the GHQ, and responded in a general sort of way to the index and control patients. My evidence is that in this particular setting of prepaid health plan, the recorded rate of mental disorder was somewhere around 3 per cent in the first study that was done. In the next study, in which the GPs also received no feedback, the GHQ screened the population and the patients were then interviewed to yield an estimate of prevalence. The recognition rate went up something like 5 per cent. For both control and index patients, the overall rate of detection of emotional distress was 15 per cent.

I would recommend that in any further test of the effectiveness of screening, comparison groups of physicians need to be evaluated with respect to their ability to use this information, and that they should not be in the same clinic, where contamination can so readily occur.

PART 3

PROFESSIONAL TEAM ROLES

J. Horder

Professional team roles

A CASE HISTORY

Mr Robinson, a milkroundsman, with a face deformed by a long-standing nerve paralysis on one side, had by 1970 six children, ranging in age from 4 to 14. This was the situation when his first wife died of cancer at the age of 38. The husband coped alone for a year, but could not both work and look after the younger children. Economics forced him to put the children into care and go to work himself. He soon met a divorced woman who had one child of her own and he married her rather quickly, taking some of the children back.

Two major disasters of a different sort then ensued. A heavy package fell on Mr Robinson's neck at work and this left him permanently weak in both legs and arms. He was unable to work at all for two years, but has now been retrained and is doing a clerical job. In 1976 the fourth child at the age of sixteen was involved with two other boys in the murder of an old man who was a sexual deviant. All three boys were convicted of murder and are now serving long sentences. It was perhaps not surprising that the new wife was by now making suicidal gestures and attributing her trouble to the behaviour of her stepchildren; they were indeed rebellious.

By this time three doctors out of our group of seven were involved with the family, together with a health visitor and social worker from the same health centre, a child psychotherapist who visits weekly and a family therapy group of social workers from the nearby area office. One doctor was seeing Mr Robinson regularly, another his second wife (the same doctor had looked after his first wife). The social worker played a large part in getting Mr Robinson his new job as a clerk. The heaviest task was with Sarah, the youngest daughter of the first marriage; she saw the child psychotherapist at the health centre weekly over two years. Then the mother said to the psychotherapist 'Now that you have talked some sense into Sarah, will you see Glyn instead?'

Sarah was by now accepted back into the family. But it is really the family that has changed. Previously the parents had made very rigid rules which the children either had to obey or be excommunicated; if older, they were thrown out altogether. The family had been a little island, isolated and defended against an outside world which its members had seen as hostile since the time of their tragedies. Some of the children had never been allowed to mourn for their mother. The two social workers from the family therapy group had penetrated this fortress. They went weekly over two years seeing the whole remaining family in the home, but reporting back to a group which included the social worker attached to our practice. There is no doubt that change has been achieved in this family – change for the better.

Here is a factual example of one multi-professional team in action.

THE TEAM

When I started as a GP, I worked in a team which consisted of three doctors, one receptionist and a housekeeper. When I finished thirty years later, apart from seven doctor principals, there were two district nurses, three treatment room nurses, a school nurse, three health visitors for children, two for over-sixty-fives, a midwife, half of a social worker and half of a community psychiatric nurse. In addition, there were regular visits from a psychiatrist and a child psychotherapist and a marriage guidance counsellor. That still leaves the group of receptionists, secretaries, and administrator until last: they too were important to patients. Members of all these professional groups were regular attenders at the twice-weekly lunchtime meetings: shared clinical problems were the main subject of discussion. One of the meetings was devoted entirely to psychosocial problems and, indeed, they featured largely in the other. Anyone whose problem was nagging most urgently or most interestingly would present it. Less often it would be a nurse or geriatric visitor, more often a health visitor, social worker, GP or GP in training. The psychiatrist or psychotherapist would comment on the free exchanges. The regulars at those meetings would have been coming for anything between two years and the twenty years since such discussions started.

We hoped and believed that these meetings, through sharing information and points of view, would help the individuals and families discussed, while adding something to our own capacity to help other people. I cannot produce evidence that this was so or that we solved many problems that could have been solved in no other way. What seems more certain is that we frequently helped each other by providing emotional relief and by the support of knowing that others, too, found a difficult problem to be difficult. We often picked up new information and sometimes new understanding. In the face of the uncertainties and disappointments of dealing with mental illness such support is very valuable. In any case these meetings were crucial to holding so large a team together.

Here then was one example of a large primary care team working together in the forefront of mental health care.

TASKS OF THE TEAM

What overall were the team's tasks in this part of medicine? I believe that the most important task was to be *available*, to be available quickly when necessary and to carry on being available. In other words, that being there was at least as important as doing things – a principle which it takes most doctors some time to learn. But was it good enough to be there as a team? No. It was better than nothing, but, when people are ill in this way, they want the availability and continuity of one person, and that can be frightening for the one person concerned. We make much of the dangers of patients becoming dependent, but it seems to me that we are talking at least as much about a dangerous burden for ourselves as about doing harm to patients. Everybody needs to depend on someone else, and there are some people who have nobody more reliable than a medical person to depend upon.

Second to availability, our chief task was to assess – to assess urgency, our own ability to cope, and, as far as possible, the form of disturbance and its causes, in terms of body, long-term personality, and the immediate circumstances and relationships. Starting from the assumption that it was our job to cope ourselves if possible, we needed to determine the likelihood of help from discussion, drugs or social interventions of some sort. We expected an exploration which could seldom be achieved in one interview and in which diagnosis and treatment went on together, as both the team member and the patient tried to align their understanding of what was going on. Very often, of course, our hopes of creating change had to yield to acceptance of things that could not be changed.

These were the obvious tasks, but there was an earlier one than assessment. Doctors and nurses frequently had to detect the mental problem hiding behind a physical disguise. Health visitors would need to detect it hiding behind difficult parent/child relationships, where the child in particular might be acting as a symptom of trouble elsewhere.

We also hoped that our increasing understanding might allow us sometimes to prevent trouble and even to promote mental health. Undoubtedly the opportunities were there in baby clinics and when we saw people at the usual transition times like puberty, adolescence, marriage, first child, and so on. Is it too much to imagine, for example, that there is some broad agreement about the needs of small children – 'continuity of care in a loving, familiar and stable environment where the child is valued for his or her uniqueness' (Hood 1976)?

I have tried to summarize the tasks of the team as a whole. In doing so, I have left out the relation of this, the primary care team, to relatives and families on the one hand and to the specialist psychiatric team on the other. The primary care team depends on both, but the title allotted to me here rules the psychiatric team out of court. Suffice it to say that the boundary between primary care teams and psychiatric teams is increasingly fuzzy, with uncertainties about the role of community psychiatric nurses, about psychiatrists visiting primary care teams, and about hospital outreach unrelated to primary care, all of them very important issues at present.

PROFESSIONAL ROLES

Turning now to the different professions working within the team, do they have distinct roles? I suggest that job descriptions, separate trainings and professional boundaries are of no importance; what counts is the personality, understanding and behaviour of the individual worker.

To make this clearer: dealing with the mentally ill seems to demand qualities that not all medical or social workers possess, despite training. I am thinking of the capacity to listen, the value which different people put on mental suffering compared to physical, the extent to which they can accept strange or troublesome behaviour and the way in which they can temper involvement with detachment. These were the qualities which seemed to count, as judged in our group discussions. The longer someone had been in the team, the less conscious one became of their label or their training. Sometimes it became obvious that professional straitjackets can be a menace.

To test the hypothesis it had to be asked were different sorts of workers seeing the same sort of patients with similar problems? Were they eliciting the same sorts of information? Were they making assessments in the same way, and offering similar sorts of treatment?

Clearly not. Some were seeing people in limited age groups, for example, the two sorts of health visitors. It was the receptionists, nurses and doctors who dealt with most acute crises; marriage guidance counsellors and psychiatrists were seeing only referred cases. The community psychiatric nurse was seeing mostly very disturbed patients who had been in hospital.

As for information, I shall never forget how our first attached health visitor described a family which I did not recognize until she mentioned the name; I then realized that I had known them for ten years and thought that I knew all about them. She had picked up an entirely different set of facts and an entirely different impression of their problems.

There were some differences between professionals in assessment and treatment, notably between doctors on the one hand, social workers and health visitors on the other. It would come out most clearly over the nature of a depressive state. To the doctors the other two groups seemed reluctant to recognize the possibility of a constitutional, hereditary or physical factor, or that some depressive states could 'just happen' or be disproportionate to any precipitating event. To them, the doctors seemed too much concerned with diagnostic labels and too ready to use drugs to relieve anxiety and depression.

There were obvious differences in duration of involvement between receptionists and most of the others, even if a lot can go on in those interchanges in the waiting room. There were even differences in purpose or emphasis. Health visitors aimed more than any other member to promote health through their observation and discussion with mothers.

These were all differences which stemmed from professional roles, differences in training and from the way in which patients think of a nurse, a doctor or a social worker. And yet the overlaps were very great and there were large personal variations within one profession: one need think only of the various ways in which different doctors would deal with a patient with phobias.

I cannot, therefore, test my hypothesis sufficiently. Professional roles are *not* without some importance in the primary care team, even if personal qualities count just as much. But I would find it quite impossible to define totally distinct purposes, types of patient or methods of assessment and treatment attaching to a particular professional group. We must accept overlapping roles mixed with contributions derived from personality, partly from specific training.

Before finishing, I want to say something of our experience with visiting psychiatrists and psychotherapists; and about the role of the GP in the team.

Two distinct patterns emerged. In one a consultant or senior registrar would see two or three patients already in the care of a team member, usually because they were raising particular problems. The main question was usually: 'Have we understood the problem and are we doing all we should be doing?' An hour's interview would be followed by a written report and often a discussion, either one-to-one with the team member or at the lunchtime meeting. If the upshot was no more than 'carry on in the same way', this was a great help. But there would often be new interpretations and insights; less frequently some new course of action. Taking over the case, or referral elsewhere, was rare (Brook 1976).

The other pattern was quite different, namely a psychotherapist offering up to six sessions for the patients referred to her, but in the familiar surroundings of the health centre. This, of course, provided both larger slices of time for some patients and usually greater skill. Dramatic successes were nevertheless uncommon and at the end some new decision about management would have to be made.

The child psychotherapist worked alongside the doctor or health visitor in the baby clinic, often in the same room, acting as observer and commentator (Dawes 1985).

Most of these activities were sustained over fifteen years and we would have been very sorry to see them lapse, even if there were sometimes disappointing discussions without revelation or without resolution of any problem. The cumulative educational value both to team members and to the visitors would not be questioned by any of them.

It seems appropriate to leave the GP until last. I see him/her as the mortar between the bricks, as well as being one of the bricks in the wall. Somebody has to hold the team together, to ensure that it has a sense of direction, to draw out special viewpoints and bind them into a shared whole. The task of integration is now a major clinical characteristic of the general doctor in a specialized medical world; it is a role which can be transferred into a team setting, providing the responsibility is accepted. Other members of the team may matter more to particular patients or families, but the GP does seem to be the professional around whom all the others are organized in primary medical care. It is not very difficult to see why this is so at present, but it will not necessarily remain so. There is a demand for more sharing. How far the GP will retain a central role will depend, I think, on how far he or she sustains the characteristics of being available, going on being available and being able to make integrated and well-balanced assessments on a very broad front, which covers body, mind, and relationships. These are rather difficult tasks to sustain.

ACKNOWLEDGEMENT

I am grateful to Dr Caryle Steen, my former partner, for permission to quote a case.

REFERENCES

Brook, A. and Temperley, J. (1976) 'The Contribution of a Psychotherapist to General Practice'. *Journal of the Royal College of General Practitioners*, 26: 86–94.
Dawes, D. (forthcoming) 'Standing next to the Weighing Scales.'
Hood, C. (1976) Children under three and their families. Winnicott Memorial Lecture (unpublished) (Bedford College, University of London).

Margot Jefferys

Professional team roles

INTRODUCTION

Group practice with employed and attached non-medically qualified professional staff, whether or not it functions from a district-owned health centre, is
now the modal form of general practice unit, having in this respect replaced in
the last two decades the simpler organization composed of one or two medical
practitioners with at most some paid secretarial and receptionist help. The
increasing organizational and occupational complexity of this modal unit
provides more human resources than the single-handed practitioner can
muster and these may be of significance in the handling of mental illness and
emotional distress. It may also bring with it the development of formal
bureaucratic rules intended to define roles and competencies, and these may
be inimical in their very essence to the task of helping disturbed people.

In developing my theme, therefore, I propose to consider not only the
appositeness to the care of mentally ill people of the training, experience, and
life qualifications of some of the non-medically qualified members of the
typical group general practice unit. I also intend to review the inter-
occupational relationships within such units because such relationships can
affect the quality of care given to patients.

TYPES OF PRIMARY CARE SETTING

Before embarking on the analysis, I want to make several points about the
place of group general practice in the gamut of community services for the

mentally ill. Reading the medical journals, one could be forgiven for thinking that the care of most physically and mentally ill individuals devolves entirely on the formally organized health services of hospital and general practice, and more particularly on doctors in these organizations. It would be a pity if this myth were to be perpetuated. It exists largely because so much professional training and practice encourages tunnel vision and egocentrism. In reality, kith and kin generally spend much more time and energy in caring for the mentally as well as the physically ill than the professionals do in their brief, episodic encounters with patients. We might begin, therefore, by asking whether kinsfolk are given enough support in the often thankless tasks they perform? Giving kin and friends more material resources and emotional support could well be more effective than increasing the input of professional time. This is of course merely a hypothesis which needs testing, as does much else in the field we are discussing today.

Apart from kith and kin, there are bodies other than the official National Health Service (NHS) ones which also play some part in helping the mentally ill. The personal social service departments of local government employ trained and untrained social workers in a variety of community settings with an express duty to assist individuals and famiies in all kinds of social distress including that occasioned by mental illness. These departments often encourage the formation of self-help groups composed of sufferers and/or their relatives. Such groups may result from the initiative of volunteers attached to religious or secular associations. Other groups with the more general aim of community participation may *inter alia* concern themselves with the support of lonely and unhappy people. Some of the bodies may see their role as supplementing the endeavours of the NHS and mainstream medical practice. Others represent themselves as offering alternatives to orthodox medicine. For example, they may totally reject the use of drugs or physical treatment.

There was a time when it was common for medical people to ignore, discount or dismiss the efforts of all those who were not medically qualified or acting under the direct aegis of someone who was. Fortunately, this is much less likely to occur today. Most doctors are now aware of the fact that many of their own practices have not been subjected to rigorous scientific examination; nor has their efficacy been demonstrated beyond all possible doubt. The awareness may have led them, in turn, to be more tolerant of the efforts of non-medically qualified practitioners of the healing arts, especially if the latter are dealing with problems which have proved intractable and are using methods which do not endanger life or risk side effects as serious as the condition being treated. Certainly, there are no grounds for imposing restraints on all grassroots innovations in the care of mentally ill patients initiated by non-medically qualified people, given the evidence of much unmet need for help and the inelasticity in the supply of NHS resources of man and woman power.

Nor are there grounds as yet for advocating that all available non-medical personnel resources in the shape of social workers and health visitors should be located in general practice units rather than dispersed among such units and the social service departments' area offices or the district health authorities' community nursing units. It is true that Corney's study (Clare and Corney 1982) demonstrated substantial differences between the work undertaken by social workers in an intake team in a social service department area office and that of social workers attached to a general practice in the same district. However, it did not establish the relative effectiveness of the work carried out in the two settings in modifying the presenting conditions or problems of the two groups of patient/client. Indeed, the problems of setting up an experimental situation to test the relative effectiveness and efficiency of similar workers in two kinds of organizational setting are formidable. It is to be hoped that the DHSS will encourage researchers somewhere to tackle such a task, which would involve the co-operation of general practitioners, social workers and administrators.

GENERAL PRACTICE AS A SETTING FOR MULTI-OCCUPATIONAL TEAMWORK

The effect of the re-thinking about the proper field of work of the general practitioner which has gone on in the last twenty years has been to establish him/her in the eyes of the medical profession as a whole as the professional person, in contrast to the hospital-based specialist, best able to assess the patient in the broadest possible terms. The GP is now seen as someone who can gauge how far the patient's life style, personality, and family relationships as well as his/her genetic constitution and past pathological experiences are (a) factors in his/her presenting symptoms or covert condition, and (b) place constraints on or provide resources for his/her treatment and ultimate prognosis. Furthermore, current thinking, largely influenced by Balint's work (1964) and some sociological studies of the doctor–patient relationship (e.g. Parsons 1951; Stimson and Webb 1975), emphasizes the importance of the quality of that relationship in the therapeutic process, especially when the patient suffers from anxiety or depression.

Given this designation of general practitioners as the people ideally fitted to meet patients' needs at the primary level by virtue of their training and of the mantle of affective authority which descends upon them, whether they like it or not, in their encounters with patients, what role is there left for members of other occupational groups who are employed by or attached to the symbolically significant eponymous unit to play?

In the first instance, the commonsense answer would seem to be that other occupations should only perform those tasks in direct patient care which, as a result of their training and experience, they are better able to do than the general practitioner, and which are likely to be performed more effectively and efficiently if done in close collaboration with the latter. Some such, often unspoken, principle lay behind the first decisions to employ surgery nurses. They were usually seen as possessing more expertise than doctors in dressing wounds, giving injections and syringing ears, and as able to do these things without intruding upon the intimacy of the doctor's subtle relationship with his/her patient. Similarly, health visitors were recognized as possessing more systematic knowledge of nutrition and baby care and hence able to give preventive services in these fields which the doctors would do only indifferently. By the same token, some doctors wanted to see social workers attached to their practices because they possessed detailed information on the available social resources of the community and could be relied on to mobilize them more effectively on behalf of a doctor's patient if they were working alongside him/her rather than from a remote area-based office. None of these three groups was at first credited by doctors with the capacity to play a part in the management of mental illness.

Such essentially *supplementary* roles for nurses, health visitors and social workers were on the whole welcomed by most general practitioners. They did not disturb the doctor's freedom or challenge his/her authority in the broad territory over which he/she was now claiming competence. Indeed, their presence in the team could relieve the doctor of the necessity of undertaking some of the work which he/she was apt to label as routine or uninteresting and not 'proper medicine'. At the same time, it allowed the doctor to have more control over its performance than if it had taken place elsewhere by individuals over whom he/she had no authority. As Bennett asserted in an international symposium on the Greater Medical Profession 'doctors have the authority to direct and evaluate the work of others without in turn being subject to normal direction and evaluation by them' (Josiah Macy Jr Foundation 1973: 86).

The idyllic image of 'convex and concave surfaces fitting to form the complete pattern of planned patient care' (1973: 141) did not survive for long in sharp focus. Instead, as Skeet, a nurse suggested: '. . . our roles have been so twisted, altered, amplified and changed, that a considerable number of people in both the hospital and community service field are confused, insecure, frustrated and unhappy.' (1973: 141)

Why did roles become twisted, altered, amplified and changed? Has the result inevitably been professional confusion, insecurity, frustration and unhappiness? And what are the implications of occupational mix in general practice settings for patients with mental illness?

OCCUPATIONAL ASPIRATIONS

The tidy picture of complementary, smoothly interlocking occupational roles pursued in complete harmony in general practice units was always likely to be a gross over-simplification, if not a pipe dream, because it ignored many aspects of the social reality of Britain in the 1970s. It was based on the still widely held but false assumption that, although the general practitioner's role was changing, the roles of members of other occupational groups would remain the same or adapt automatically to fit the changes occurring in medicine.

In practice, during the 1960s and 1970s, each of the three occupations involved was undergoing a process of re-evaluation of its own functions and the part it wished to play in caring for dependent people. All of them were to a greater or lesser extent discontented with the roles to which they had been assigned and were seeking to change them. Moreover, all of them were seeking more autonomy, more control over their own tasks and the capacity to use their own discretion to a far greater extent. This involved challenging the right of another occupational group – the medical profession – to circumscribe their functions and lay down the ground rules for their performance.

Social workers

The social workers, for a number of reasons, were in a more favourable position than the nurses and health visitors to achieve their professional independence. They succeeded, thanks to the 1970 implementation of many of the recommendations of the Seebohm Report (1968), in establishing social worker controlled departments in local government and in ending the last remnants of their subordination to the medical officer of health. If their members served in NHS hospitals or general practice units, they did so as seconded staff with responsibility to their local authority social service department.

On the other hand, their very important political successes had the paradoxical effect of making them more vulnerable to scape-goating both by the general public and other professional groups. They reigned over departments comparatively starved of resources at a time when public expectations of better and more extensive statutory welfare provision were rising. The rapid expansion in social service department personnel which did take place could only be done by recruiting many young, untrained social worker assistants who could then be asked to exercise the judgement of Solomon and get pilloried when they got it wrong.

The NHS was also experiencing a growth in demand; but in contrast to the social service departments, its resources were also expanding, the number of general practitioners was growing annually, their patient lists were contracting, and they did not have to restrict the most visible and costly part of their service to patients – their drug prescriptions – which were still not subject to cash limits. Indeed, with the attachment of more professional workers to their practices and the employment of more receptionists and administrative staff, the resources which they were able to offer patients would appear to have exceeded the often low public expectations of the general practice service.

These differences in the institutional settings and public images of the two professional groups of general practitioner and social worker need to be borne in mind when considering the part which social workers placed in general practice units can play in the treatment of the mentally ill. So too do the points made by Huntington (1981) in her study of the background social and cultural factors affecting the relationships between the two occupational groups when they work within the same unit. She drew attention (1) to the social status disparities between the independent contractor/employer on the one hand and the salaried employee on the other; (2) to the customary gender and age differences between the two occupational groups; and (3) to the primacy given by one to the physiological, organic manifestations of illness and by the other to the emotional.

Given an insensitive general practitioner, unaccustomed to having judgements challenged by members of another professional group, used to giving orders to subordinates, and influenced by the not uncommon view that social work at its best is the commonsense provision of material services or down-to-earth practical advice and at its worst pseudo-psychiatric nonsense, there is little hope that social workers can make any contribution to the care of the mentally ill from a general practice setting. This picture may resemble a caricature of an extinct species of general practitioner, and it is true that he/she is not likely to be found in the group practices most likely to seek a social worker attachment. But there is still the possibility of inter-occupational tension even when the general practitioner is aware that patients' lives and relationships may be important factors in the conditions for which they consult and that they may need more help in sorting out these difficulties than he/she has time to give. In a study which Hessie Sachs and I have recently published (Jefferys and Sachs 1983) we found that it was the general practitioner most aware of the inter-connectedness between his patients' physical and mental health and their social lives who was the most reluctant to refer to the social worker attached to his group practice. He knew that she wanted to have a psychotherapeutic role and not merely be regarded as a mobilizer of external services. Yet he felt that her skills in psychotherapy were no greater than his. Furthermore, this last was the aspect of his own work from which he obtained most satisfaction. He could and did argue cogently, moreover, that the patient might regard referral to a social worker as a rejection by him, yet another perhaps in a long list of such rejections which could have punctuated the patient's history. For her part the social worker was aware that the doctors saw it as part of their own role to help patients suffering from anxiety or depression with more than drugs and courtesy. She also was prepared to acknowledge that the slow rate of referrals to her initially was due to a correspondingly slow and cautious build-up of doctors' confidence in her. But when this had eventually been accomplished, she was hurt when it appeared that general practitioners' referrals depended primarily on 'what they had on their plate at the moment'. One doctor, after referring a patient to her, had insensitively taken him back when his own caseload slackened (1983: 150).

Health visitors

Health visitors form a resource which is located increasingly in a general practice setting. Their work is still predominantly with families where there are young pre-school children. Their statutory obligation to visit mothers of new-born babies gives them opportunities of identifying women at risk of post-natal and more general depression (Brown and Harris 1978; Oakley 1980). Their training is now geared to preparing them to recognize the forms of behaviour which indicate a worrying level of depression and/or anxiety, and the kind of situation, for example, a poor marital or extra-marital relationship, which may lie behind them.

Health visitors attached to general practice units are more likely than those with a district-based responsibility to be asked to make house calls to the very old, especially when they live alone or merely with other old people. Here, too, they are acquiring the knowledge and skills to alert themselves and others to incipient crises or chronic conditions in which depression, confusion and anxiety play a part.

There was a time in the 1950s when there was a good deal of evidence of general practitioner antagonism to health visitors, not least perhaps because they were then under the aegis of medical officers of health employed by local government. That antagonism appears to have diminished during the 1960s, when attachment schemes began (Warin 1968). Health visitors, for the most part, appeared contented with their redeployment and closer association with general practitioners (Jefferys 1965). They were still, however, part of the area (later district) health authority labour force and accountable to their nursing officer superiors for their work and not directly to the general practitioners whose patients they served.

Such a situation can lead to conflict if general practitioners see health visitors as a resource at their disposal to deal with problems which they have encountered and regard as urgent and not as independent fellow professionals. There is some evidence, for example, which the Court Committee (Department of Health and Social Security 1976) considered, that the work of health visitors attached to general practice units was more attenuated, and by implication less effective, than the work of unattached visitors who were able to concentrate more on the problems of young families.

There is also the potential for direct conflict between health visitors and social workers when they are both attached to general practice. They may well compete with one another for the kinds for work which both see as challenging and within their competence, while accusing the other of an unwillingness to take on work which is intellectually undemanding, performed at unsocial hours, or administratively time-consuming.

Nurses

Like health visitors, the district or home nurses employed by the district health authorities are now quite frequently attached to general practice (Reedy, Philips, and Newell 1976). They spend the greater part of their time in people's homes. They are there to give traditional bedside nursing services at the behest of general practitioners or of the hospitals who have discharged patients for care in the community. They are seldom if ever, called to assist patients with frank mental illness and, until recently, almost no attention was given in their training to the emotional problems which their patients and patients' relatives were likely to encounter in the chronic or terminal illnesses which they, the nurses, were mainly treating.

Since the implementation of the Family Doctors' Charter (British Medical Association 1965), most general practice groups have employed nurses mainly to work in their surgeries on a full- or part-time basis (Reedy, Philips, and Newell 1976). In the first instance, they undertook work for which they had had as much if not more training than the doctors, such as the dressing of wounds. In theory, this would leave the doctors with more time to undertake the diagnostic and psychotherapeutic work for which the nurses were not trained.

In practice, however, surgery nurses found themselves in a position to play a greatly extended version of the customary doctor's handmaiden role, if they so wished and were able to secure the doctors' approval. Patients with some chronic conditions which required regular monitoring or periodic treatments (e.g. those with skin complaints or high blood pressure) could use the nurse as a source of information and support. Anxious mothers also might learn that they could by-pass the often hasty consultation with a doctor for a more relaxed and reassuring chat about their symptoms and home circumstances wth the nurse.

There has been considerable reluctance on the part of the national representative bodies of both doctors and nurses to countenance the development of a specific nurse practitioner occupation in this country comparable to that which has grown up in the USA. At the grass roots level, however, many community-based nurses are trying actively to create conditions for themselves which would make them increasingly into general health counsellors to patients who would not dream of seeking help from a social service department or who would hesitate to 'waste the doctor's time' with their self-defined 'trivial' problems. In the very nature of things, it is impossible to gauge how much help of this kind is given and how much saving of doctors' time it represents. Such incidental work should not be ignored, however, as a source of potential emotional support for those patients with chronic physical complaints who are also anxious and depressed. It has the additional benefit of enhancing job satisfactions for many nurses who want to take more responsibility on their shoulders in the totality of care which can be offered in the general practice setting. Many of them are willing to undergo in-service further education in order to improve their understanding of complex human behaviour in health and illness and their capacity to help. Regular case conferences held in the practice at which they are asked to present their 'cases' can be of great importance in helping to extend their knowledge and their self-confidence.

IS PRECISE JOB DESCRIPTION THE SOLUTION TO
POTENTIAL INTER-OCCUPATIONAL RIVALRY?

In reviewing the development of group general practice as a setting for the work of members of three occupations besides medicine, I have drawn attention to the knowledge and skills which they are likely to possess to deal with depressed, anxious and confused patients and to the situational opportunities which their major occupational role objectives – social work, nursing and health visiting – give them to identify and help such patients. At the same time, I have pointed to the existence of potential inter-occupational rivalries which may prevent the thorough utilization of the resources which members of these three occupations represent.

Precise job description has in recent years become a central tenet of business management theory and a recent book suggests that it could contribute substantially to the effectiveness and efficiency of multi-disciplinary general practice units (Bowling 1981). In the international symposium on the Greater Medical Profession, to which I have already referred, Pellegrino, for example, argued: 'if volume medical care is to be delivered with some substance of quality and with consideration, the question of who does what, by whose order and agreement, must be resolved consciously and not left to happenstance, as is now the case' (Josiah Macy Jr Foundation 1973: 68) and Skeet, a representative of the nursing profession, made a similar plea: 'if we are to avoid the overlappings that are often interpreted as trespassing and that cause jealousies' (1973: 141).

In my view, however, we should think carefully before we suggest that general practitioners should seek to set out precise boundaries for the work of all those now working in their units, including themselves. Such a bureaucratic course may well be appropriate in a large, hierarchically structured organization like a hospital, although too great a rigidity may be injurious to patients even there, as well as to staff whose capacities to contribute to patient welfare may be restricted.

In the multi-disciplinary general practice setting, however, there is a conjunction of independent professionals whose knowledge and skills overlap to a considerable extent. That is the reality. In pursuing their core work, they will inevitably encounter opportunities to use knowledge and skills derived from the holistic view of health and illness which now informs general practice as a major primary health care facility.

Indeed, the attempt to set discrete boundaries around the work of any of the three occupations if done unilaterally by general practitioners would cause great offence and be counter-productive. Even if it were done in concert with all the occupations involved, it might have the effect of entrenching assertive professional stances rather than diminishing them.

Another cogent reason for avoiding rigid job descriptions, especially where the care of depressed and anxious people and their relatives is concerned, is that we have no clear evidence of the value of different forms of non-drug therapy undertaken by different professions or laymen and women in the alleviation of distress. While this is the case, we had better go along with Bennett who states: 'the knowledge and capacity to intervene successfully does not reside in any profession, individual or service, but in the person who is on the spot when needed' (Josiah Macy Jr Foundation 1973: 86).

General practitioners, therefore, should recognize the potential of the other occupational groups who have joined them, especially in the prevention of anxiety and depression and its management in the very different guises which they take on. By encouraging mutual exchanges, without implying occupational hierarchies of knowledge and skills, they can maximize situational advantages. They can also lay the foundations for a high level of inter-occupational harmony and of job satisfaction. These, although not ensuring automatically a contribution to the primary health care objectives of caring for the mentally ill, are necessary pre-conditions for patients' welfare.

REFERENCES

Balint, M. (1964) *The Doctor, His Patient and the Illness*. Revised 2nd edn. London: Pitman Medical.
Bowling, A. (1981) *Delegation in General Practice*. London: Tavistock Publications.
British Medical Association (1965) *A Charter for the Family Doctor*. London: British Medical Association.
Brown, G. W. and Harris, T. O. (1978) *Social Origins of Depression*. London: Tavistock Publications.
Clare, A. W. and Corney, R. H. (1982) *Social Work and Primary Health Care*. London: Academic Press.
Department of Health and Social Security (1976) *Fit for the future*. Report of the Committee on Child Health Services. Vol. 1. London: HMSO.
Huntington, J. (1981) *Social Work and General Medical Practice*. London: George Allen and Unwin.
Jefferys, M. (1965) *An Anatomy of Social Welfare Services*. London: Michael Joseph.
Jefferys, M. and Sachs, H. (1983) *Re-thinking General Practice: dilemmas in Primary Medical Care*. London: Tavistock Publications.
Josiah Macy Jr Foundation (1973) *The Greater Medical Profession*. Report of a Symposium sponsored jointly by the Royal Society of Medicine and the Josiah Macy Jr Foundation. New York: Josiah Macy Jr Foundation.

Oakley, A. (1980) *Women Confined: Towards a Sociology of Childbirth*. Oxford: Martin Robertson.

Parsons, T. (1951) *The Social System*. London: Routledge and Kegan Paul.

Reedy, B. L. E., Philips, P. R., and Newell, D. J. (1976) Nurses and Nursing in Primary Medical Care in England. *British Medical Journal* 2: 1304–306.

Seebohm Report (1968) *Report of the Committee on Local Authority and Allied Personal Social Services*. Cmnd 3703. London: HMSO.

Stimson, G. V. and Webb, B. (1975) *Going to see the doctor*. London: Routledge and Kegan Paul.

Warin, J. F. (1968) General Practitioners and Nursing Staff: a complete Attachment Scheme in retrospect and prospect. *British Medical Journal* 2: 41–5.

Roslyn Corney

Discussant

In this area there are basically two questions that need to be answered. First, are there major advantages to be gained by reinforcing general practice with the attachments of other professionals rather than having these professionals placed in other settings? Second, if we decide that there are such advantages, which is the best way to organize the team so that it works both effectively *and* efficiently.

The close relationship between social problems and health, both physical and mental, indicates the need for different professionals to collaborate closely with one another. In addition, it has been found that people with psychosocial problems are more likely to visit their GP than any other social agency, presenting their problem either covertly or overtly. On the basis of my own work on social problems I would point out a number of obvious advantages to having social workers at the surgery. There is much stigma attached to visiting a social services department for help, partly due to the shame associated with having social problems and partly due to the statutory nature of local authority social work. A depressed mother, for example, may be too frightened to go to the social services department for help because of the stories she has heard of children being taken away from their parents. Health problems are generally much more socially acceptable and the surgery is usually more accessible and familiar to the patient. Some or all of these advantages would also hold for the attachments of other professionals, such as psychiatric nurses, psychologists, health visitors and psychiatrists.

Apart from such considerations, it is also essential to find out whether 'attachments' actually benefit the patient. There is little doubt that when good working relationships are built up, the attachments benefit the professionals concerned, as in John Horder's account and that of others (Goldberg and Neill 1972; Graham and Sher 1976; Bowen et al. 1978; Williams and Clare 1979). But what about the patient or client? As Margot Jefferys has pointed out, independent measures of outcome have not been obtained between social work carried out in a general practice setting and that carried out in a local authority setting. In addition, with other professionals, there has been very *little* research carried out comparing outcome between settings.

In our unit, we have attempted to compare the work done by attached social worker with local authority social workers by comparing referrals and the resulting social workers' interventions (Corney and Briscoe 1977; Corney 1980; Clare and Corney 1982). We have also asked clients from the two settings for their views of the service and whether it has helped (Corney 1983a). Overall, the results come out in favour of the attachment service, with the attachment social workers being far more thorough in their work and offering a more personal service. The clients in this setting were much more satisfied, and a higher proportion felt that they had been helped. The evidence strongly suggests that when the attachment scheme was working well (and this was not always the case), the social workers, being in close contact with other team members, took more professional pride in their work and felt more responsible to these others (Bowen et al. 1978).

We have also carried out two clinical trials of social workers operating in attachments, but unfortunately no similar trials have taken place in social services departments. The results of these trials suggest that the involvement of social workers had a beneficial effect only on certain groups of patients. These patients tended to be the more chronic cases with more long-term neuroses or depression, who also had many social problems requiring practical assistance (Cooper et al. 1975; Corney 1984). Clearly, in this area, there is much more research that needs to be done.

More recently, a member of the General Practice Research Unit, Monica Briscoe, has begun to evaluate the role of health visitors in the identification and management of psychosocial problems. She is also investigating the relationship between health visitors and other members of the primary care team (Briscoe and Lindley 1982).

It should also be pointed out that there are certain disadvantages to the patient when a number of professionals are all in under one roof. They do not have so much chance to pick and choose between different agencies, and if they acquire a bad reputation it will follow them around. It is also true that these benefits to patients and professionals only accrue when the working relationships developed are free from conflict, aggravation and misunderstanding. Where relationships are poor, the communication system will usually break down, leading to inappropriate referrals, little feedback and much dissatisfaction on all sides (Gilchrist *et al*. 1978).

This leads us to the second question. If these advantages only occur in schemes free from professional conflict, which is the best way to make the attachments work? Both previous speakers have considered this question and Margot Jefferys discusses whether a stricter allocation of tasks between team members would lead to less conflict. Certainly, where there is a stable division of work, there is less possibility for inter-occupational rivalry and misunderstanding. John Horder, however, suggests that the personality and aptitudes of an individual are as important as his training, implying that strict demarcation of tasks is neither feasible nor efficient. This is particularly pertinent to the field of mental illness. For example, a social worker who has been widowed may be especially gifted at counselling the bereaved, while a health visitor may find she is particularly good at group work.

However, for professionals to work together effectively as a group, some changes from the present system will have to be made to reduce some of the antagonisms and conflict. The reasons for these problems have been documented elsewhere (Huntington 1981; Clare and Corney 1982; Corney 1983b); they are generally greater when attachments involve non-medically qualified staff members, such as social workers, as they are not used to the hospital situation where doctors professionally dominate. I feel that the major barrier to communication is the differing status differentials between the professions. However, with the present situation, where GPs are independent contractors with overall responsibility and other members of the team are salaried members of other organizations, it is difficult to see how such equality can come about. While many hopes have been pinned on educational reform with more joint training at the undergraduate and postgraduate level, leading to a better understanding of each other's roles and skills (Ratoff, Rose, and Smith 1974; BASW/RCGP 1978), the results of these training courses are very mixed (Schenk 1979; Samuel and Dodge 1981). Further, others consider that education is largely irrelevant without dramatic structural change (Dingwall 1979). If decisions are made to encourage attachments of other professionals in a routine manner, some major changes in training and organization will have to take place.

REFERENCES

BASW/RCGP (1978) Some suggestions for teaching about co-operation between social work and general practice. *Journal of the Royal College of General Practitioners* 28: 96, 670–73.
Bowen, B., Davies, Y. A., Rushton, A., and Winny, J. (1978) Adventure into health. *Update* 6: 1512–515.
Briscoe, M. E. and Lindley, P. (1982) Identification and management of psychosocial problems by health visitors. *Health Visitor* 55: 165–69.

Clare, A. W. and Corney, R. H. (1982) *Social Work and Primary Health Care.* London: Academic Press.

Cooper, B., Harwin, B. G., Depla, C., and Shepherd, M. (1975) Mental health care in the community: an evaluative study. *Psychological Medicine* 5: 372–80.

Corney, R. H. (1980) A comparative study of referrals to a local authority intake team with a general practice attachment scheme and the resulting social workers' interventions. *Social Science and Medicine* 14A: 675–82.

—— (1983a) Social work in general practice. In *Research Highlights – 7, Collaboration and Conflict – Working with Others.* Aberdeen: Department of Social Work, pp. 94–125.

—— (1983b) The views of clients new to a general practice attachment scheme and to a local authority social work intake team. *Social Science and Medicine* 17: 1549–558.

—— (1984) The effectiveness of attached social workers in the management of depressed female patients in general practice. *Psychological Medicine* (Monograph Supplement 6) Cambridge: Cambridge University Press.

Corney, R. H. and Briscoe, M. E. (1977) Social workers and their clients: a comparison between primary health care and local authority settings. *Journal of the Royal College of General Practitioners* 27: 295–301.

Dingwall, R. (1979) Problems of teamwork in primary care. In T. Briggs, A. Webb, and F. Lonsdale (eds) *Teamwork in the Health and Social Services.* London: Croom Helm, pp. 111–37.

Gilchrist, I. C., Gough, J. B., Horsfall-Turner, Y. R., Ineston, E. M., Keele, G., Marks, B., and Scott, H. J. (1978) Social work in general practice. *Journal of the Royal College of General Practitioners* 28: 675–86.

Goldberg, E. M. and Neill, J. E. (1972) *Social Work in General Practice.* London: George Allen and Unwin.

Graham, H. and Sher, M. (1976) Social work and general medical practice: Personal accounts of a three year attachment. *British Journal of Social Work* 6: 233–49.

Huntington, J. (1981) *Social Work and General Medical Practice.* London: Allen and Unwin.

Ratoff, L., Rose, A., and Smith, C. (1974) Social workers and GPs: problems of working together. *Social Work Today* 5: 16, 497–500.

Samuel, O. W. and Dodge, D. (1981) A course in collaboration for social workers and general practitioners. *Journal of the Royal College of General Practitioners* 31: 172–75.

Schenk, F. (1979) A course on collaboration between social workers and general practitioners during their vocational training. *Medical Education* 13: 31–3.

Williams, P. and Clare, A. W. (1979) Social workers in primary health care: The general practitioner's viewpoint. *Journal of the Royal College of General Practitioners* 29: 554–58.

General Discussion

Dr L. Ratoff: For 10–15 years we have been operating a team practice similar to Dr Horder's and have been struck by the role-perception of the professional workers involved. This was demonstrated strikingly when our senior health visitor was replaced by a younger health visitor and we found that cases formerly referred to the health visitor were going to the social worker. This reflected the perception of roles and abilities by other team members.

Joint training at an early stage is imperative because so many interprofessional misunderstandings arise from the lack of contact in the undergraduate years.

A sociological survey of our own practice brought out the status hierarchies in a way that we had not appreciated. For example, we came to understand that not only were doctors financially better off, but they were all in posts many years longer and had vested interest and ownership in the properties which the other workers had not. In all team work one needs to be aware of the status hierarchies which exist.

Dr H. L. Freeman: I should like to ask whether the relatively sophisticated experience described by Drs Horder and Ratoff can be applied more widely in general practice?

Dr J. Horder: This is a very difficult question to which I have no satisfactory answer. We have hitherto put most of our hopes in education and have given up expecting that such developments occur quickly. It has taken thirty years to have vocational training made available and necessary for every general practitioner. However, none of us has found the way to reach all general practitioners who are not reachable, as Professor Morrell's unpublished work has shown.

Dr A. R. K. Mitchell: Several speakers have expressed the commonality of the sharing of experience in team work. I should emphasize the fact that each member of the team has a unique task and that no other members of the team perceive this uniqueness. It seems that the more people there are working in teams, the more it is necessary to be clear about their individual roles.

Professor Jefferys: One cannot go through life without labels of some kind. An occupational label makes sense, especially in an inequal world when the reality of the situation is that the general practitioner frequently owns the premises, employs some of the staff and accepts attachments from the Social Services Department, District Health Authority, etc. Such factors certainly influence the whole pattern of relationships. I am not sure, however, that job descriptions and job analyses in themselves can solve problems. In the small-scale teams that we are trying to develop – and one of the problems is the eponymous nature of the setting which is called general practice, where the general practitioner is seen by everyone, including patients, as the central figure – we have to accept and recognize that the situation raises problems for those occupational groups who are there in various capacities. Whether we can allocate tasks by consensus judgement remains uncertain.

On the other hand, to have the general practitioner impose a pattern of duties and tasks, and have the authority to judge and evaluate the work which is done by other people would also clearly not meet the aspirations of occupational groups who see themselves as independent, autonomous workers with responsibility for the tasks which they themselves undertake, and who use the general practice setting only as a setting in which they claim professional freedom. It seems to me that attempts to make rigid distinctions in a situation with all sorts of conflicts, will either court disaster or breed people who tolerate a degree of authority and do not want any kind of personal growth and independent contributions. Ideally, one would prefer a team of lively people who are all growing together, so to speak, and taking problems from each other.

Dr H. Tegner: As a general practitioner I should like to raise the question of patient participation. There are now several groups throughout this country where primary health care teams and their patients meet together informally on a regular basis, which gives the opportunity for the patients to enlighten us to some extent about what they see to be their needs, and for us to express what we believe to be our role. This often opens new doors for patients and perhaps enables them to understand that the GP's role is wider than they thought. Because the whole team takes part in these discussions – health visitors, social workers, receptionists, nurses – we are able to give a much clearer view of what we do to our patients. The concept of patient participation also includes open meetings to which other people are invited and with a certain amount of appropriate publicity I think a lot of good can be done.

Dr A. Brook: Over a number of years, I have been involved with general practitioners and their teams, working in their premises and have often asked myself why patients with psychological difficulties go to their doctor. It seems to me that about half of them see their problems as illnesses and go to their doctor because they want specific remedies. The other half go because they want some understanding of their problems, their difficulties and their conflicts. That means they want the doctor to listen, not to talk, and to listen is not easy. In short, I think many people want counselling appropriate to the setting of general practice.

Although, as has been pointed out, there has to be a differentiation of roles, it is in this area of counselling appropriate to general practice that there can be a real sharing between the various disciplines. The type of group where a whole practice meets with a visiting specialist psychiatrist or psychotherapist is able to share information and the individual members can get together, pool their resources and know more about their patients. It also acts as a support group so that the professionals can tolerate anxiety more effectively and are so more able to give the patients experience and understanding.

Dr D. L. Crombie: The basic problem of the general practitioner is his inherited professional isolation. The GP rapidly finds himself in an intellectually isolated situation and very often it is a self-selected role.

With regard to the team, I am not sure that its effectiveness arises from the reasons that have been discussed. I feel that it is much more to do with the fact that the general practitioner cannot get away and has to abandon his/her isolated position. Some of the things about the team are in a sense counterproductive. We often talk about efficiency and effectiveness: for instance, in our practice we say: one problem, one problem solver. The crux of working with health visitors and social workers, however, is the need to sort out on an *ad hoc* basis which parts of a problem belong to individual team members. The demarcation of responsibility cannot be viewed in industrial terms.

I would also suggest that for the same reasons John Horder's type of frequent sessions are, in effect, case conferences. Further, I take the old-fashioned view that one of the greatest effects perpetuating intellectual isolation in general practice is the lack of a case conference culture; even today it does not exist, and it is very difficult to create. There is no equivalent to the hospital setting where you cannot get away from your colleagues; they look over your shoulders and they are in a position to comment and see what you are doing. If professional isolation is indeed the central problem, then team work may be a very elaborate and expensive way round it.

Mr A. C. Adams: Dr Corney forgot to mention that when patients go to see GPs it is not only because of their accessibility but also because they help obtain benefits under the National Insurance Fund. This is a vital function. A visit to social services departments does not confer any such benefits. General practitioners, through their certificates, spend a very large portion of the total national insurance budget.

Mr B. Kat: Professor Jefferys used the word 'colonizing' in relation to the area of integration of work. With regard to counselling, it is interesting to see the developments being made by a significant number of professions to 'colonize' the counsellor's role. They include social work, in some places health visiting, community psychiatric nursing, occasionally nurse therapy, and occasionally clinical psychology. There are also developments in the work of general practitioners themselves. It should be asked whether this is an area where rational decision-making is possible, or just an evolutionary process where there will be some kind of natural selection. In that event the process might lead to one or two professionals concentrating on this area of work, or, perhaps, the emergence of a community mental health specialty which is either an integration of existing professions or a new profession entirely.

Dr P. Tyrer: However one regards collaboration, there is no doubt that many general practitioners are not keen on participation with patients or on long consultations with doctors. Nor do they have the facilities described by Dr Horder. In good health centres where GPs get on well with each other and with other staff, it is possible to bring them together and undertake collaborative ventures. However, GPs are independent contractors and many of them choose to work on their own or in small groups. Layer forms of collaboration are not for them. The primary care setting is only one of the places where the mental health work in the community should be going on. Similarly, I have found it necessary to by-pass the general practitioner and see the patient on premises away from the surgery. I have yet to find an effective way of persuading the general practitioner to collaborate against his will.

Professor Jefferys: There is an evolutionary process operating in all team work. Teams are created by people coming together and trading off with one another the kinds of work which they want to do; trying to obtain work of greater intrinsic interest and greater external rewards. We have seen the processes of fission and fusion of occupations to form new occupations, and this is still going on. We have, for example, rejected the nurse practitioner in this country but in practice, nurse practitioners are beginning to evolve from the grass roots.

Dr Horder: It is principally the business of the representative professional body to ensure standards in general practice. We have been trying to deal with this issue ever since its inception, but with independent contractors you cannot impose authority, you can only exercise influence. Most of the efforts of the Royal College of General Practitioners has been through education, whether through vocational training or, increasingly, through continuing education, where we are demanding that half of the general practice profession think increasingly of standards. We are also encouraging them as much as possible to form small groups where they all contribute in order to maintain their enthusiasm and their intellectual activity, and to develop habits of mutual criticism and, above all, self-criticism.

PART 4

TREATMENT
EFFECTIVENESS

G. W. Ashcroft

Treatment effectiveness

To reduce this topic to manageable proportions I shall confine the discussion to the drug treatment of depressive and panic attack syndromes. The paper will be in two parts. First, there is a general outline of the problems encountered in assessing the effects of treatment; second, an account of some specific studies in which we have examined response in general practice studies.

ASSESSING THE EFFECTS OF TREATMENT

Selection for treatment

Many depressive reactions in a general practice population are clearly an appropriate reaction to adverse life events. No simple rules are available to decide at what point the depression is to be regarded as excessive or inappropriate. A number of criteria are combined in arriving at such a decision; severity, duration, nature and intensity of precipitating events, presence of psychological symptoms. Too rigid a selection for any treatment may exclude patients who would benefit. However, in clinical trials of anti-depressant therapy it is essential that standardized interview techniques are used to describe the symptom profiles and severity of the depressive syndromes included in the trial.

Natural history of the disorders

There is little information available on the duration of and nature of spontaneous recovery from these minor affective syndromes. The assumption is often made that recovery is rapid and complete. This assumption may be unjustified, and many patients may suffer months of severe dysphoria without treatment. In the absence of clear information on natural history it can be argued that placebo groups should be included in all studies of treatment in this population.

Nature of response

Rating scales, such as the Hamilton Rating Scale, measure the response to treatment in terms of the disappearance of symptoms. A complete assessment would, however, include other measures, for example, recovery of social functioning and the recovery of activities, interests and other aspects of positive well being.

Non-drug factors in determining response to treatment

In general practice studies the patients are in their home environment, which carries additional possibilities for both adverse and favourable effects on response to treatment. Adverse factors will include the effect of additional adverse life events and the continuous effect of an unsatisfactory environment. As the patient starts to improve, the response may be facilitated by the opportunity for new activities and explorations in the presence of supportive relatives. In future studies it is desirable that we attempt to measure these variables, although if the methods for such assessment are too complex they may reduce patient co-operation in the overall investigation.

Acceptability of drug treatment and other treatment options

A drug may effectively relieve symptoms but have unacceptable side effects, or toxicity or other risks. The patients' response to side effects is often to stop taking the drugs, and in studies of anti-depressant treatment in general practice low compliance has been shown to be a serious factor in reducing the response to otherwise effective drugs. In such a setting the ideal drug might be one with fewer side effects than those used in hospital, even if pharmacological effects on depression are reduced and the treatment regime in terms of dosage and duration of treatment may also differ from that used in severe or recurrent disorders.

With the introduction of non-drug treatments for depression and anxiety, e.g. cognitive therapy, it will be essential to compare these treatments with drug treatments. It is essential here that such studies should be concerned with the practicability of the treatments in normal treatment settings.

Specificity of drug treatment

It is important to attempt to match the treatment regime to the needs of individual patients. The search for drug specificity for particular depressive syndromes will continue, although to date the results of such studies have been disappointing, the specificity of the tricyclic drugs for the panic attack syndrome being an exception. Groups of patients, for example, the elderly, may also require drugs with particular characteristics. Sex differences in response must also be considered.

EXPERIENCE WITH GENERAL PRACTICE STUDIES

Over the past seven years I have been involved in a number of drug trials in a general practice setting. I shall concentrate here on describing some of the puzzling and anomalous findings from these studies which I believe may provide a challenge to some of our accepted beliefs.

The treatment of depression in general practice: a comparison of L-tryptophan, amitriptyline and a combination of L-tryptophan and amitriptyline with placebo[1]

One hundred and fifteen patients from five general practices participated in this twelve-week double blind study.

1. The results of treatment as assessed by observer and self ratings are shown in *Figures 1* and *2*. There are interesting discrepancies between the two methods of assessment. Self assessment of mood showed a higher placebo response with a more rapid response in the amitriptyline groups and less response to tryptophan alone.
2. Compliance was assessed in this study by measurement of amitryptyline plasma levels. Compliance overall was 80 per cent over the period of the study. An important subgroup of patients, 20 per cent of those on amitriptyline, failed to take the drugs from the fourth week of the trial onwards. This subgroup showed the same response rate to treatment as the patients who had continued to take amitriptyline.
3. Symptom profiles on the Present State Examination and on the Hamilton Rating Scale (HRS) were examined in relation to response both to placebo and to active drugs. No predictions of placebo or of drug response were found from an examination of symptom profiles. No overall correlation was found between plasma levels of amitriptyline and response to the drug.

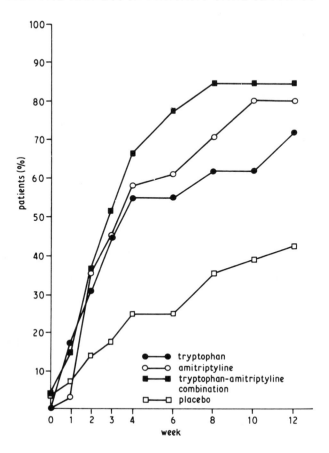

Figure 1   Comparison of treatments showing the cumulative percentage of patients in each group in remission, defined as reaching a score of 0 (not depressed) on the global rating scale

Zimelidine and amitriptyline in the treatment of depressive illness in general practice[2]

This report describes a double blind study of 56 patients, 25 receiving zimelidine and 31 amitriptyline.

Comparable responses were obtained to treatment with the two drugs, with regard to relief of depression and anxiety symptoms. Some specificity of action was, however, seen in relief of sleep disturbance (*Figure 3*) and with regard to weight change (*Figure 4*). These effects might have made zimelidine a valuable addition to the drug treatment of some depressed patients if it had

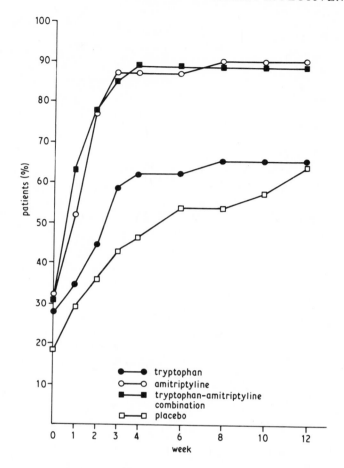

Figure 2   Comparison of treatments showing the cumulative percentage of patients in each group reaching a score of 50 (normal mood) or more on the visual analogue scale

not been withdrawn subsequently because of reports of cases of Guillain Barré Syndrome.

While the common side effects of the anti-depressants were less prominent with zimelidine (*Table 1*), it is interesting to note that a new syndrome of nausea and headache proved troublesome in this (*Table 2*) and other studies and should be looked for in trials of other drugs with similar pharmacological actions.

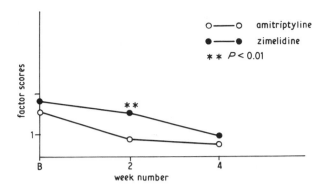

Figure 3 Sleep disturbance as measured by the Hamilton scale in the amitriptyline and zimelidine treated groups

Source: Factor VI as derived by Clearly and Guy (1977)

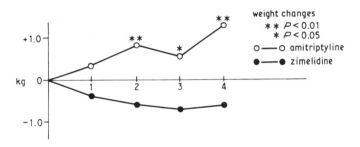

Figure 4   Weight changes in the amitriptyline and zimelidine treated groups

Screening of an elderly rural population for physical and psychiatric illness with an investigation of the role of anti-depressant medication in the treatment of those suffering from depressive illness[3]

In this study all patients aged sixty-five and over registered with one of the eight doctors working at Inverurie Health Centre were visited in their homes by a research worker. Screening for depression was carried out using the General Health Questionnaire and the Leeds Scale for self assessment of anxiety and depression. Patients scoring above cut off scores were then interviewed by a psychiatrist using the Standardized Psychiatric Interview for use in community surveys. Out of 1,800 patients screened, 50 were identified as suffering from depression and 32 entered a double blind study of the

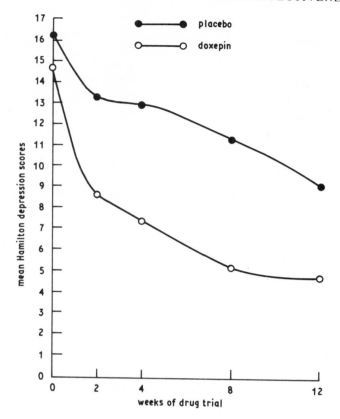

Figure 5   Weeks of drug trial

efficacy of doxepin. Both groups improved during the course of the trial, improvement being greater in patients on doxepin (*Figure 5*).

An investigation into the nature of panic attack symptoms and their response to either a tricyclic anti-depressant or behavioural treatment[4]

This study was recently completed in a general practice setting. Sixty patients in four equal groups were treated with:

1. placebo clomipramine plus placebo behaviour therapy;
2. active low dose clomipramine plus placebo behaviour therapy;
3. placebo clomipramine plus active behaviour therapy;
4. active low dose clomipramine plus active behaviour therapy.

Only preliminary results are available so far, but already some challenging and interesting facts are emerging, for example *placebo response* seems to be virtually non-existent in the first month of treatment. Furthermore, *response to 30 mg. or less of clomipramine* daily is rapid and complete: 70 per cent have lost their panic attacks within one week and remain free of these symptoms after one month. Unlike the study in depression, it seems possible that drug treatment may need to be continued for up to six months to avoid subsequent relapse.

OVERALL CONCLUSIONS AND SUGGESTIONS FOR FURTHER STUDIES

This series of studies suggest the following tentative conclusions which require testing in further studies.

1. It is possible to define a group of depressed patients (age 18–65) in general practice with a poor short-term response to placebo but a good response (75 per cent) to full doses of a standard tricyclic anti-depressant. These patients will have been depressed for longer than five weeks and will have an HRS score of twelve or over.
2. It is possible that in most of these patients a short period of treatment – four weeks – with full doses (150 mg. amitriptyline) of the drug will be adequate to treat the episode, but further studies are required to assess the risks of recurrence.
3. In the elderly, compliance is severely reduced if the drugs have a high incidence of side effects. The search for the best drug regime in these patients should be continued.
4. The role of environmental factors in response to treatment requires further investigation.
5. The dramatic response of panic attacks to certain tricyclics is important both practically and theoretically and can be studied in general practice populations.

REFERENCES

1. Thomson, Joan, Rankin, H., Ashcroft, G. W., Yates, Celia M., McQueen, Judith K., and Cummings, S. W. (1982) The treatment of depression in general practice: a comparison of L-tryptophan and amitriptyline with placebo. *Psychological Medicine* 12: 741–51.
2. Loudon, J. B., Tiplady, B., Ashcroft, G. W., and Waddell, J. L. (1981) Zimelidine and amitriptyline in the treatment of depressive illness in general practice. *Acta Psychiatrica Scandinavica* Suppl. 290. 63: 454–63.
3. Blackwood, G., Beattie, J. A. G., and Ashcroft, G. W. (in preparation)
4. Waring, H. L. (personal communication).

Anthony Ryle

Efficacy of treatment of mental illness in primary care settings

The efficacy of the treatment provided in primary care settings can be considered in terms of the degree to which treatments of known power are available, the degree to which they are skilfully delivered to patients, and the degree to which the setting either enhances or reduces either the effectiveness or the cost of the treatment, or avoids the potential cost of, or harm done by, treatment in specialist centres. This paper considers the treatment of major and minor mental illnesses (excluding the disorders of childhood or old age) with reference to the general practice setting, the Community Psychiatric Nursing Service and Consulting Mental Health Centres.

MAJOR MENTAL ILLNESSES

Effective pharmacological treatments are available for both depressive and schizophrenic illnesses. However, many patients do not find their way to treatment or do not maintain their medication after discharge from hospital care. Psychosocial factors that provoke illness or relapse are now well documented (Brown and Harris 1978; Leff and Vaughn 1980), but the implications of these findings for prevention and treatment are little applied; this is true both of the psychotherapy of depression and of the use of family intervention in schizophrenia (Leff et al. 1982).

Depression, of varying severity and aetiology, is a commonly encountered symptom in general practice, but the effectiveness of general practice treatment is uncertain. One paper described the difficulty experienced by a psychiatrist in finding new cases of depression, and postulated that this was the result of effective anti-depressant treatment by general practitioners (Little, Kerr, and McClelland 1978). In a study of five selected practices, however, Johnson (1973) showed that of 73 patients with depression, mostly stress-provoked, few had felt helped by the doctor–patient relationship, only two had been offered psychotherapy and the dosage and duration of drug therapy was often insufficient, with poor patient compliance. That effective psychotherapy of depression is possible in the general practice setting has been demonstrated in two recent studies of cognitive psychotherapy (Blackburn *et al.* 1981; Teasdale *et al.* 1984). Such therapy is not normally available and would need the attachment of therapists to general practices.

In the case of schizophrenia, effective management of medication and of the psychological and social aspects of treatment is beyond the scope of the GP working alone. Community psychiatric nurses, working in relation to practices and from hospital, are cost-effective (Dawes 1980), acceptable to GPs (Leopoldt 1979; Shaw 1977; Harker, Leopoldt, and Robinson 1976) and welcomed by patients (Mangen and Griffith 1982). They have an essential role to play in the effective management of both medication and of the family and social problems that play such an important part in preventing relapse.

The community mental health centre represents another approach to the improvement of the primary care of mental illness. These centres offer ease of access compared to hospitals, with less risk of institutionalization, while providing a wide range of professional skills. The success of these centres is disputed. The United States experience is reviewed by Feldman (1979), who points out the complexity of assessing a service that has evolved rapidly in a changing social context. Feldman suggests that the changes in attitude expressed by, or emerging from, these centres may prove more durable than the particular structures evolved. In this country the debate is by no means closed, and at least one centre has reported considerable reductions in hospital admission and mean bed occupancy rates following the setting up of a mental health centre (Brindle House, undated; see also Bouras and Brough 1982).

In summary, as regards major mental illnesses, there is reasonably good evidence to show that work in general practice would be strengthened by the addition of more professionals from other specialties to the team; that community psychiatric nurses working with GPs and from hospital bases are effective; and that these approaches and the development of community mental health centres are able to improve care and reduce hospitalization. The evidence is, of course, incomplete and the problems of evaluation will never be fully solved, but there seems no reason to doubt that the wider application of the better practices that have been described and to some degree assessed would be beneficial.

MINOR MENTAL ILLNESS

The neuroses and personality disorders often termed 'minor' are frequently disabling and personally costly, and their incidence is very high. Only a small proportion of individuals suffering from chronic neurotic symptomatology are under professional care at any one time. A medical consultation is often associated with changes in the associated marital, family and social stresses that are more prevalent in these individuals, and is best seen as an episode in a long-term career. Success in intervention is best measured in terms of stable improvements in personal and social functioning rather than by changes in symptomatology. Such considerations are, however, often ignored by research workers, especially those working in hospital contexts and with drug treatments.

It might be expected that the general practitioner, with his long-term contact with patients, often in the context of their families, would be particularly effective in treating these conditions, but in general the response of GPs to neurotic and psychosomatic patients is based on the attempt to provide symptomatic relief with medication. While the minor tranquillizers offer short-term relief for many symptoms, there is no evidence that they influence the long-term course. Moreover, they often produce dependency and side-effects and, by labelling the patient's problem as medical, may actively discourage patients from taking responsibility for their lives or seeking to control their symptoms by psychological means.

While some GPs develop skills in the psychological management of this sort of patient, and while many provide long-term support (though this dependency too can be disabling), it is likely that more skilful application of psychological and social work skills will require the attachment of other professionals to practices. Community psychiatric nurses, as already discussed, play a role here when working in GP attachments. Paykel et al. (1982) and others have described the attachment of social workers (Ratoff and Pearson 1970; Cooper 1971; Graham and Sher 1976; Goldberg and Neill 1972), of psychotherapists (Temperley 1978) and of clinical psychologists (Johnston 1978; Clark 1979; Koch 1979; Bhagat, Lewis, and Shillitoe 1979; Rosen and Wiens 1979; Ives 1979; McPherson 1981; Burns 1981; Dewsbury 1982; France and Robson 1982; Butler and Davidson 1982; Jerrom et al. 1983; Spector 1984). These reports tend to suggest satisfaction with the service provided among both the patients and the GPs and many also describe a reduction in consultation rates and in prescribing. However, studies with no-treatment or treatment-as-usual controls are rare and the follow-up is usually brief. Such studies as do exist (for example Earll and Kincey (1982) for behavioural interventions; Blackburn et al. (1981) and Teasdale et al. (1984) for cognitive therapy and France and Robson (1982) for unspecified clinical psychological interventions), tend to show more rapid recovery with psychological treatments, but less certain long-term benefits. This has led some authors to question the enthusiasm among clinical psychologists for work in primary care settings (McPherson 1981; Spector 1984) and to underline the need for more careful evaluation of the work. Such evaluations need to attend both to the effective use of the attached professionals in primary care settings. Direct clinical work with patients tends to be over-valued in both practice and research, while the potential value of educating primary care workers, of modifying practice, and of promoting the opportunities for research, are neglected.

THE EVALUATION OF PSYCHOTHERAPY

As regards the evaluation of treatment methods, I believe that the need for rigour in research should be matched by a scrupulousness in argument and I feel called upon to comment on some of Professor Shepherd's recent statements on this topic. His pointing (Shepherd 1979) to the failed Maudsley–Tavistock trial (Candy et al. 1972) as evidence for 'the reluctance on the part of professional psychotherapists to have their activities subjected to independent evaluation' is a very idiosyncratic interpretation of that rather poorly conceived trial which, like the camel, bore the marks of having been designed by a committee. It is also a remark that ignores the embarrassingly copious, if very uneven, flood of work in this area. Nor is it fair to go on to quote from one of the better studies in the field – that of Sloane et al. (1975) – a conclusion that the trial favoured the behavioural approach, when this is explicitly denied by the authors, while failing to report the considerable efficacy demonstrated for both approaches in the study. Wilkinson (1984) has clearly indicated the ultimate conclusion of such arguments. Basing his argument on the currently fashionable but controversial technique of meta-analysis (Andrews and Harvey 1981; Prioleau et al. 1983), this author calls for the protection of 'unhappy and at times desperate people' from 'unscrupulous practitioners of psychotherapy' and links this with a call to the reader to digest the 'disturbing piece of information' that consultant psychotherapists have increased in numbers by 350 since 1975. I note that this increase, of which I am a part, was in an army originally numbered 18, and note too that the present numbers are still less than half the ratio of one per 400,000 population recommended by the Royal College of Psychiatrists.

I do not believe that the treatment of patients or the design of services will be helped by this kind of discourse. Psychotherapy is poorly evaluated but so too is psychiatry; on the basis of the Northwick Park studies of ECT (a well standardized treatment for a well defined condition) (Clinical Research Centre 1984) one might ask: 'How many unhappy and at times desperate people without delusions have had unnecessary ECT?', but one would not propose the disbanding of the psychiatric establishment.

The phenomena which psychotherapy seeks to change are more complex than those treated medically, and the nature of the influence brought to bear on the patient more difficult to isolate and define. The patient lives his/her life in a social context on the basis of cognitive structures organizing hierarchies of aims, assumptions and strategies. At each level in this hierarchy, action involves intention, perception, recall, planning, execution and the evaluation of the action.

Different therapies influence different levels in the hierarchy and attack different points in the sequence, but any changes will be incorporated by the patient into his/her system, so that similar inputs may produce different outcomes or different inputs may produce indistinguishable change (Ryle 1984).

To attempt controlled trials of therapy often results in designs like the comparison of 'a random assortment of psychotropic tablets swept off the floor at each of two busy pharmacies, and administered in random assortments to unspecified patients' (Shapiro 1980). Our efforts might be better directed to demonstrating the effects of specific interventions on single cases or in groups of single cases, as was argued by Shapiro (1966) twenty years ago. This approach demands the specification of goals directly related to the patient's dysfunction, which is also good for the therapy, and it is particularly suitable for work in primary care settings, where short-term treatments are given to heterogeneous collections of usually long-term patients. It can, in such settings, be contrasted with a treatment-as-usual control condition. The specification of goals can go beyond the focus on symptoms and behaviour to a concern with beliefs, assumptions and the patient's ineffective life procedures, thus incorporating areas of concern to dynamic psychotherapists. A small series of cases treated in a primary care setting with this approach has been reported (Ryle 1980) and a larger outpatient sample is currently under investigation. I believe that future evaluation of psychological treatments in primary care settings should follow this model of a single case or a small series of single cases. The aim will be to develop methods capable of producing relevant change at minimum cost. I doubt, on the basis of research so far, whether any one approach will emerge with a clear advantage over all others, though I have a prejudice in favour of the unprejudiced therapist capable of integrating ideas and methods from the whole span of current therapies.

THE ROLE OF THE SPECIALIST IN PRIMARY CARE

Finally, a word about the role of the specialist working in primary care settings. Psychiatrists, psychotherapists or clinical psychologists, whether working in new organizations such as Community Mental Health Centres or in relation to existing organizations such as general practices, are clearly called upon to do more than simply shift the location of their clinical work. Given the size of the problem posed by the chronic, severe mental illnesses and the long-term distress of the more common disorders, a principal concern must be the support and development of the work of the primary care practitioners and the evaluation of the processes of case referral and of the effectiveness of the treatment provided. Such research is rare and difficult and we should be grateful when it is attempted even though the methodology is likely to be flawed. But here, as in the clinical setting of work with patients, we could strive towards the ideal of 'no intervention without evaluation' and so move nearer to firm knowledge in this complex field.

REFERENCES

Andrews, G. and Harvey, R. (1981) Does Psychotherapy Benefit Neurotic Patients? *Archives of General Psychiatry* 38: 1203–208.
Bhagat, M., Lewis, A. P. and Shillitoe, R. W. (1979) Clinical Psychologists and the Primary Care Team. *Update* 479–88.
Blackburn, I. M., Bishop, S., Glen, A. I. H., Whalley, L. J., and Christie, J. E. (1981) The Efficacy of Cognitive Therapy in Depression: A Treatment Trial Using Cognitive Therapy and Pharmacotherapy each Alone and in combination. *British Journal of Psychiatry* 139: 181–89.
Bouras, N. and Brough, D. I. (1982) The Development of the Mental Health Advice Centre in Lewisham Health District. *Health Trends* 14: 65–9.
Brindle House Community Mental Health Centre, Hyde, Cheshire. Undated cyclo-styled documents.
Brown, G. W. and Harris, T. (1978) Social Origins of Depression. London: Tavistock Publications.
Burns, L. E. (1981) The Role of the Clinical Psychologist in Primary Care – An Analysis of Current Practice. In Main, C. J. (ed.) *Clinical Psychology and Medicine: A Behavioural Perspective*. London: Plenum.
Butler, R. J. and Davidson, R. J. (1982) A Psychological Service in General Practice. *Update* 497–503.
Candy, J., Balfour, F. H. G., Cawley, R. H., Hildebrand, H. P., Malen, D. H., Marks, I. M., and Wilson, J. (1972) A Feasibility Study for a Controlled Trial of Formal Psychotherapy. *Psychological Medicine* 2: 345–62.
Clark, D. P. (1979) The Clinical Psychologist in Primary Care. *Social Science and Medicine* 707–13.
Clinical Research Centre, Division of Psychiatry (1984) The Northwick Park ECT Trial. Predictors of Response to Real and simulated ECT. *British Journal of Psychiatry* 144: 227–37.
Cooper, B. (1971) Social Work in General Practice. The Derby Scheme. *Lancet* 539–42.
Dawe, A. M. (1980) A Case for Community Psychiatric Nurses. *Journal of Advanced Nursing* 5: 485–90.
Dewsbury, A. R. (1982) Psychologists in the Practice. *Update* 1057–061.
Earll, L. and Kincey, J. (1982) Clinical Psychology in General Practice: A Controlled Trial Evaluation. *Journal of the Royal College of General Practitioners* 32: 32–7.
Feldman, S. (1979) Community Mental Health Centres in the United States. *Journal of the Royal Society of Medicine* 633–34.
France, R. and Robson, M. (1982) Work of the Clinical Psychologist in General Practice: Preliminary Communication. *Journal of the Royal Society of Medicine* 75: 185–89.

Goldberg, E. M. and Neill, J. E. (1972) *Social Work in General Practice*. London: Allen and Unwin.

Graham, H. and Sher, M. (1976) Social Work and General Practice. A Report of a three-year attachment. *Journal of the Royal College of General Practitioners* 26: 95–105.

Harker, D., Leopoldt, H., and Robinson, J. R. (1976) Attaching Community Psychiatric Nurses to General Practice. *Journal of the Royal College of General Practitioners* 26: 666–71.

Ives, G. (1979) Psychological Treatment in General Practice. *Journal of the Royal College of General Practitioners* 29: 343–51.

Jerrom, D. W. A., Simpson, R. J., Barber, J. H., and Pemberton, D. A. (1983) General Practitioners' Satisfaction with a Primary Care Clinical Psychology Service. *Journal of the Royal College of General Practitioners* 33: 29–31.

Johnson, D. A. W. (1973) Treatment of Depression in General Practice. *British Medical Journal* 2: 1593–594.

Johnston, M. (1978) The Work of the Clinical Psychologist in Primary Care. *Journal of the Royal College of General Practitioners* 28: 661–67.

Koch, H. C. H. (1979) Evaluation of Behaviour Therapy Intervention in General Practice. *Journal of the Royal College of General Practitioners* 29: 337–40.

Leff, J. P. and Vaughn, C. (1980) The Interaction of Life Events and Relatives Expressed Emotion in Schizophrenia and Depressive Neurosis. *British Journal of Psychiatry* 136: 146–53.

Leff, J. P., Kuipers, L., Berkowitz, R., Eberlein-Vries, R., and Sturgeon, D. (1982) A Controlled Trial of Social Intervention in the Families of Schizophrenic Patients. *British Journal of Psychiatry* 141: 121–34.

Leopoldt, H. (1979) Community Psychiatric Nursing. *Nursing Times* 75: 57–9.

Little, J. C., Kerr, T. A., and McClelland, H. A. (1978) Where are the untreated depressives? *British Medical Journal* 2: 1593–594.

Mangen, S. P. and Griffith, J. H. (1982) Patient Satisfaction with Community Psychiatric Nursing: a prospective controlled study. *Journal of Advanced Nursing* 7: 477–82.

McPherson, I. (1981) Clinical Psychology in Primary Health Care: Development or Diversion? In I. McPherson and A. Sutton (eds) *Reconstructing Psychological Practice*. London: Croom Helm.

Paykel, E. S., Mangen, S. P., Griffith, J. H., and Burns, T. H. (1982) Community Psychiatric Nursing for Neurotic Patients: A Controlled Trial. *British Journal of Psychiatry* 140: 573–81.

Prioleau, L., Murdock, M., and Brody, N. (1983) An Analysis of Psychotherapy Versus Placebo Studies. *The Behavioral and Brain Sciences* 6, 275–310.

Ratoff, L. and Pearson, B. (1970) Social Case-work in General Practice: An alternative approach. *British Medical Journal* 2: 475–77.

Rosen, J. C. and Wiens, A. W. (1979) Changes in Medical Problems and use of Medical Services following Psychological Intervention. *American Psychologist* 34: 420–31.

Ryle, A. (1980) Some Measures of Goal Attainment in Focussed Integrated Active Psychotherapy: A Study of Fifteen Cases. *British Journal of Psychiatry* 17: 475–86.

—— (1984) How Can We Compare Different Psychotherapies? Why Are They All Effective? *British Journal of Medical Psychology* 57: 261–64.

Shapiro, M. B. (1966) The Single Case in Clinical-Psychological Research. *Journal of General Psychology* 74: 3–23.

Shapiro, D. A. (1980) Science and Psychotherapy: The State of the Art. *British Journal of Medical Psychology* 53: 1–10.

Shaw, A. (1977) CPN Attachment in a Group Practice. *Nursing Times* March.

Shepherd, M. (1979) Psychoanalysis, Psychotherapy and Health Services. *British Medical Journal* 2: 1557–559.

Sloane, R. B., Staples, F. R., Cristol, A. H., Yorkston, N. J., and Whipple, K. (1975) *Psychotherapy versus Behaviour Therapy*. Cambridge, Mass.: Harvard University Press.

Spector, J. (1984) Clinical Psychology and Primary Care: some Ongoing Dilemmas. *Bulletin of the British Psychological Society* 37: 73–6.

Teasdale, J. D., Fennell, M. J. V., Hibbert, G. A., and Amies, P. L. (1984) Cognitive Therapy for Major Depressive Disorders in Primary Care. *British Journal of Psychiatry* 144: 400–06.

Temperley, J. (1978) Psychotherapy in the Setting of General Medical Practice. *British Journal of Medical Psychology* 51: 139–45.

Wilkinson, G. (1984) Psychotherapy in the Market-place. *Psychological Medicine* 14: 23–6.

E. S. Paykel

Discussant

One of these two interesting papers has focused particularly on pharmacology and the other on psychotherapy. I will briefly address both issues. Like Professor Ashcroft I will mainly confine my comments to depressive disorders, which form a large part of the spectrum of morbidity needing treatment and illustrate the wider issues.

In reviewing treatment efficacy in primary care we need to keep at the forefront two major questions: What is the general evidence of efficacy for the treatment, and what is there special about general practice settings in terms of patients and service organization which renders separate evaluation necessary? For anti-depressant drugs, there is a large body of general evidence of efficacy outside general practice; the drugs are superior to placebos, although the gain is often not very marked. Endogenous depressives may tend to respond better, but this is not very clear cut and there is good evidence of efficacy in neurotic samples (Paykel in press). Drug prescription is not time consuming and it easily fits the organization of general practice. The problem lies in the paucity of evidence from adequate placebo controlled trials that the drugs actually have any beneficial effects in the types of patient seen in the primary care setting. Professor Ashcroft's studies have led the way in this country.

Separate evaluation in general practice patients is very important. Lester Sireling, Paul Freeling, Bridget Rao and I have recently carried out at St

George's a survey of symptom and diagnostic characteristics of depressives seen in general practice, using explicit psychiatric criteria and rating scales. We studied 95 patients started on a new course of an anti-depressant drug by the general practitioner, 48 patients identified as depressed but given treatment other than an anti-depressant, and 24 patients not identified as depressed by the GP, but by General Health Questionnaire (GHQ) screening and subsequent interview found to fit the Research Diagnostic Criteria for major depression (Spitzer, Endicott, and Robins 1978). The subjects were interviewed by means of a composite interview including the Research Diagnostic Criteria, the Present State Examination (Wing, Cooper, and Sartorius 1974), and the Clinical Interview for Depression (Paykel, Klerman, and Prusoff 1970).

The majority of these patients in all three samples were 'cases' on the PSE Index of Definition, but tended to be at the threshold level of 5. On the Research Diagnostic Criteria (RDC), among the anti-depressant-treated sample 56 per cent received a diagnosis of major depressive disorder, 23 per cent a diagnosis of minor or intermittent depressive disorder, and the remaining 21 per cent had other diagnoses. Among those receiving other treatment, 19 per cent were major depressives, 31 per cent minor or intermittent depressives, 21 per cent anxiety disorders, 21 per cent had other diagnoses and 8 per cent were not deemed to be mentally ill by these criteria (Sireling, Paykel, Freeling, Rao, and Patel in press). The missed depressives were, by definition, all major depressives: comparisons of them with major depressives identified by GPs showed a little less overt depressive symptomatology, but the differences were quite small. Comparison of the anti-depressant sample with drug treated depressed outpatients showed the general practice patients to be much less severely ill with a lower proportion of endogenous depressives (Sireling, Freeling, Paykel, and Rao in press). Most anti-depressant trials in psychiatric settings now specify RDC major depression with a minimum Hamilton Score of 17. Among the anti-depressant treated primary care subjects, only 56 per cent satisfied the first criterion and 37 per cent the second.

We are clearly dealing with a different range of depression in which separate evaluation is mandatory. Professor Ashcroft's study of amitriptyline and tryptophan had a minimum Hamilton entry score of twelve. With Dr Julie Hollyman we are currently carrying out a large comparative trial of amitriptyline against placebo in general practice patients covering a considerable range of severity including patients even more mildly ill. The same rating and diagnostic assessments are being applied, with the ultimate aim of identifying the groups of patients who show drug-placebo differences and those who do not and for whom the drug treatment conveys no benefit.

There will remain another problem related to the setting – that of low dose prescribing and patient non-compliance. In our first study, as in many others, only a minority received a dose equivalent to 75 mg or more of amitriptyline daily for as long as four weeks. This seems mainly to be an issue of treatment practices: both in Ashcroft's studies and in ours it has been possible to achieve considerably higher doses by aiming for them.

For psychotherapy the principles are the same, but the points at issue currently are rather different: is there evidence for efficacy of the treatments in general, can they be applied efficiently within primary care organization and do the benefits outweigh the costs? Dr Ryle raises the pertinent issue of the degree to which psychotherapies have been shown to be effective. In the field of depression there is, in fact, better evidence than is sometimes realized.

For psychodynamically orientated psychotherapy the evidence comes mainly from a series of US outpatient studies published in the 1970s and supported from the Psychopharmacology Research Branch of NIMH. They represent successful transplantations of drug trial methodology, all employing randomized comparisons of psychotherapy and low contact in factorial designs which also involved drug treatment and placebo (or no drug). Our own study (Weissman et al. 1974; Paykel et al. 1975) in depressed women found that individual therapy by psychiatric social workers produced significant benefit compared with low contact on social role performance and interpersonal relations, although it did not prevent symptomatic relapse following early drug withdrawal. Friedman (1975) found that marital therapy significantly improved marital relationships and produced some symptomatic improvement, although considerably less than amitriptyline. Covi et al. (1974) found small effects from group therapy on social function and none on symptoms, but there was a lack of good social adjustment measures in this study. These investigations support Jerome Frank's earlier views that the main effects of drugs are on symptoms and those of psychotherapy on social effectiveness. The most recent study (DiMascio et al. 1979) differed in that the symptomatic response to individual psychotherapy by psychiatrists was comparable with that to amitryptyline, although the psychotherapy appeared to act especially on situational depressives and the drug treatment on endogenous depressives. In all the studies the two treatment modalities combined well and the greatest advantage was derived from the administration of both.

The evidence concerning the effects of cognitive therapy in depression comes partly from outpatients and partly from general practice. In US outpatient studies, Rush et al. (1977) reported it to be marginally superior to imipramine, and Murphy et al. (1984) found no difference from amitriptyline. Two studies in this country have involved general practice. Blackburn et al. (1981) in Edinburgh studied both outpatients and general practice patients. Their results were somewhat complex, but in outpatients cognitive therapy and drug therapy appeared approximately equivalent, while in general practice cognitive therapy appeared superior. In Oxford, Teasdale et al. (1984) found cognitive therapy superior to the GP's usual treatment.

Obviously more work needs to be done. A major unanswered question for both psychodynamic and cognitive approaches is the extent to which they may produce benefits by the non-specific influence of the increased time associated with therapist–patient contact, rather than by specific effects of the treatments. Although the findings are promising, neither efficacy nor place can yet be said to be clearly established in general practice.

Granted that efficacy be established there remain the large questions of how to apply them in practice and of costs versus benefits. Both psychodynamic psychotherapy and cognitive therapy are time-consuming and do not fit well into the busy series of time-limited consultations which comprise the average surgery session. Also if drugs and psychotherapy are equally effective, then drugs would be preferable because less expensive. What if they are not equally effective? If the psychotherapies confer particular benefits on social role performance and interpersonal relationships which, by and large, drug treatments do not, then the cost might in the long run be more than recouped by more people in work, fewer days off, fewer children in care, less public expenditure on social security and welfare payments.

A practical answer could lie in the use of other members of the larger multi-disciplinary primary care team, and in moving away from traditional psychotherapy to briefer and more focused approaches. Within the specialized field of behaviour therapy, more applicable to phobic and obsessional disorders than to depression, Marks and colleagues have shown the value of behaviourally trained nurses. We, too, found community psychiatric nurses efficacious and cost effective in the care of neurotic patients (Paykel and Griffith 1983). Though our study was concerned with psychiatric teams, the patients were in many respects comparable with chronic neurotic patients in primary care. Studies have also been reported of social workers, psychologists and counsellors.

In the long run the disorders of which we have heard today present to the doctor because of distress and disability. They either remit spontaneously or require treatment. I believe that the two papers in this session point the way towards what will have to be an increasing series of treatment evaluative studies in general practice. There will also need to be some innovation in the application of psychotherapeutic and social treatments. Such studies will need to address themselves to the question of efficacy, selective treatment choice, realistic applicability to the conditions of general practice and cost effectiveness.

REFERENCES

Blackburn, I. M., Bishop, S., Glen, A. I. M., Whalley, L. J., and Christie, J. E. (1981) The efficacy of cognitive therapy in depression: a treatment trial using cognitive therapy and pharmacotherapy each alone and in combination. *British Journal of Psychiatry* 139: 181–89.

Covi, L., Lipman, R. S., Derogatis, R., Smith, J. E., and Pattison, L. J. H. (1974) Drugs and group psychotherapy in neurotic depression. *American Journal of Psychiatry* 1131: 191–98.

DiMascio, A., Weissman, M. M., Prusoff, B. A., Neu, C., Zwilling, M., and Klerman, G. L. (1979) Differential symptom reduction by drugs and psychotherapy in acute depression. *Archives of General Psychiatry* 36: 1450–456.

Friedman, A. S. (1975) Interaction of drug therapy with marital therapy in depressive patients. *Archives of General Psychiatry* 32: 619–37.

Murphy, G. E., Simons, A. D., Wetzel, R. D., and Lustman, P. J. (1984) Cognitive therapy and pharmacology. *Archives of General Psychiatry* 41: 33–41.

Paykel, E. S. (1986) How Effective are Antidepressants? In S. Iversen (ed.) *Psychopharmacology: Recent Advances and Future Prospects.* London: Oxford University Press, pp. 3–13.

Paykel, E. S. and Griffith, J. H. (1983) *Community Psychiatric Nursing for Neurotic Patients.* The Royal College of Nursing, London.

Paykel, E. S., Klerman, G. L., and Prusoff, B. A. (1970) Treatment setting and clinical depression. *Archives of General Psychiatry* 22: 11–21.

Paykel, E. S., DiMascio, A., Haskell, D., and Prusoff, B. A. (1975) Effects of maintenance amitriptyline and psychotherapy on symptoms of depression. *Psychological Medicine* : 67–77.

Rush, A. J., Beck, A. T., Kovacs, M., and Hollons, S. (1977) Comparative efficacy of cognitive therapy and pharmacotherapy in treatment of depressed outpatients. *Cognitive Therapy Research* 1: 17–37.

Sireling, L. I., Freeling, P., Paykel, E. S., and Rao, B. M. (in press) *Depression in General Practice: Clinical Features and Comparison with Outpatients.*

Sireling, L. I., Paykel, E. S., Freeling, P., Rao, B., and Patel, S. P. (in press) *Depression in General Practice: Case Thresholds and Diagnosis.*

Spitzer, R. L., Endicott, J., and Robins, E. (1978) Research diagnostic criteria: rationale and reliability. *Archives of General Psychiatry* 35: 773–82.

Teasdale, J. D., Fennell, M. J. V., Hibbert, G. A., and Amies, P. L. (1984) Cognitive therapy for major depressive disorder. *British Journal of Psychiatry* 144: 400–06.

Weissman, M. M., Klerman, G. L., Paykel, E. S., Prusoff, B. A., and Hanson, B. (1974) Treatment effects on the Social Adjustment of depressed outpatients. *Archives of General Psychiatry* 30: 771–78.

Wing, J. K., Cooper, J. E., and Sartorius, N. (1974) *The measurement and classification of psychiatric symptoms.* Cambridge: Cambridge University Press.

General Discussion

P. J. Tyrer: With regard to Dr Ryle's comments on psychotherapy, I am sure Professor Shepherd and Dr Wilkinson can look after themselves, but I think one of the major points they were making was the cost-effectiveness and the time involved. I think that, particularly in the setting of primary care, it is very difficult to justify recommending many forms of psycho-therapy unless we can show them to be greatly superior in efficacy. I think the evidence of the recent work that Dr Ryle quoted is that the amount of time involved does not justify the small increase in benefit that they confer beyond that given by placebo measures. Dr Ryle referred to giving instructions to patients in general practice and finding that this was highly effective and perhaps prevented the further need for medication. I think the argument is more that one should be giving low-cost, minor forms of psychotherapy rather than some of the major forms.

I should also like to comment on the evidence that the cognitive and behaviour therapies come out much better than the classical psycho-therapies as to efficacy, certainly as to primary care, because they are time limited, depend upon specific training, and can also be given by non-medical and non-trained staff. Currently, I think that Nottingham is the only health authority in the country which has organized a course of training for these new therapies for community nurses. I think this is the sort of line we ought to be adopting; of using the less complicated psychotherapies, and training staff in these methods so that they can administer them in primary care settings.

Dr Ian Falloon: I am at present setting up a community mental health service entirely within the framework of general practice. One of the things which general practitioners in this area have said to me is that they do not really want someone to give an attachment to them; they do not want to have a psychotherapy clinic or people 'doing their thing' in their practice; they want to keep the patients very much under their case management, and they are looking more towards a consultation effort where they are taught to do as much as they can and are quite willing to put in extra time, as many of them will do, to give case conferences and to deal with particular problems, provided their skills are being appreciated and being added to. One of the things we can do – and a lot of the things we do in psychiatry have to be revised when we go into the general practice setting and see the constraints that colleagues there work under – is to help in some of the early detection of cases which might become severe problems. This can be achieved by being five minutes away from a GP when he has a patient in his surgery, so that you can run along and give a quick consultation.

Similarly, when we translate some of the psychotherapy and drug therapy literature into the general practice context, we often find that patients of equal severity, with quite severe endogenous depression, for example, are very responsive to time-limited and very small amounts of skilful and specific treatment. Many of the behavioural methods can go a long way, and they come directly from the specific psychotherapy techniques which we have used, taking a much greater time span, when we work in psychiatric clinics. So, my suggestion is that psychiatrists might want to work in general practice in this kind of way, by trying to increase the skills of the general practitioner and his team in their practices.

Dr Ryle: I think the general assumption that psychotherapy lasts for ever really does need to be challenged. But I do not think that we should allow the issue of time to be introduced as if there were an enormous differentiation between cognitive and behavioural approaches, or between those and pharmacological approaches, particularly if we can show that the changes produced by therapy are long term. This has not yet been shown. It is potentially researchable and it does need to be done in the setting of general practice, and I think that is a high priority.

Dr Essex: We have been concentrating on the effectiveness of drugs or psychotherapy, but I should like to make a plea for mounting studies on the effectiveness of delivery of mental health care. For example, at present we are very poor at following up psychotic patients who are discharged from mental hospitals. I should like to see studies which look at the use of the practice register of psychotic patients, studies that compare the effectiveness of follow-up of such patients by the health visitor compared with the GP, or by the nurse compared to the general practitioner or the social worker. I should also like to see studies which look at something which is analogous to what the obstetricians do with general practitioners. They have a shared case card, and I see every reason to do studies that evaluate such shared care between psychiatrists and general practitioners for the management of long-term patients who need long-term support and follow up in the community.

PART 5

PATTERNS OF
COLLABORATION

Geraldine Strathdee
and Paul Williams

Patterns of collaboration

INTRODUCTION

One of the most significant developments in British psychiatry in the past few decades has been the recognition of the extent of psychiatric morbidity in the community. Shepherd *et al.* (1966) demonstrated that, of some 15,000 patients at risk each year, just over 14 per cent consulted their doctor at least once for a condition diagnosed as entirely, or largely psychiatric in nature. In addition to this 'conspicuous' morbidity, identified by the general practitioner, Goldberg and Blackwell (1970) have cited evidence that a further 7–10 per cent of patients form a hidden undetected pool of psychiatric morbidity.

However, although between one-fifth and one-quarter of all patients presenting to the GP suffer from significant psychiatric disorder, no more than one in twenty are referred to specialist mental health facilities (Shepherd *et al.* 1966). These findings have presented a major challenge to psychiatrists, general practitioners, non-medical specialists and health services planners alike, in their attempts to determine ways in which they can collaborate to best meet the needs of this substantial pool of psychiatric morbidity.

MODELS OF COLLABORATION

Williams and Clare (1981) have outlined three models of collaboration whereby this general practice–psychiatry interface can be bridged. The first of these, the *replacement model*, refers to the notion that the psychiatrist should replace the GP as the 'doctor of first contact' for patients with psychiatric/ emotional problems (Fink and Oken 1976). It has been suggested that Great Britain emulate the US strategy of placing the psychiatrist in specialist settings outside hospital, for example, community mental health centres (Jones 1979). However, it has also been argued (Clare 1980) that some of the aims and deficiencies of the US Community Mental Health Center Program make it unlikely that this is the strategy which is best suited to British primary care needs. Furthermore, it is at variance with the strongly held international view promulgated by the World Health Organisation, that primary care physicians should be strengthened in their role as the cornerstone of community psychiatry (World Health Organisation 1973).

The second model of collaboration is termed the *increased throughput model*, and refers to the idea that GPs, while retaining their role as primary physicians, should be encouraged to refer more patients to psychiatrists. In practice, there is evidence that this strategy does not meet the requirements of the community (Williams and Clare 1981). The 28 per cent increase in consultant psychiatrists, and 35 per cent increase in non-consultant psychiatric staff, between 1970 and 1975, did not result in any increase in the extent to which general practitioners referred new patients to psychiatrists. In fact, the total number (and rate) of referrals to the psychiatric services remained constant over the years studied, and the average number of new patients per consultant psychiatrist decreased sharply.

The third identified model of collaboration is the *liaison-attachment* model. Its theoretical framework can best be described by the conclusions of Shepherd *et al.* (1966), from their survey of psychiatric illness in general practice that:

'administrative and medical logic alike, suggest that the cardinal requirement for the improvement of the mental health services in this country, is not a large expansion and proliferation of psychiatric agencies, but rather, a strengthening of the family doctor in his therapeutic role'.

In public, this model has appeared to receive a small measure of support from a few isolated psychiatrists over the past twenty years, with occasional reports in the literature of individual psychiatrists forming attachments, and working in direct collaboration with general practitioners in the primary care setting (Gibson *et al.* 1966; Brook 1967; Lyons 1969; Hunter and McCance 1983; Tait 1983; Mitchell 1983). However, the full and surprising extent of support for this liaison-attachment model among psychiatrists and general practitioners remained unknown until the study described below was undertaken.

A SURVEY OF LIAISON ATTACHMENT SCHEMES –
THE DISCOVERY OF A SERVICE

We conducted a survey of all consultant psychiatrists in England and Wales. The four-fold aim of this was:

1. to provide basic data on the extent to which psychiatrists in Great Britain are involved in the liaison-attachment model in general practice;
2. to obtain information on patterns of collaboration associated with the styles of working adopted in these attachments;
3. to elicit the views of the involved psychiatrists as to the advantages and disadvantages of working in this way;
4. to place these data in context of what is already known about the provision of psychiatric care for the community, and to assess their implications for psychiatric practice, training and research.

The survey was conducted by the administration of two questionnaires in two stages. The initial questionnaire, administered to all consultant psychiatrists in England and Wales listed in the 1981 Medical Directory (n = 1,133), yielded an 88 per cent response rate. From this list, 811 psychiatrists were identified as general adult psychiatrists and/or psychotherapists and therefore suitable for inclusion in the survey. Of these, 154 – almost one-in-five – indicated that they, or their junior staff, spent on average one session per week, in addition to their other commitments, working in the general practice setting. In the second stage of the study, 109 of these psychiatrists completed the second questionnaire, which elicited details of several aspects of their work in the general practice setting.

HISTORICAL DEVELOPMENT OF LIAISON
ATTACHMENT SCHEMES

Figure 1 demonstrates that, while a few of these schemes were commenced in the 1950s and 1960s, the major growth of this collaborative activity is a development of the last decade. The discovery that one in five of these survey psychiatrists are engaged in the provision of a relatively new nationwide service is, in itself, a striking finding. Furthermore, this service has materialized, not as a result of any central organizing body, but as a consequence of the initiative of numerous individual psychiatrists and general practitioners. In addition, the growth of this movement (*Figure 1*) appears to be gaining momentum.

These observations raise a number of fundamental questions concerning the reasons for the commencement of the service and the attractions and advantages of liaison-attachment schemes as a form of collaboration. These questions can be partly answered by examination of the working patterns of liaison and collaboration adapted by the participants and by study of certain

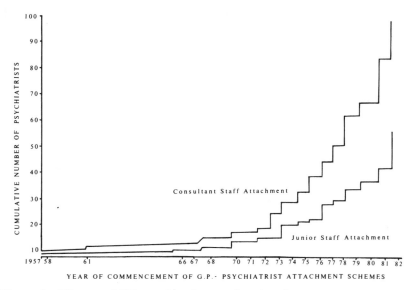

Figure 1   History of GP-psychiatrist attachment schemes

organizational aspects of the individual schemes. These facets will be examined individually and have been summarized in *Table 3*.

Organizational aspects of liaison attachment schemes: regional location of schemes

As can be seen in *Table 1*, the liaison attachment schemes have been under-taken nationwide most intensively in the West Country and East Anglia and least frequently in London and the South East and Wales. These regional differences may be related to geographical factors, such as population density and the availability or otherwise of road and travel networks. Other important considerations must be the availability of local community care facilities, the format of the local psychiatric services and individual regional health authority policy with respect to the provision of community care.

The psychiatrists

The involved psychiatrists tended to be significantly younger in terms of length of consultant experience, with 22 per cent of consultants appointed within the past ten years engaged in such work (*Table 2*). Only 17 per cent of those appointed ten to nineteen years ago were involved and 15 per cent of those appointed twenty or more years ago. This trend reaches statistical significance at the 5 per cent level (Bartholomew's Test).

Table 1   *Location of GP liaison attachment schemes*

region	no. of attachment schemes	% of psychiatrists in region involved in attachment schemes
North	32	(20)
Midland	30	(17)
East Anglia	8	(25)
London and South-East	41	(15)
West Country	39	(30)
Wales	4	(8)

Table 2   *Correlates of psychiatrist involvement in GP liaison-attachment schemes*

variable	no. attachment psychiatrists	% attachment psychiatrists
facilities		
beds in District General Hospital unit	58	(15)
beds in psychiatric hospital only	84	(22)
no beds or not known	12	(29)
length of experience		
appointment to consultant (or equivalent) post:		
within the past 10 years	84	(22)
10–19 years	53	(17)
20+ years	16	(15)
not known	1	

There was also a statistically significant relationship between the location of the consultant's base hospital facilities and his/her proclivity to become involved in a general practice attachment scheme. Of psychiatrists whose inpatient facilities were entirely in psychiatric hospitals, 22 per cent were involved in such work, compared with about 15 per cent of consultants who had inpatient facilities in district general hospital units. These two findings would appear to reflect the changes in psychiatric philosophy and training in recent years, with a resultant change in psychiatric practice of greater emphasis on the provision of community based psychiatric care.

The enthusiastic commitment of many of the psychiatrists can be gauged by the finding that two-thirds of them undertake their work in the general

Table 3   *Factors influencing the development of GP liaison attachment schemes*

Factors in psychiatry
1. Recognition of the psychosocial nature of many disorders.
2. Philosophical focus on community care
3. Interaction with GPs on Vocational Training Schemes.
4. Development of the multi-disciplinary team approach.
5. Dissatisfaction with clinical care provision within the hospital outpatient setting.

Factors in general practice
1. Introduction of GP Vocational Training Schemes.
2. Establishment of health centres.
3. Development of multi-disciplinary links.

Factors in health service organization
1. Development of health centres.
2. Trend towards closure of psychiatric hospitals.

---

practice setting *in addition* to other commitments. For the remaining one-third, the work largely replaced hospital outpatient clinics. Of the 109 respondents, 50 (46 per cent) were consultant psychiatrists working alone in the GP setting. In 11 instances junior staff, mostly senior registrars, worked alone. Junior psychiatric staff worked with the consultants in 47 (43 per cent) of the schemes. In the main, these were of senior house officer grade, many being GP trainees on Vocational Training Schemes.

The practices

The majority of psychiatrists were involved with one to two practices and, on average, there were just over seven GPs per attachment scheme. Of the 177 practices involved, 147 (83 per cent) were based on health centres. When this figure is viewed in the context of statistics (Statistics and Research Department, Department of Health and Social Security, October 1982) which indicate that nationally only 26 per cent of GPs work in health centres, it permits the inference that the establishment of health centres was an important influential factor in the development of liaison attachment schemes.

There are a number of possible explanations for this marked preference for attachments to be based in health centre premises. Psychiatrists may regard it as more valuable and cost effective to see patients in health centres where the potential number of referrals is necessarily increased with the larger number of incumbent doctors. Administratively, the provision of accommodation is less problematical in health centre premises which are, in general, larger than the traditional general practice premises.

In addition, health centres tend to attract younger GPs, many of whom will have been involved in GP vocational training schemes. This may create increased awareness of psychiatric morbidity, with the resultant desire to seek consultation with specialist colleagues. The move by the GPs into health centres has necessarily led to more collaboration between disciplines, and has perhaps facilitated the practice of multi-disciplinary teamwork, a trend which is more common to both general practice and psychiatry than to other specialities.

PATTERNS OF COLLABORATION – WORKING
STYLES ADOPTED IN LIAISON ATTACHMENT
SCHEMES

In spite of the spontaneous and unco-ordinated nature of the development of this service, three clearly distinguishable working patterns can be identified from the survey psychiatrists' reports of their work: the 'consultation' pattern; the 'shifted outpatient' pattern; and the 'liaison attachment' team pattern.

Twenty-eight per cent of the psychiatrists chose to adopt the 'consultation' pattern of collaboration. This consisted for psychotherapists, in not seeing any patients but in spending time with the GPs, giving Balint-type seminars, and studying with them the nature of the doctor–patient relationship with the aim of changing attitudes and developing new diagnostic and therapeutic skills. For those psychiatrists who acted in a consultative role and saw patients, their working method consisted of the assessment of patients, liaison and discussion of management with the referring GP, and treatment undertaken by the GP.

However, the majority of psychiatrists (64 per cent), adopted the 'shifted outpatient' pattern of working, whereby they undertook both assessment and treatment of patients. This session in the general practice, while regarded as an alternative to a hospital outpatient clinic was, however, seen as facilitating the provision of a qualitatively different standard of clinical care from that which can be offered in the conventional hospital outpatient setting.

The ability to form a close liaison with the GP appeared to be the fountainhead from which this improved clinical care stemmed (*Table 3*). This liaison enabled the psychiatrist to acquire a knowledge of the patient's medical and social background which is rarely transcribed in the traditional referral letter, but is readily contributed by the GP in either personal discussion or via access to his/her records. Many of the psychiatrists asserted that the increased access to the patient's background and the ability of the GP to participate in the assessment process allowed a better identification of the presenting problems, with a clearer understanding of the reasons for the referral, and thus in a sense it provided the psychiatrist with an opportunity to adopt a new work style which could be broadly classed as a patient-centred approach.

Continuity of care was noted to be improved with the ability to involve the GP and other members of the primary care team, not only in the assessment of the patient, but in the decision-making relative to the management of the patient. The ongoing collaboration inherent in the schemes rendered the joint specialist-primary care team treatment of patients a reality rather than a desirable but intangible objective.

The third pattern of collaboration adopted by a small number (5 per cent) of the psychiatrists was the liaison attachment team pattern of working. In these attachments the psychiatrists instituted working and training links with members of other disciplines, e.g. social workers, community nurses, health visitors and psychologists attached to practices. This working pattern appeared to have evolved in the longer-standing attachments, and in some cases had enabled the psychiatrist to reduce his/her own services to minimal levels, with the adaptation of a largely supervisory and training role.

In addition to the advantages in terms of clinical care offered by the collaborative patterns outlined above (*Table 4*), other significant advantages for patients and doctors were cited by the liaison participants (*Table 5*). Patients benefited in terms of the perceived decrease in stigma afforded by a consultation with the psychiatrist in the familiar setting of their general practice. Indeed, in some cases it was the only setting where patients were prepared to see a psychiatrist.

Both general practitioners and psychiatrists were felt to benefit by the process of mutual education ensuing from their close collaboration. The psychiatrists saw a wider spectrum of psychiatric disorder than that which they traditionally encountered in hospital practice, and they had an opportunity to view some of the management strategies adopted by GP colleagues in coping with their large caseload of psychosocial disorder. In turn, the GPs gained an increase in their knowledge of psychiatric disorder and treatments.

In addition to their clinical work, some of the psychiatrists noted that they occasionally performed two other roles. First, they *provided support* for the primary care team. This consisted of acknowledging the difficulties and frustrations encountered by the GPs in dealing with some of their patients, particularly those with chronic or intractable problems. A forum for discussion was also provided where the GPs could express their own emotional reactions to certain patients and colleagues.

Approximately one-third of the surveyed psychiatrists also provided a formal *educative* function. This was done by giving lectures and seminars and conducting formal case conferences. Many psychiatrists, however, stressed the value they placed on the informal discussions which they held with their GP colleagues. The usefulness of the attachment as a learning experience for junior staff was a frequently reiterated theme.

Disadvantages of the schemes

Administrative problems were rated by 60 per cent of the survey psychiatrists to consitute the major disadvantages of working in the GP setting. These

Table 4   *Perceived advantages of clinical care provision in GP liaison attachment schemes*

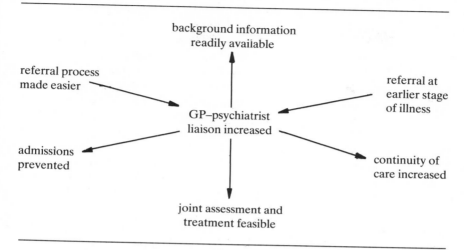

Table 5   *Perceived advantages to doctors and patients of GP liaison attachment schemes*

advantages stated by psychiatrists	survey psychiatrists	
	No.	%
advantages to patients		
familiarity of setting	27	(26)
ease of access	27	(25)
stigma decreased	23	(22)
admissions prevented	11	(10)
continuity of care	7	(7)
relatives more accessible	5	(5)
compliance increased	5	(5)
advantages to GPs		
increased psychiatric knowledge	30	(27)
improved awareness of psychiatrist's role	18	(17)
earlier referral possible	9	(9)
advantages to psychiatrists		
improved liaison with primary care team	70	(65)
ease of access to background information	24	(23)
administration advantages	13	(12)
wider spectrum of disorder seen	11	(10)
ability to involve GPs in treatment	10	(9)

disadvantages included the difficulty of establishing a good record-keeping system, lack of secretarial and other clinical facilities, and accommodation problems in some instances. Some psychiatrists felt that the attachment was time-consuming in terms of travel between hospital and the practice. Other psychiatrists felt frustrated by the constraint that a single session placed on their ability to offer certain treatments, for example, psychotherapy.

Just over one-fifth of the psychiatrists felt that the demand for their services was excessive. Less than one-tenth of the respondents, however, considered that they received inappropriate referrals. Relationship difficulties arose infrequently (noted by only 6 per cent of respondents). They appeared to be a consequence of either administrative difficulties – that is, when the psychiatrist could only be accommodated in a room when the GPs were absent, thus making liaison very limited – or where the psychiatrist found it difficult to readjust his attitude to the differences in professional roles in the absence of the typical hospital hierarchical relationship in the GP setting.

THE FUTURE OF LIAISON ATTACHMENTS –
GROWTH AND ORGANIZATION OF THE SERVICE

In discussing the findings of this paper with colleagues, the most striking feature has been the surprise expressed at the unexpectedly large number of psychiatrists involved in this new service. The unprecedented growth in this area in the past decade, the factors with which it appears to be linked, and the fact that it is the result of numerous like-minded individuals acting separately without any central organization makes it highly likely that this growing trend will continue, even in the present climate of restricted resources.

In terms of service-organization, many of the psychiatrists declared that the relative isolation in which they worked made any useful interchange of ideas difficult, if not impossible. They felt that the lack of a formal co-ordinating body rendered this necessarily unavoidable. The major drawbacks of this form of collaboration were noted to be administrative. In any future expansion of the service, consideration should be given as to how the above problems should best be overcome. From the comments of the participants it would appear that the institution of a formal and co-ordinated approach to future development would be helpful.

IMPLICATIONS – PATTERNS OF COLLABORATION
AS WORKING PATTERNS FOR THE FUTURE?

The existence of this liaison attachment service, its spontaneous spread and the likelihood of its future growth have important implications for many aspects of psychiatric practice and training. The psychiatrists involved in the liaison attachment schemes expressed a great deal of enthusiasm for what they viewed as the numerous advantages accruing from them. The key advantage was noted to be the improved GP–psychiatrist liaison, which in turn resulted in major benefits both clinical and administrative for patients and doctors alike. This enthusiasm, and the view of the benefits derived from these patterns of collaboration, must be placed in the context of what is documented about existing GP referrals to the specialist services, particularly the hospital outpatient clinics. Major areas of interest in this context are:

The spectrum of psychiatric referral

The majority of psychiatric referrals to outpatient clinics are from GPs. In 1975, some 185,000 new patients were seen in psychiatric clinics in England and Wales. It has been shown that a selective referral process takes place; Shepherd *et al*. 1966 demonstrated that there is a preferential referral of younger patients. Kaeser and Cooper (1971) and Johnson (1973) have shown that, despite the almost twofold sex difference in the prevalence of psychiatric disorder in general practice, there is little difference in the number of men and women referred to outpatient clinics. Although there is a preferential referral of patients with psychoses, approximately two-thirds of the cases seen by consultants in outpatient clinics present with personality disorder and psycho-neurotic complaints.

Psychiatrists involved in liaison attachment schemes noted that they saw a broader spectrum of psychiatric morbidity than that which they encountered in hospital practice. Further research is necessary to ascertain the nature of this broader spectrum. It may be a function of the additional observation that the patients are seen at an earlier stage of their illness. Alternatively, it may be that GPs refer patients whom they would traditionally treat themselves but that with the ease of referral within the schemes they feel more enabled to seek advice on management and treatment issues.

The referral process and reasons for referral

Studies have revealed several diverse reasons for referral of patients to psychiatric clinics by GPs. Kaeser and Cooper (1971), in a study of London GPs, found that a primary reason for referral was the desire for responsibility to be taken over by the hospital. In contrast, Johnson (1973), in a study in Manchester, found that in 50 per cent of cases the GPs wanted advice only from the hospital, with treatment to be continued by them. The Manchester GPs specified the need for a diagnostic opinion in 63 per cent of referrals and special investigations in 46 per cent of patients. Three other important reasons for referral were identified in Kaeser and Cooper's findings: the presence of behavioural disturbance, serious social problems, or the possibility of suicide; the failure to respond to general practitioner treatment; and the patient request for specialist referral. The reasons for referral are therefore not only clinical in nature, but include a variety of other factors –

administrative factors, factors inherent in the doctor–patient relationship, factors linked to the GP's perception of his role and the role of the specialist in the treatment of morbidity, and the training and expertise of both doctors in the management of psychiatric disorder.

The liaison attachment patterns of collaboration as a working system offer substantial opportunities for clarification of the GP's reasons for referral and for an extension of the nature of referrals. The increase in face-to-face contact allows GPs to make more explicit their requirements in terms of what they wish the specialist to provide in the way of advice, investigation, diagnosis, assumption of responsibility, and follow-up. The nature of referrals can be extended to include not only (1) those patients whom the GP wishes to refer to the specialist; but also (2) patients for whom the GP is uncertain of the need for referral and can discuss the appropriateness or otherwise of referral with the psychiatrist, and (3) patients whom the GPs wish to continue treating themselves but on whom they wish to seek advice without having to refer. Corser and Ryce (1977) have attempted to assess the implications of this new service for existing facilities utilization with particular respect to hospital outpatient utilization.

A major influence on the perception of the referral process must be the communication patterns between GP and psychiatrist. It has been shown that there are numerous deficiencies in the information transmitted between the two. Williams and Wallace (1974) conducted a study wherein they asked both psychiatrists and GPs what information they considered most important in letters exchanged between them. Examination of a sample of the letters revealed that the psychiatrists generally obtained the information they considered pertinent, i.e. the nature and duration of the present symptoms, current medication and past psychiatric history. However, the GPs often received a different set of information from that which they wanted. While they were usually given an account of the diagnosis and treatment of the patient, they were not informed of suicide risk and prognosis. They considered that the voluminous information on the patient's family and social background which they received was not appropriate, as they were already well acquainted with most of it.

In the liaison attachment setting, with its inherent facilitation of liaison and communication, some of the above-mentioned problems in the referral process must necessarily be diminished. Obviously, this improved communication has important implications for the educative function of specialist-generalist contact and thus ultimately for the roles of both in the treatment of psychiatric disorder. A possible impact on the psychiatrist's role has been demonstrated by the progression to the liaison attachment team pattern of collaboration in the longer established attachment schemes, where the role has shifted from that of direct clinical involvement to a more supervisory/training function.

Referral outcome

Examination of patients referred to outpatient clinics reveals that the majority of new patients are discharged or lapse from treatment after relatively few consultations, and that a high proportion of referrals (approximately one-third) fail to keep their initial appointment with the clinic at all. (Baldwin 1971, Wing and Hailey 1972). Of the patients referred, Kaeser and Cooper (1971) and Johnson (1973) have shown that between 10–20 per cent of the new psychiatric outpatients are recommended for hospital admission and that a similar proportion are referred back to the GP for treatment and the majority are retained for outpatient treatment. Johnson (1973) found that over half of the patients were treated by the psychiatrist alone, with psychotropic drug therapy playing a major role in the treatment. His conclusion was that:

'although the expertise of the consultant psychiatrist may be required for diagnosis and advice on treatment or management, in a substantial proportion of outpatients, the hospital does not offer any form of treatment that is not equally available in the setting of general practice'.

Some of the attached psychiatrists have intimated that within the GP setting patient compliance, both in terms of attendance at appointments and with treatment, was increased. It may be that the decrease in stigma associated with a visit to the familiar setting of the local general practice, coupled with the greater facility for the GP to be involved in the decision-making process, makes patient care and satisfaction generally better.

Training implications

If the trend towards these patterns of working collaboration continues, there are obvious implications for the training of both psychiatrists and GPs. Most psychiatrists are hospital based and see a very specific spectrum of psychiatric morbidity. General practice contains a much wider range of disorders with a greater prevalence of psychosocial disorder and minor psychiatric morbidity.

Many GP trainees have commented that, although their postgraduate training in hospital-based psychiatry had proved useful in increasing their ability to identify and treat certain forms of psychiatric disorder, it was, nevertheless, not entirely suitable and, at times, inappropriate as a preparation for the problems they encounter in dealing with psychologically disturbed people in general practice. Likewise, many of the study psychiatrists noted the deficiencies of their hospital-based training in dealing with the spectrum of illness seen in general practice. As Lesser (1983) has commented:

'if a successful partnership is to occur, not only must the psychiatrist come equipped with a knowledge-base and eclectic experience suitable for general practice and its patients, but general practice must be prepared to identify and treat the problems of 39.6 per cent of their patients who are emotionally disturbed at any given time.' (p. 617)

The establishment of greater links between psychiatry and general practice in terms of vocational training, both for psychiatrists and GPs, would seem necessary for the effective promotion of this partnership to occur. This could be achieved by inclusion of a GP liaison-attachment scheme into psychiatric rotation schemes. Similarly, the inclusion of more formal teaching in GP-based psychiatry, in both undergraduate and postgraduate training schemes, would be beneficial.

Psychiatrists need to consider the ways in which they can best adapt and modify their assessment and treatment techniques to the needs of general practice. These techniques must be developed with an awareness of the extent of the psychiatric morbidity presenting to GPs, the severe constraints of the limited time available in general practice consultations and the limitations of many treatments applied to the general practice setting.

REFERENCES

Baldwin, J. A. (1971) *The Mental Hospital in the Psychiatric Service.* London: Oxford University Press.

Brook, A. (1967) An experiment in GP/psychiatrist co-operation. *Journal of the Royal College of General Practitioners* 13: 127–31.

Clare, A. (1980) Community mental health centres. *Journal of the Royal Society of Medicine* 73: 75–6.

Corser, C. M. and Ryce, S. W. (1977) Community mental health care: a model based on the primary care team. *British Medical Journal* 2: 936–38.

Fink, P. J. and Oken, S. (1976) The Role of Psychiatry as a Primary Care Speciality. *Archives of General Psychiatry* 33: 998.

Gibson, R., Forbes, J. M., Stoddart, I. W., Cooke, J. T., Jenkins, C. W., Mackeith, S. A., Rosenberg, C., Allchin, W. H., and Shepherd, D. (1966) Psychiatric care in general practice: an experiment in collaboration. *British Medical Journal* 1: 1287–289.

Goldberg, D. and Blackwell, B. (1970) Psychiatric Illness in General Practice. A Detailed Study using a New Method of Care Identification. *British Medical Journal* 2: 439–43.

Hunter, D. and McCance, C. (1983) Referrals to the psychiatric services by general practitioners in relation to the introduction of sessions by psychiatrists in health centres. *Health Bulletin (Scotland)* 41: 78–83.

Johnson, D. A. (1973a) A further study of psychiatric outpatient services in Manchester. *British Journal of Psychiatry* 123: 185–91.

Johnson, D. A. (1973b) An analysis of outpatient services. *British Journal of Psychiatry* 122: 301–06.

Jones, K. (1979) Integration or disintegration in the mental health services. *Journal of the Royal Society of Medicine* 72: 640–48.

Kaeser, A. C. and Cooper, B. (1971) The psychiatric patient, the general practitioner, and the outpatient clinic: An operational study and a review. *Psychological Medicine*, 1: 312–25.

Lesser, A. L. (1983) Is training in psychiatry relevant for general practice? *Journal of the Royal College of General Practitioners* 39: 617–18.

Lyons, H. A. (1969) Joint psychiatric consultations. *Journal of the Royal College of General Practitioners* 18: 125–27.

Mitchell, A. R. K. (1983) Psychiatrists and GPs: working together. *Psychiatry in Practice* October: 15–19.

Shepherd, M., Cooper, B., Brown, A. C., and Kalton, G. (1966) *Psychiatric Illness in General Practice*. London: Oxford University Press.

Tait, D. (1983) Shared care between psychiatry and general practice. *Update* 26: 177.

Williams, P. and Wallace, B. (1974) General practitioners and psychiatrists – do they communicate? *British Medical Journal* 1: 505–07.

Williams, P. and Clare, A. (1981) Changing patterns of psychiatric care. *British Medical Journal* 282: 375–77.

Wing, J. K. and Hailey, A. M. (1972) *Evaluating a Community Psychiatric Service*. London: Oxford University Press.

World Health Organisation (1973) Psychiatry and Primary Medical Care. Copenhagen: World Health Organisation Regional Office for Europe.

H. N. Grindrod

Patterns of collaboration

Croydon has a long tradition of collaboration between different services in the field of health care. This goes back at least as far as the Community Psychiatric Service established jointly between the Mental Health Section of the Public Health Department and the Warlingham Park Hospital Management Committee in the early 1960s. This was an initiative between the London Borough of Croydon and Warlingham Park Hospital whereby (1) there was a sustained input by London Borough of Croydon Social Workers (or Mental Welfare Officers) to work alongside medical staff in Warlingham Park Hospital in the care of patients, and (2) to work alongside and with them, when patients left Warlingham Park Hospital and started to attend day hospitals, live in homes/ hostels, or were boarded out in the town and eventually – some of them – reached independence.

Today a large number of ex-Warlingham Park Hospital patients live in our old people's homes, our elderly mental infirm homes, our homes/hostels or are boarded out and may also attend our day centres.

At the end of the 1960s the General Practice Research Unit itself mounted a pilot study aimed at identifying the needs of the elderly in their own homes. This study was the precursor of the action research in which the Croydon Social Services Department was associated with the GPRU in the attachment of social workers to general practices in South Norwood and Woodside. These projects have been written up in detail and will not be discussed here in detail, although attention will be drawn to a number of salient issues.

From the GPRU study several important lessons have been learnt which it is worth mentioning. These lessons stem not only from the Croydon experience, but also from my knowledge and recollection of the social work attachment to the Ratoff practice in Liverpool which was next door to one of my district offices during my time in Liverpool. Seven issues may be noted.

First, doctors on the whole do not usually know what social workers do, or are, until they meet with them and work with them. When they work alongside them, I think they learn to value, respect and trust them and use the complementary services they can provide – either themselves, or through 'taps' they can turn on.

Second, I suspect that the availability of the social worker in an adjacent room gives doctors more confidence in their own ability to cope with the less obvious sources of trouble in patients – the emotional and social dimensions of patients' lives – than might otherwise be the case.

Third, because social workers know of all the available options in their Social Services Department or in the housing, Department of Health and Social Security, or voluntary market, they can be a real resource to the doctor who might otherwise think only in terms of, say, an old people's home.

Fourth, I can understand why it is too much trouble to ring up an area office, get some unknown person at the other end, or find that the person they spoke to previously has either left or is at a meeting. Because the social worker is in an adjacent room they are used far more often.

Fifth, it seems to be an accepted view that patients referred to a social worker in a health centre or general practice will make contact with the social work resource earlier than they would otherwise. The same patient, or the same sort of patient, seems to turn up at our area offices later on in their careers when their problems are more chronic.

Sixth, I suspect that social workers have to be hand-picked for this type of work, but so do doctors. It may be that there are probably many GPs about still who have a 'written off' view of social workers and would not be motivated to try and work alongside them. Notwithstanding this, there are many GPs up and down the country who would welcome the opportunity of having a social worker attached to their practice if the local Social Services Department would give them a chance. Despite the obvious financial stringencies we must try to continue to increase the availability of this service.

Seventh, as Professor Clare reminded us when looking at the attitude of doctors and social workers in general practice, judgements are made and decisions implemented on the basis of attitudes to and perception of information, rather than on information itself, and some doctors still have a strange view of social work and what it can do: we have still quite a long way to go before we can overcome this particular hurdle.

At present, my department and the Health Service are working together to make available the skills and resources of multi-disciplinary groups of staff to people for whose care and assistance we both have a responsibility. These schemes range from the tightly knit and very formal structures of the Community Mental Handicap Team to the much less formal, yet equally serious-minded, attempts to develop effective localized networks for support and care. These schemes are probably too young to evaluate, so that I will not comment on them in detail. But there are difficulties. To take just the community mental handicap team, social workers and mental handicap nurses are having to learn from and about each other, and I think Croydon are doing quite well. The great difficulty though is to get the two systems to work together. The health service seems to me to be more hierarchical and rigid than we are, and I do not have the impression that the same view of easy collaboration is reflected at the top as it is at the bottom. I really do not think that I have any problems about social workers and community nurses working together but I am less clear whether that is the view of the nursing professions.

I think the factors governing the relationship between doctors and social workers in this setting are similar to those in the Health Centre – once people know each other, trust each other and understand what the other can do, then there is fertile ground for collaboration.

What I next wish to do is to sketch out what in my view are those areas in which collaboration over issues of primary health care can arise and, second, to make a few general remarks about the spirit in which collaborative work should be approached. Further, I want to approach these matters from my own point of view as a Director of Social Services.

1. *As a chief officer of the local authority* I meet with the other Chief Officers in the corporate management structure of the authority. I also work directly with the council as a whole, with several of its committees and with individual councillors. Here my concerns are with advice and recommendations for policy and planning with collaborative work with other departments, very often on matters to do with the local authority's contribution to issues of common concern with the Health Service.

   In Croydon we have what is known as a Joint Chief Officers Group which meets about twice a year, and a mini Joint Chief Officers Group which meets more often. We try to set broad agreed objectives which others in our respective authorities seek to implement. In my judgement, neither authority has in the past been good about consulting the other about its plans and strategies. We have, for example, adopted a Special Sheltered Housing policy without consulting the Health Authority and they decide to close beds without consulting us. We are now trying to do better, but it is extremely difficult even in coterminous areas. The organizations and accountability are so different. We are a political organization and they are not. Our funding is even more precarious than theirs. They have consensus management – though not for much longer – and we do not.

2. *In my own department I am responsible for*:
   (a) staff working with Health Service primary care staff on individual cases;
   (b) staff with overlapping responsibilities with Health Service middle managers, where the shared concerns may either be for an area of the borough or for groups of clients and patients with common difficulties;
   (c) senior staff working closely with colleagues in the Health Service in the planning and monitoring of joint services for which both have responsibility.

In Croydon, one of the most difficult issues with which we are having to contend is not in the primary care field, but in the large mental handicap hospital for which we both have responsibilities. Hundreds of patients – though nobody seems to know how many – are, it is thought, capable of leaving the hospital and coming to live in the town. However, they come from a score of local authorities, some of whom do not want to know about them. The selection of patients for discharge and preparation plans for their discharge are proving formidable obstacles to collaboration. It is extremely difficult for the two organizations and groups of professionals to work effectively alongside each other. We have certainly not yet learnt the lessons of collaboration there that we learnt at the GPRU.

3. Thus my concern in all these areas has to be that of ensuring: first, that the framework of management and communication exists in which the skills and resources of my department can be used appropriately in all the fields of collaboration, not least in the field of primary care; and second, that the necessary skills are developed for different kinds of work involved.
4. With regard to the style, attitudes, aspirations with which collaborative work is approached, there are three general notions which strike me as being of fundamental importance: First, there is the way in which staff at all levels, whatever their training and experience, approach the importance of their work. In collaborative work of any kind, especially when one is working with other professionals in the service of fellow citizens, it is necessary to keep in mind distinctions between:
   (a) those activities which I can do, those matters which I can attend to, on my own, with my own skill, from my own experience and using the resources which I have directly to hand; and
   (b) those circumstances in which I can be of assistance, but where my contribution is made much more effective when it is combined with the efforts of one or more other persons possessing different skills, insights, etc.

It is this latter area which seems to be such an uphill struggle. People tend to be defensive and often prickly about territory. For my own part, by contrast, I am unconcerned about territory. It does not much matter to me, as long as patients or clients get what they need, but I sometimes wonder whether patients, pupils, clients really do come first any longer.

In addition to the situations where I can do something useful, it is necessary for all of us to recognize that there are circumstances when there is *nothing* to be done. If I insist on remaining involved, I am going to get in the way; I had better see that this person, this family, this group are as quickly as possible put in touch with those that do possess the requisite knowledge and skills. This does not just apply to me or my social workers but to all of us. Not too easy a lesson to learn. I think there is no doubt that there is only a very limited number of circumstances in which any of us, or indeed any one organization, has all, or even most, of the necessary answers. Far more often than not we need to work with colleagues in one discipline or another to deliver the most effective package that the particular patient needs. Second, and this is to do with honesty, both as truthfulness and in the sense in which one uses the word when talking about an 'honest' well-crafted piece of work, we must accept other people doing the best they can with whatever resources they have. In these straitened times, we can no longer afford the rivalries and suspicions in which it was once possible to luxuriate. The rivalries and suspicions are, alas, all too often still there. Third, even before entering into collaborative work of any kind, any individual or organization must first feel secure in its own skills and resources. Without this, what started off as collaboration may very quickly become discontented subordination.

In conclusion, my feeling about the GPRU, the Ratoff exercise in Liverpool and the slight knowledge I had about the Woodside Health Centre in Glasgow is that the potentials for the good of the patients or clients are so vast that we must continue to try and find means of extending this service provision wherever possible. In my view, the local surgery or health centre is still one of the natural places for people to go to whether they are unwell or upset, whereas the Social Services Department area office is plainly *not* one of the natural places for people to go to when they are looking for help or want someone to talk to. I hope, therefore, that despite the formidable constraints facing all of us we may continue to move gradually to a more widespread use of social work attachment in general practice, as I think it is one of the most hopeful and effective ways of helping the very large number of people who need and could benefit from personal, social and counselling support. Most people, I suspect, are unlikely to receive help except in this familiar context, which most still see as the natural place to go to when we are anxious or upset – the doctor's surgery.

D. C. Morrell

Discussant

I was surprised and pleased to hear from Dr Strathdee how collaboration between general practitioners and psychiatrists has grown in the last decade. I was particularly interested to hear her say that this arose, not from any edict from above, not as the result of the activities of a planning team or of a special working party, but simply because some like-minded individuals got together and thought it would be a good idea. That, of course, is why by and large it has succeeded.

I have some ten years experience of this type of development in the field of community antenatal care and diabetic care in the St Thomas' District. This occurred because the Professors of Obstetrics, Diabetes and General Practice were personal friends, because they thought the existing system was pretty unsatisfactory, and because they happened to be in a position to introduce change. Interestingly we found, as did Dr Strathdee, that in the early stages of the scheme, patients tended to be referred to the specialist for an opinion, 'the shifted outpatient pattern', but very soon the educational potential of this arrangement was realized and the general practitioners, health visitors and nurses came to think so closely with the specialists and their nursing staff that referral became uncommon, and care was planned largely by mutual discussion. The situation now is not unlike that described by Dr Horder, except that we meet over tea after our antenatal or diabetic clinics.

We encountered another problem evident in Dr Strathdee's paper, namely accommodation, which is so often the crucial factor in determining the course of such liaisons. In London we have special problems, with many doctors working in single-handed practices and from inadequate premises. In psychiatry I am sure that one of the reasons why the liaison schemes have developed so well in East Anglia and the West Country, and so poorly in London, is this accommodation problem.

I would like to leave this point, however, and return to the statement about like-minded individuals producing change, and the role which the hierarchy in the Health Service plays in these developments. In the late 1950s, Swift and McDougall in Wessex suggested that it would be more efficient if general practitioners, nurses and health visitors looked after common populations of patients, if possible working from common premises. This led to the attachment of nurses and health visitors to general practices. For some years all went well, and attachments were worked out between like-minded individuals. Then the hierarchies became concerned. Questions were asked about accountability. Attachments were made from above without proper discussion between the doctors and nurses who were going to have to work together, and it was not long before research in a London borough demonstrated that attachments did not work. What the research in fact demonstrated was that unless there is free and open discussion between those who are planning to work together, then any partnership in care is almost certain to fail. In my own area accountability has been a rock on which many attachments have foundered.

This brings me to the paper by Mr Grindrod. If collaboration is to work, those involved must be so secure in their roles that they respond to a challenge by exploration of the problem and not by retreating into defensive positions. This I believe to be at the very heart of problems of collaboration and team work in primary care. So many who work in this field seem to have a need to have their roles clearly delineated and then to defend them at all costs. If we stop looking at ourselves, however, and at the roles we think we fulfil and look instead at the needs of patients in primary care, we will see that this is nonsense, as I think we concluded yesterday afternoon.

This is what Mr Grindrod is saying when he refers to the skills of the individual worker in terms of the patient's needs, but I would push this further and say that it is not just the skills of the worker, but existing and potential relationships between the worker and client, and the worker and the other professionals involved, which are often paramount to a successful therapeutic outcome. Which brings us back once more to our discussion on the fact that personality can be more important than training.

And this brings me back to the psychiatrists who work in the community. Dr Strathdee has demonstrated that it is not the clinical diagnosis which determines whether or not a patient is referred to a psychiatrist. In the light of the discussion yesterday morning none of us can be surprised. There are many other factors and it is sometimes not easy, in a referral letter, to spell them out or even to be quite clear about them oneself. General practitioners may be able to obtain help and support and continuing education much more easily from the sort of liaisons described in Dr Strathdee's paper than by referral of patients to hospital. I feel she is asking how can these liaisons be further developed because they seem extremely desirable in so many ways. I would suggest that they should continue to evolve, and I suspect that the new generation of general practitioners and psychiatrists will ensure that they do. And as they do, this information should be leaked to other general practitioners who do not have psychiatrists. It is said that 'jealousy gets you nowhere' but in bringing about change in general practice a little envy works wonders. What I would suggest you do not do is seek approval from professional committees, because this produces polarization. And finally, as Mr Grindrod has explained, managers can play an important role in removing restraints which often hinder the development of new ideas and can facilitate initiatives which encourage collaboration.

General Discussion

Dr P. J. Tyrer: We have heard about the benefits of psychiatric clinics in primary care. There are also certain disadvantages of such clinics, and these apply to all three forms of clinic that Dr Strathdee discussed. Psychiatric clinics in primary care tend to be preferred by patients because of easier access but this also means that the psychiatrist has to spend more time travelling. He must also come to terms with the loss of his 'specialist' image: in primary care all doctors are regarded as equal. The consultant is not cushioned by junior staff and other hospital personnel and often receives plain talking from patients in surroundings that are more familiar to them.

By improving services to primary care there is a danger that the main hospital may be short of cover, and there could be a fall in the standard of hospital medical services. If it is perceived that many of the patients seen in primary care are suffering from trivial disorders that do not require specialist psychiatric attention or can be dealt with equally well by the general practitioner, a feeling of resentment can build up in the hospital. It is therefore important to demonstrate a beneficial effect of psychiatric services in primary care or the hospital services. The simplest way in which this can be demonstrated is by a fall in admissions to hospital or a shorter duration of stay. A significant fall in the number of admissions from areas covered by general practice psychiatric clinics has been demonstrated in Nottingham, but this improvement has to be maintained if continued deployment of hospital based medical and nursing staff to primary care psychiatry is to be justified.

The best form of delivering psychiatry to primary care has still to be decided, but it is likely to involve a mixture of the models that Dr Strathdee has discussed. In all of them, the psychiatrist will need to take the initiative in the first place and, in consequence, take on a slightly increased workload. With the expansion in the numbers of community psychiatric nurses and greater awareness of community psychiatry in the nursing curriculum other trained staff should be able to follow this lead, but they cannot take it independently. At present there is no incentive for psychiatrists to stimulate the development of psychiatric clinics in primary care apart from the satisfaction of providing a better service. If this movement is to develop, more attention needs to be paid to general practice psychiatry in psychiatric training and in job descriptions.

Dr D. C. Watt: First of all, over the question of co-operation between social service departments and psychiatric departments, Mr Grindrod pointed out the difficulties with co-operation at the top. In Buckinghamshire we have a joint care planning team which includes representatives of social work departments. Its original *raison d'être* was the rehabilitation of long-stay patients, but it has undertaken the question of psychiatrists co-operating with general practitioners.

On the issue of social workers liaising with general practitioners, it seems to me that they are going to do very little for psychiatry unless they have some experience in training for psychiatry. As you know, the lack of experience in training of many social workers in psychiatry has given rise to a great deal of difficulty, not least in implementing the new Mental Health Act.

Dr E. M. McLean: I have not been able to set up a follow-up study of clinical outcome because that required more resources than I could provide, but I have counted how much patients referred to me as a consultant psychiatrist working in a primary care clinic, how much they bothered their GPs before they had seen me and how much they bothered them afterwards. I followed up 19 of the 25 patients that I saw in one year; in the six months before they saw me they bothered their GPs 112 times, and in the six months after they saw me they bothered their GPs 87 times. The other thing it was easy to count out of this work was how efficient was the use of my time in that clinic compared with the use of my time in a hospital clinic. In the year in question there were 41 new patients booked in at the hospital clinic, but only 30 patients turned up; whereas, for 21 attendances at the general practice, 25 new patients turned up. I think that this is worth showing.

Dr A. H. Mann: Dr Strathdee gave reasons why psychiatrists might want to change their practice and work with general practitioners. Because of the Short Report, our district in North London is going to lose a large number of junior staff in exchange for something like half a consultant, so most consultant psychiatrists will have to rethink how they practice. One way of making consultant time much more effective is to work in collaboration in general practice.

Professor I. Marks: Of the 20 per cent of psychiatrists working in primary care, how many sessions on average are they doing per week and is there any data on how much their travel time increased by virtue of doing primary care work? What about the proportion of failed appointments in primary care clinics as opposed to hospital clinics? We have found that where nurses are working in primary care settings, the proportion of failed appointments has gone up quite considerably, so the efficiency seems to go down by that criterion.

Dr Strathdee: Most psychiatrists are working for one or, at most, two sessions per week in the practices. We have no data on their travel times. If one looks at the regional variation of schemes, they are more common in the West Country than in East Anglia, rather less common in London than the South East. There may be a number of reasons for this. It may be that there are fewer health centres in the inner city areas to perhaps it is easier for psychiatrists to go into areas which have good facilities. On the other hand, it may be that the psychiatrists in some of the regions actually find it more effective for them to do the travelling rather than have the patients do it.

We do not have specific information on failed appointments. From my own experience, working in general practice, I find that the failed appointment rate is extremely small – very much less than in the equivalent hospital outpatient setting, and that seems to be a general impression from most of the psychiatrists who work in general practices.

Dr L. Ratoff: We published our work at the height of the enthusiasm for social work/general practice attachments. When the Department of Health and Social Security grant ran out and the social worker left us, we then had a liaison social worker from the Social Services Department next door, in the same building as us. Ten years later, there is no such attachment in Toxteth. The social workers next door are not willing to come round to see us and there remains the sort of hostility that is general throughout social work/GP collaboration. I am fully aware that GPs are just as bad as social workers in the hostility they have for each other; my belief is that we have got to start at the undergraduate level in order to get things going.

Dr B. Essex: Rather than looking at the collaboration between GPs and psychiatrists, I should like to concentrate on looking at the collaboration between patients and families and the multi-disciplinary workers that are involved in mental health care. The Corner Report stressed that in order to collaborate we need to develop a common language, and Corner recommended that we develop problem-oriented classifications which are equally applicable to primary health care and the social worker fields, so that by means of these classifications the GP, social worker, relatives and voluntary carers could begin to be able to classify problems and disabilities.

In the area of mental handicap, it is very difficult to collaborate with the multi-agency and multi-disciplinary areas which are involved, but in some parts of the country, for example the Wessex region, they have ten years' experience of overcoming some of these difficult collaborative problems. We need to look at the areas in the country where they have successfully innovated, and then experimented, rather than trying to start in each region all over again.

Dr D. Wilkin: I am somewhat depressed when I hear people saying that collaboration is essentially down to the personalities of the people involved, whether it is in teams or between agencies. I think that probably what that reflects is a lack of any systematic knowledge about the structural conditions, the ideological conditions, or the personal characteristics of people which make for good collaboration. We have heard a little this morning about some systematic research along these lines. There is a need for much more fundamental research into the structural characteristics and the personal characteristics which facilitate collaboration. It is all very well to say members of a primary health care team should work together and have flexible roles, but they work under completely different organizational structures, and they work with disparate salary levels and backgrounds. There is very little research which says much about the outcomes of effective or ineffective collaboration in terms of the clients themselves, whether they be psychiatric patients or any other client group. I think it needs to be recognized that collaboration itself has a great deal of cost attached to it; it actually occupies a lot of service time and we need to be looking at what the outcomes of that are, in terms of client characteristics and client contact.

Mr B. Kat: The pattern of numerous individual initiatives which Dr Strathdee reported for psychiatrists parallels the developments since 1974 in clinical psychology. I was one of those who began the process of closer contacts with general practitioners by clinical psychologists. They had a number of motives. Certainly, one of them was to do with shortening the referral route for behaviour therapy, which was a particular emphasis of psychologists' work at that time. There were also the issues of psychologists' understanding patients better by seeing them earlier and seeing their problems closer to home; and, patients being able to see psychologists for psychological problems without the stigmatization of involvement in psychiatric services. The fact that we are using non-drug treatments, behavioural, and cognitive therapy methods has been valued highly by both general practitioners and patients. As a profession we have been struck by the problems of rehabilitation, the elderly mentally ill, patients with severe acute problems, and forensic services; which have constrained developments in clinical psychologists' work in general practice.

PART 6

THE VIEW
FROM ABROAD

J. H. Henderson

Health for all:
one common goal

The enjoyment of the highest attainable standard of health is one of the fundamental rights of every human being without distinction of race, religion, political belief, economic or social condition.

(World Health Organisation Constitution)

The World Health Organisation (WHO) and 163 countries co-operate in the field of health and have set themselves a common goal, 'Health for All by the Year 2000' (HFA/2000). The goal is that, by the end of the century, people everywhere should have access to health services which will enable them to lead socially and economically productive lives. The Global Strategy for Health for All, adopted in May 1981, represents a solemn agreement between the governments and WHO.

HEALTH FOR ALL STRATEGY

The HFA/2000 strategy calls for concrete action in the health and related socioeconomic sectors. For it to succeed, the commitment of political, economic and social decision makers is essential to bring about the necessary co-ordinated efforts mobilizing public support and involvement. The application of managerial processes is also critical for the implementation of the strategy.

'Health for All by the Year 2000' does not mean that by then disease and disability will no longer exist, or that doctors and nurses will be taking care of everybody. What it does mean is that resources for health will be evenly distributed, and that essential health care will be accessible to everyone, with full community involvement. It means that health begins at home, in schools and in factories, and that people will use better approaches than they do now for preventing disease and alleviating unavoidable disease and disability. It means that people will realize that they have the power to shape their own lives and the lives of their families, free from the avoidable burden of disease, and aware that ill-health is not inevitable.

PRIMARY HEALTH CARE

In 1978, the International Conference on Primary Health Care, jointly sponsored by WHO and UNICEF and held in Alma-Ata, USSR, declared that primary health care is the key to attaining the goal of Health for All by the year 2000. Primary health care is based on practical, scientifically sound and socially acceptable methods and technology. It should be made universally accessible to individuals and families in their community through their full participation and at an affordable cost on a continuing basis. Primary health care takes place at the first contact between individuals and the national health system, as close as possible to where people live and work. It is the first element in a continuing health care process and forms an integral part of the country's health system.

The Alma-Ata declaration

The declaration of Alma-Ata, in defining the essential elements of health care, stressed that primary health care should focus on the main health problems in the community, but recognized that these problems and the ways of solving them would vary from one country and community to another. Accordingly, Recommendation 5 of the Conference included promotion of mental health as one of the desirable elements of primary health care.

The role of the World Health Organisation

As the United Nations specialized agency for international health, WHO is a co-operative organization with policies and programmes representing the collective expression of the health aspirations and actions of its member states as a whole, and in which WHO is the partner of each one. Under the global health for all strategy, the member states and WHO have resolved to place special emphasis on the developing countries. Nevertheless, the benefits of WHO's international health work are reaped by all countries, including the most developed.

WHO's main functions can be summed up as follows: to act as directing and co-ordinating authority on international health work; to ensure valid and productive technical co-operation; and to promote research.

An important aspect of WHO's function is the generation and international transfer of valid information on health matters. WHO serves as a clearing house, absorbing, distilling, synthesizing and disseminating health information of many kinds.

Besides providing technical co-operation for individual member states, WHO facilitates technical co-operation between them, whether they are developed or developing.

The structure of the World Health Organisation

The central authority in WHO is the World Health Assembly, which determines the organization's policies. It meets once a year in May and is attended by national delegations from all Member States. The WHO Executive Board, which meets twice a year, is made up of thirty people who are designated by their countries for three year periods of office; however, they act in their personal capacity as public health experts. The Executive Board advises the World Health Assembly and gives effect to its policies.

The World Health Organisation is divided into six regions, in each of which there is a regional committee. Each regional committee meets once a year and is attended by representatives of the member states in that region. It formulates policies of a regional character and monitors regional activities.

The secretariat of WHO is headed by the Director-General, the chief technical and administrative officer, elected by the World Health Assembly. The headquarters is in Geneva. In each region a regional office acts as the administrative organ of the regional committee which elects its Regional Director.

Expert committees and scientific groups provide WHO with technical advice on most aspects of its work, including medical research, for which advisory committees have been established in each region and at the global level. These bodies ensure the close association of leading representatives of the scientific community with WHO's activities.

Regional strategy for health for all in Europe

In order to translate the WHO's global strategy and objectives for HFA/2000 into a strategy with a regional character and to develop subsequently activities at regional and national levels, the European Regional Committee approved in 1980 a regional strategy for health for all. Basically, this strategy contains three main thrusts for action in health in the region: promotion of more healthy lifestyles; intensification of efforts to reduce preventable illnesses; provision of adequate health care accessible to all. Henceforth, the programmes of the European Regional Office are based on the WHO general policies for HFA/2000, the Alma-Ata Declaration and the Regional Strategy for HFA.

Primary Health Care (PHC) is seen to be the key to the attainment of HFA, but it is clear that there has been doubt in some industrialized or developed countries about the importance and meaning of these issues for long-established and relatively well functioning systems of health care.

Mental health for all by the year 2000

Within the mental health systems in many countries of Europe the policy issues outlined in HFA and PHC are comparatively well known, well accepted and embedded already to a greater or lesser degree in current policies and practice for delivery of mental health care.

Mental Health Services in Europe have been characterized in their policies and development by aiming to provide comprehensive community based mental health care. Thus it is no new philosophy to emphasize that health care should be related to the needs of the population; consumers should participate, indirectly and collectively, in the planning and implementation of health care; primary health care is not an isolated approach but the local component of a comprehensive care system.

What is novel and challenging to many governments and professions and communities is the need to enlarge the primary *medical* care concept to the primary *health* care concept. Just as familiar and just as difficult perhaps as that implied in the transition of widening the *mental illness* concept to that of *mental health*. This shift and thrust means a strengthening of the horizontal activities at the local level, linkages of health with education, welfare, law enforcement, public services, etc. At a national level, too, it means a creation or a strengthening of intersectoral or interdepartmental co-operation within government.

PRIMARY HEALTH CARE IN EUROPE

Judging from developments in the member states up to 1983, primary health care seems to be getting off the ground. Greece is moving towards establishing a network of health centres. France and Spain decided to establish pilot health centres. Legislative reform (effective as of 1 January 1984) in Norway decentralized services and brought the decision-making power closer to the community. Italy has already some experience from a similar decentralization effort. Sweden emphasized in its new basic health law (effective as of 1 January 1983) the concept of the right to health and the integration of health services at local levels. Important national meetings dealing with PHC have been organized in Belgium and Turkey. Algeria, Morocco and Turkey have accorded high priority to PHC in their national plans and are developing their

PHC services. PHC-related training courses have been organized in Austria, Belgium and Yugoslavia and are planned in Finland and the Soviet Union.

In spite of these encouraging developments, the promotion of PHC has also met with difficulties. Many countries still equate primary health care with primary medical care. Surprisingly few members of the various health professions have ever heard of the Declaration of Alma-Ata. PHC team work has not always been developed and the collaboration between various health related sectors, particularly health services and social services may be deficient. Certainly not enough research is carried out in this field. The WHO regional programme in PHC is undergoing a change from developing a conceptual framework to providing assistance in organizing PHC services and training. Many of the past activities have aimed at clarifying and promoting the concept. Papers in learned and professional journals and participation in scientific and professional, international and national meetings have played a key role in this respect. Studies on management problems in PHC and community participation mechanisms are now approaching completion. Other studies were launched during the year on: the effectiveness of primary care; indicators for monitoring the development of PHC; information systems for PHC; and different approaches to organizing PHC services (with special reference to south European countries with health care systems based on social security).

A Conference on Primary Health Care in Industrialised Countries was held in November 1983 in Bordeaux, France, and was attended by representatives from twenty-six countries, and fourteen delegates from non-governmental organizations representing general practitioners, medical students, nurses, and from UNICEF. Observers from several countries outside the region, and members of the press were also present.

The Conference was intended to reaffirm the Declaration of Alma-Ata as relevant health policy guidance for the industrialized countries, to take stock of national developments in the implementation and development of primary health care since Alma-Ata, to review concrete examples of successful implementation of the Alma-Ata principles and to identify obstacles to implementation.

While practical application of the Alma-Ata principles has been influenced by economic, social and political realities, progress has been made in the integration of public and private medicine, the control of the hospital costs and the re-allocation of financial and human resources to the isolated, deprived, vulnerable, and politically powerless. Teaching of the principles of PHC has increased at professional and non-professional levels, as have opportunities for individuals and communities to participate in the health care process. The role of prevention is recognized, and legislative support for control of environmental and personal risk factors is widespread.

However, a number of constraints have also become apparent. Attitudinal differences between health professionals and lay people, the technical nature of many health issues, variations in willingness or ability to co-operate, and rigid administrative structures make intersectoral collaboration and community participation difficult goals to achieve. While the integration of health services would improve the quality and continuity of care, constant attention to the needs of individuals and communities rather than health professionals is needed. Finally, instead of increasing health expenditures, the development and application of technology should support PHC and help to stabilize or reduce costs.

The Conference recommended that governments, health professionals and lay people acknowledge the central role of PHC in improving the accessibility and quality of care by: controlling the expansion of the hospital sector; promoting the appropriate use of health and communication technology and ensuring the allocation of resources according to need; co-ordinating multi-sectoral, community and individual efforts to improve the physical, social, political and economic 'prerequisites to health'; stimulating, particularly at community level, health promotion, disease prevention, and health care activities related to the needs of vulnerable groups and the elderly.

Finally, it was recommended that health professionals recognize their responsibility to provide comprehensive, continuous *health care* rather than just *medical* care; take steps to improve the undergraduate and postgraduate teaching of PHC principles and increase their efforts to re-orientate the practice patterns of licenced practitioners; acknowledge their responsibility to improve data collection, information transfer and monitoring procedures; increase teamwork; and communicate more effectively with health care users.

MENTAL HEALTH IN PRIMARY HEALTH CARE

A Working Group on First Contact Mental Health Care was convened in Tampere (Finland), April 1983, as part of WHO's medium-term programme for developments in mental health care, particularly in relation to primary health care. The working group was composed of fourteen temporary advisers from Bulgaria, Finland, Greece, Italy, Morocco, Netherlands, Norway, Spain, Sweden, the United Kingdom, USSR and Yugoslavia.

A previous report of a WHO working group that met in Lysebu, Oslo in 1973 focused on psychiatry in general practice, and the role of the general practitioner in mental health services. The present working group was concerned primarily with the roles and functions of mental health teams operating in the context of primary health care with emphasis on the ways in which specialists in mental health could give support to primary health care workers, and work directly at community levels with self-help groups and other voluntary agencies who were already contributing to mental health. Four main topics were considered in some detail.

General policy and organization of mental health in primary health care

The principal aim must be to provide access to mental health care for as many people as possible by making clear all the potential contact points with the primary health care system. First contact mental health care can be provided at four different levels: by specialist mental health services including inpatient facilities in the hospital units; by specialist centres provided in the community such as day centres and outpatient departments; by general practices or health centres in the form of primary health care; by self-help and voluntary bodies in the community.

It is deemed important at each level to provide the minimum degree of intervention that will allow individuals and their families to maintain their self-regard and independence.

The nature of the first contact for mental health care

Several basic questions were raised: first contact with whom and by whom, where is it to be undertaken and what is its purpose? Recognizing the importance of this first contact between the services available and those seeking help, great sensitivity is required to structure and handle the potential interpersonal relationship so that there is the most favourable outcome. The role of the specialized mental health service is seen, therefore, to guide and support primary health care givers in their work at this first point of contact.

Membership and functions of mental health and primary care teams

The terms of reference or job description of each of the participating professionals and volunteers define the potential membership of each team. It will have a core group of colleagues working regularly together, and an extended group of others who will join in the work of the core group from time to time as circumstances and occasion demand. It is vital that the quality of status of all those working in these mental health care teams is fully recognized and practised. Each team should work out its own procedures for consultation among its members, and for the referral of problems and specialized tasks to each other. When many people are involved in this work at the various levels described, communication systems require careful definition and discipline if there is not to be confusion, frustration and wasteful overlap.

Training and research

To enable people to work in this way, training should be extended into the community, using established methods that are traditionally based on the psychiatric hospital or district general hospital psychiatric unit. Such training schemes should allow potential members of future mental health care teams to receive their training and education together as a team. The educational aims should be directed not only towards the acquisition of required technical knowledge, but also towards shaping the attitudes of the students, developing their sensitivity and providing basic management skills such as the establishment of priorities and the identification and utilization of resources. University departments and academic institutes have a vital part to play, but they too must become community-orientated and participate in training schemes located directly in the primary care setting.

Research should focus not only on epidemiological studies as such, establishing prevalence rates of disorder, etc., but should also determine indicators of change in health parameters, which can then be used in evaluating the provision and utilization of services.

Certain basic conclusions emerged from the discussions of the working group:

1. that the promotion of mental health is a vital component of primary health care;
2. that the decentralization of mental health services is essential to bring them into the community where people live and work;
3. that at all times an attempt must be made to supply the minimum level of care required, according to the needs and existing resources of individuals and their communities, so as to give them back their self-regard and the capacity to be responsible for themselves and their own futures; and
4. that mental health care skills and resources should be closely integrated into primary health care and social welfare systems, for the purposes of education, support and consultation.

Recommendations were prepared and offered to WHO and governments. These were:

1. A working group should be set up to study the organization and provision of psychiatric emergency services given their importance as points of first contact with mental health care.
2. Inter-country training should be developed in mental health practice in the primary health care setting, based initially on designated WHO collaborating centres.
3. A multi-disciplinary study group should be set up to examine the consultative relationship between mental health care and primary health care systems.
4. National authorities with responsibilities for health planning should relate shape and form of mental health services to the population size of the localities to be served.
5. Voluntary bodies such as mental health and psychiatric patient associ-

ations in lay care and community health programmes should examine the ways in which users of mental health services are able to find out what is available, and what values they attach to these services. Consideration should be given in this context to the contribution of the mass media to health education programmes.

6. To promote active mental health care in primary health care settings, links are recommended in national and international activities wherever there are areas of joint interest and concern. Such links are already identifiable between mental health and health care of the elderly, health economics, drug utilization programmes, health information systems, and country-wide programmes of preventive practices in chronic diseases.

REFERENCES

World Health Organisation Regional Office for Europe (1973) *The development of comprehensive mental health services in the community*: report on a conference. EURO 5414 I. Copenhagen: WHO Regional Office for Europe.

—— (1978) *Alma-Ata 1978: Primary Health Care.* Health for All Series, No. 1. Geneva: World Health Organisation.

—— (1978) *Constraints in mental health services development*: report on a working group. ICP/MNH 030 II. Copenhagen: WHO Regional Office for Europe.

—— (1978) *Formulating Strategies for Health for All by the Year 2000.* Health for All Series, No. 2.

—— (1978) *The future of mental hospitals*: report on a working group. ICP/MNH 019 11. Copenhagen: WHO Regional Office for Europe.

—— (1978) *Global Strategy for Health for all by the Year 2000.* Health for All Series, No. 3. Geneva, World Health Organisation.

—— (1978) *Psychiatry and primary medical care*: report on a working group. ICP/MNH 019 II. Copenhagen: WHO Regional Office for Europe.

—— (1979) *Primary Health Care in Europe*, by L. A. Kaprio. EURO Reports and Studies No. 14. Copenhagen: WHO Regional Office for Europe.

—— (1980) *Regional Strategy for Attaining Health for All by the Year 2000.* EUR/RC/30/8. Copenhagen: WHO Regional Office for Europe.

—— (1981) *Health Services in Europe, 3rd Edition.* Copenhagen: WHO Regional Office for Europe.

—— (1982) *Primary Health Care. From Theory to Practice*: report on a WHO Symposium. EURO Reports and Studies No. 69. Copenhagen: WHO Regional Office for Europe.

—— (1985) *First Contact Mental Health Care*: report on a working group. EURO Reports and Studies No. 92. Copenhagen: WHO Regional Office for Europe.

Barbara J. Burns, Carl A. Taube,
and Darrel A. Regier

A view from abroad – building primary care: mental health research in the USA

Primary care/mental health research in the USA has been directed toward assessing and improving mental health care in the general health sector. We hope to enhance the mental health diagnostic and treatment skills of health professionals and to add mental health specialists to primary care teams. The research to achieve the preceding aims combines epidemiological, health services and statistical methods. Over the past twenty years it has focused on four major areas:

1. documenting the extent and the types of mental disorder in primary care populations;
2. describing and assessing the mental health practices of health professionals and patterns of service use by the population;
3. modifying mental health practices; and
4. evaluating the impact of organizational structures and financing on health and mental health service use.

Primary care research in the USA has been significantly influenced by and, to a great extent, has paralleled such research in Britain. However, differences in the health systems of the two countries contributed to somewhat different research approaches. The emphasis on specialist medicine in the US and the historical separation of psychiatry from mainstream medicine have not reinforced the notion that mental health is an integral aspect of primary care medicine, from either the perspective of the primary care physician or the psychiatrist. The pluralistic (some say 'disorganized') US system of health care has not engendered the continuity of care of the British National Health Service registration of patients with specific physicians. The lack of a gate-keeper role in US primary care has meant that a referral is not needed to obtain psychiatric services.

These important differences in the structure and functioning of the two health systems seem to be decreasing. Changes appear to be in the direction of greater similarity (e.g. an increase in private practice in Britain and more use of prepaid health plans in the USA). In Britain, a mental health role for the general practitioner is integral to the practice of primary care medicine, while this has been a slow uphill battle in the USA. A recent survey of British GPs indicates that they may be less enamoured than previously with their psycho-social role,[1] while the USA is witnessing a return to primary care medicine and a strong bio-psychosocial emphasis.[2,3] From the perspective of emerging systems of health care, both countries can continue to benefit from under-standing changes in the other.

This paper addresses the development of primary care/mental health research in the USA within the context of social, political, economic, legis-lative and service system changes from the early 1960s to the present. The motivation for and the focus of this research sponsored by the USA Govern-ment, more specifically the National Institute of Mental Health (NIMH), has shifted over time. Two periods are traced: an early period, a time of growing mental health resources; and a more recent one characterized by shrinking mental health resources. Also, specific mechanisms available to the Federal Government for implementing such a research program are discussed.

GROWING MENTAL HEALTH RESOURCES (1960–1972)

The 1960s, a decade of strife around racial issues and the war in Viet Nam, was a time of major change in social policies in the USA. Liberal governments advocated 'the New Frontier' and 'the Great Society' in a period of perceived affluence. Major attempts were made to diminish social imbalances in educa-tion, health, employment and housing. The most significant health legis-lation, Medicaid and Medicare, increased access to health care for low income people and provided limited health insurance to the elderly; funds to support this legislation represent a major portion of the Department of Health and Human Services budget. Legislation also enabled the establishment of federally supported community health centers to provide comprehensive, continuous, family-centered health care.

The 1963 Community Mental Health Centers Act legislated community-based mental health services across the country and promised a shift away from large psychiatric hospitals. This latter aim was realized in the 1970s, along with a major shift from inpatient to outpatient care. Concurrently, the number of psychiatrists, psychologists, psychiatric social workers and psychiatric nurses increased dramatically due in part to special support for their training from NIMH.[4] Further, in the late 1960s and early 1970s, psychiatric benefits were added to health insurance plans, with many states mandating at least minimal inpatient and outpatient coverage. During that period, little attention was given to mental health services in the general health sector by those recommending major alterations in the mental health system.[5]

The NIMH National Reporting Program, which documented use of specialty mental health services in outpatient specialty mental health clinics and public and private psychiatric hospitals, expanded in the late 1960s to collect data on psychiatric units in general hospitals and the new community mental health centers. Despite major expansion of specialty mental health services, some public health-oriented researchers recognized the major role of primary care physicians in providing mental health treatment. Without data on mental health services provided by general medical practitioners, a national picture of mental health service use would be incomplete.

A psychiatric case register in Monroe County, New York, and the possibility of surveying physicians about mental health problems in their patients, provided a starting place for NIMH investigators, Goldberg, Locke, and Rosen. Since national surveys of health professionals at that time did not provide data on mental health practices, one county was examined to obtain a combined estimate of mental health services provided by psychiatrists and primary care physicians. Although not typical, due to the influence of an established medical school and a well-known psychiatric hospital (resulting in inflated estimates if applied to other areas of the country), the picture which emerged forced recognition of a significant mental health role for the primary care physician. In three types of primary care settings the annual prevalence of mental disorder ranged from 5.4 per cent–20.2 per cent, while only 1.6 per cent–5.2 per cent of these patients were found on the psychiatric case register.[6,7,8] The classic study of the General Practice Research Unit, *Psychiatric Illness in General Practice*, conducted a little earlier, revealed similar patterns and reinforced the importance of this research direction.[9]
The natural outcome of a focus on health and mental health services was a concern about the effect of their interaction in both countries.

Interest in assessing whether psychiatric services were economically feasible in prepaid health plans was evaluated by examining the impact of psychiatric treatment on health services use. The health plans studied (the Health Insurance Plan of New York and Group Health Association of Washington, DC) offered psychiatric benefits – unusual for any health organization at that time. These studies demonstrated an association between brief mental health treatment and a reduction in subsequent medical visits.[10,11] Although there were some limitations in the design of these early studies, they opened the door to assessing the relationship between health and mental health services.

With these studies, the initial directions were set for developing a national picture of the mental health role of the general medical sector, as well as investigating ways to integrate mental health services and general health care.

SHRINKING MENTAL HEALTH RESOURCES (1973–1984)

Gains in the provision of health and human services during the 1960s and early 1970s have since been threatened by serious economic problems and increasingly more conservative governments. Proposals for national health insurance promised by 1970 by President Kennedy and others, have been tabled indefinitely. Serious concerns about the rapid increases in the cost of health care have been reflected in efforts to contain costs through (1) prospective payment, (2) a de-emphasis on specialist medical care, and (3) mandates to strengthen primary care medicine. One influential Federal official has advocated application of the principals of the market place to operation of the health care system.[12]

Within the mental health sector, funds for community mental health centers were impounded in the early 1970s and then transferred to the US in 1981 with reduced fiscal support, resulting in achievement of only 50 per cent of the goal for establishing centers in 1963. Further, support for clinical training of mental health professionals has been cut drastically and termination is likely, despite predictions of shortages in psychiatry.[13] Psychiatric benefits in insurance plans, added in the 1960s, are being reassessed and sometimes reduced. Many deinstitutionalized patients are on the streets or in nursing homes or jails in need of services. Thus, the milieu for building a program of primary care research was influenced by a strong need for the efficient and cost-effective use of general medical personnel and mental health specialists. Although responsive to the preceding needs, a long-range research agenda was proposed that would be applicable to times of either poverty or greater affluence.

BUILDING THE PROGRAM

The preceding developments highlight the importance of a strong mental health capability in primary care. Fortunately, Federal support for research has been maintained, and even slightly increased, creating the possibility of working towards resolution of these service delivery problems. In 1977, the Primary Care Research Section in the Division of Biometry and Epidemiology, NIMH, was formally organized by Darrel A. Regier who proposed the following research questions:

1. What is the prevalence of mental disorders identified in the US primary health care sector?
2. What is the validity and reliability of psychiatric diagnoses made by primary health care providers?

3. What mental health treatment services are currently being provided by primary health care providers?
4. What is the outcome or effectiveness of mental health services provided in the primary health care sector?
5. What is the optimal division of responsibility between the primary care sector and the specialty mental health sector in the treatment of patients with mental disorder.
6. What kind of mental health training programs will enable the primary health care provider to deal most effectively with his patients requiring mental health services?
7. What is the effect of different organizational and financing structures of primary health and mental health specialty services on the utilization and cost of both mental health services and other health services for patients with mental disorders?
8. What is the overall cost of mental health services provided in the primary health care sector?
9. What is the effect of different organizational and financing structures on primary health and mental health?

Two very important steps contributed to the development of the preceding research agenda. First, national surveys of health and mental health service use and case register data were combined to estimate the allocation of people with mental disorder in the US population to the service delivery sectors (health, mental health, human services) where services were received. What became known as the *de facto* paper reported that annually 60 per cent of the population with mental disorders were seen by primary care physicians, while only 20 per cent received services from mental health specialists.[14] This somewhat surprising finding, given the rapid growth of mental health professionals and facilities, was subsequently used by the President's Commission on Mental Health[15] to further enhance the mandate to conduct research on mental disorder in primary care. A second major force which shaped the early directions of the program was the use of expert consultations from outside of the government. Professor Shepherd contributed his wisdom and expertise to the proposed research agenda from his experience with the General Practice Research Unit (GPRU). He has continued to provide consultation over the years, as have other prominent British investigators, including Professors Goldberg, Cooper, and Clare.

As the Primary Care Research Section was getting underway, the impact of the 1976 Health Profession Educational Assistance Act was being anticipated. Increased support for the training of primary care physicians and severely reduced support for psychiatrists provided a strong impetus for examining the mental health education of primary care physicians. Experts from medical school departments of family practice, pediatrics, medicine and psychiatry were convened to examine the status of mental health education and to make recommendations. A meeting under the auspices of NIMH initiated communication among academic primary care physicians, psychiatrists, and governmental agencies responsible for medical training and manpower.[16] Subsequently, NIMH earmarked funds for training primary care physicians, and awareness was heightened in medical organizations regarding the need for such training; this was reflected in mandates from the respective professional academies.[17-19] A special study to improve recognition of psychological distress among residents in family medicine was designed and conducted under NIMH contract by David Goldberg at the Medical University of South Carolina.[20] A recent literature review on mental health training for primary care physicians documents increased attention to mental health, but also finds the training inadequate in many respects (e.g. lack of an organized approach to the diagnosis and treatment of specific mental disorders).[21]

With legislation greatly reducing previous funding levels for clinical training of mental health specialists, and a mandate from the President's Commission to conduct mental health research in primary care, the next major need was to identify and develop a cadre of potential investigators. A special literature review, *Mental Disorder and Primary Medical Care*,[22] commissioned by NIMH, was helpful in providing a state of the art review for future research. It also provided useful background for a conference, 'Mental Health Services in Primary Care Settings', sponsored by the Institute of Medicine of the National Academy of Sciences and NIMH. National and international investigators met in Washington, DC in 1979 to present recent research results and to interact with key governmental officials. Research issues were identified to address the mental health service needs of the population and the policy interests of the Government. Recommendations were made for epidemiological, clinically-oriented, institutionally-oriented, and health systems studies in primary care (for specific recommendations, see pp. 200–02).[23]

During the early years of the formal program, while research directions were being solidified and mandates obtained, a very active research program was pursued using the contract mechanism. Government staff design and direct the studies which are conducted in the field usually by university-based groups; analysis and publication of findings are usually a collaborative product of Government and university investigators. This is a particularly useful approach before investigators in the field are prepared to initiate such studies. Contracts are also useful for methodological projects such as development and validation of research measures. Examples include the design and field testing of diagnostic interviews, such as the NIMH Diagnostic Interview Schedule (DIS) by Robins and colleagues,[24] and an interview for clinician diagnosis, the Standardized Clinical Interview for Diagnosis (SCID), which is currently under development.

In the process of conceptualizing the extent of the problem, an early epidemiological study revealed that the prevalence of mental disorder among adults in a general medical population may be as high as 30 per cent, based on a standardized psychiatric interview (in contrast to approximately 15 per cent in the general population).[25] Problems with the mental health practices of primary care physicians, such as the low treated prevalence rates found in national surveys, were further underscored by the very low rates of recognition (around 3 per cent) and treatment or referral (also about 3 per cent) in the preceding study. Interests in the mental health problems of children was also explored. In a large study of pediatric practices in Monroe County, New York, pediatricians identified mental disorder in about 5 per cent of the children.[26] A study is in progress at the University of Pittsburgh to assess the correspondence between pediatrician recognition of mental health problems and a research diagnosis. A further reason for concern about the appropriate management of patients with mental disorder is that they make twice as many medical visits as persons without mental disorder, while also receiving more medical diagnoses (particularly of ill-defined signs, symptoms and conditions).[27,28] The issues associated with medical/psychiatric co-morbidity have been a serious concern of the General Practice Research Unit, highlighted particularly in the large-scale clinical trial of the treatment of patients with mild to moderate hypertension under the aegis of the British Medical Research Council.[29] As stated by Professor Shepherd, 'attention could be directed profitably to the relationships rather than to the difference between physical and mental disorder.'[30]

The preceding findings on clincial practice focused NIMH staff attention on identifying ways to improve clinical care for patients with mental disorder in primary care. Subsequently, studies directed toward improving the detection of emotional problems in primary care patients were designed and conducted, taking four different approaches:

1. improving interviewing skills among family practice residents;[20]
2. providing screening questionnaire and diagnostic information to physicians;[31,32]
3. developing a classification of psychological symptoms and social problems with the World Health Organisation to facilitate identification of mental disorder by general medical personnel;[33] and
4. placing mental health linkage staff in health centers to perform triage, evaluation and liaison between Federally funded community health centers and community mental health centers.[34,35]

These initial steps taken to alter detection practices represent the beginning of a long-term initiative to investigate and to improve clinical outcomes for patients treated in primary care settings. Barriers to the provision of mental health care, such as inadequate training, hospital-based role models and fiscal incentives, will be further investigated. The development of approaches to facilitate diagnosis and clinical management is critical, as is a need for guidelines to differentiate the mental health skills of primary care practitioners from those of mental health specialists.

Studies on organizational and financing structures have led the research program in several directions. Those on health settings with integrated health and mental health services have reported greater patient use of mental health services than separately organized service systems, as well as somewhat higher detection rates by medical practitioners.[36,37] There is some evidence that linkages between health and mental health organizations to better co-ordinate mental health care function as an alternate strategy.[38] This concept is similar to the British approach of attaching social workers to general practice groups as part of the primary care team.[39]

In the financing area, a series of studies has examined the impact of mental health service use on subsequent medical use.[40,41] Other studies have examined such issues as the relationship between the level of psychiatric benefits and medical use patterns,[42] and the relationship between selected medical conditions and the use of psychiatric services, finding a savings in inpatient medical care.[43] Prospective studies using randomized designs, such as a comparison of the cost of health care in a Health Maintenance Organization and a fee-for-service plan,[44] are needed to identify the most effective and efficient organizations for providing health and mental health services.

Finally, future research directed toward improving clinical practices in primary care also need to support research to develop methods to make such studies feasible (see Attachment I, No. 4).

As the field has developed, a number of health service researchers interested in the primary care/mental health interface have emerged. Thus, it is now possible to expand this area of research more rapidly with investigator-initiated studies under the grant mechanism. Grants allow investigators to compete for research funds through a peer review system. Government staff who are part of the Primary Care Research Section provide consultation to applicants to help assure that topics relate to program priorities. Over a four-year period, the quality of applications has steadily improved; studies spanning a range of topics, frequently using a 'clinical trial' design, are under way. One example of a grant which goes beyond the capability of a contract is a study comparing the adequacy of diagnosing depression in family medicine centers and community mental health centers. It would be difficult at the Federal level to obtain local co-operation to use the same protocol in both types of service settings.

In addition to the contract and grant mechanisms for Government support of research, there is another approach called a 'co-operative agreement'. This calls for greater direction by Government staff than does a grant, but less control of the investigators than a contract. Particularly useful for multi-site studies where similar designs and measures are needed, this approach has been effectively used in the Epidemiological Catchment Area studies of the Division of Biometry and Epidemiology. Data from these studies, which include research diagnoses of mental disorder and self-report of health and mental health service use, will provide an opportunity to update and replicate the *de facto* paper[14] with more detailed information. A future co-operative agreement will sample users of health and mental health services in several communities, follow their care longitudinally, and assess outcome. From this study we expect to elicit a better picture of the relative effectiveness of the health and mental health providers in managing specific types of mental disorders.

To complement the preceding types of focused studies, collaborative research activities among Governmental agencies are necessary to obtain a national picture of clinical practice and service use. For example, through interagency agreements, it has been possible to add mental health items to national health surveys of the population and of health providers, thereby gathering information over time. Rates of mental disorder diagnosis and of prescriptions of psychotropic medications in periodic surveys, like the National Ambulatory Medical Care Survey, have thus been obtained. A recent report, *The Hidden Mental Health Network, Provision of Mental Health Services by Non-psychiatrist Physicians*,[45] documented that half of the psychiatric care provided by physicians is given by non-psychiatrists who are more likely to provide mental health care to the elderly and the poor than psychiatrists. The data source is strictly physician reports, and the adequacy of the classification of patients and the treatment provided cannot be readily assessed. Particularly since a study like this has implications for manpower policies, it needs to be supplemented with more in-depth studies on the quality of care provided. In another survey sponsored by the National Center for Health Statistics, therefore, NIMH has added a mental health component to the National Nursing-home Survey which will allow comparison of a research diagnoses for mental disorder with medical record diagnoses and will document mental health care provided to nursing home patients across the country.

There are other ways to facilitate mental health research in primary care from within the Government. A plan is being developed to co-ordinate primary care research across all Public Health Service agencies through a joint PHS grant announcement. In addition, several agencies can jointly sponsor initiatives which combine research interests. For example, under the general title 'Health and Behavior', NIMH is working with the National Institutes of Health (NIH) to request grant applications on topics such as psychosocial interventions for the chronically medically ill.

SUMMARY AND CONCLUSIONS

In summary, the economic realities reflected in the social and political forces of the late 1970s and early 1980s highlighted the need for primary care/mental health research. The notion that 'the primary care team is the cornerstone of psychiatry' is an even more relevant goal in 1984 than when conceived in 1973.[46] Given the many obstacles to changing health care practices and health systems to improve mental health care, the multiple strategies available only to a government are required if some success is to be achieved.

As we look back at the primary care research program since its inception in 1977 as a distinct unit within the National Institute of Mental Health, five points emerge to account for the developments described:

1. Preparation for a new research program required assessing the readiness of the field and obtaining clear mandates. The Monroe County, New York, studies of primary care physicians, and those on mental health treatment in prepaid health organizations, opened the door to primary care/mental health research in the US. Mandates to conduct research occurred in response to the 1976 health manpower legislation, the impact of the *de facto* paper on the President's Commission on Mental Health, and the 1979 Institute of Medicine conference on primary care. The leadership of NIMH, including Bertram Brown and Herbert Pardes, as well as ADAMHA Administrators Gerald Klerman and William Meyer, also contributed significantly to providing a mandate.

2. A clearly formulated research agenda provided a long-term plan for the research program. Based on a public health rationale, questions about the prevalence of mental disorders and the settings where afflicted persons received care led to identifying primary care as the mental health service sector serving the largest number of patients. These interests moved the program naturally into issues such as training, approaches to integrating health and mental health care, and ways to improve the detection and clinical management of mental disorder in primary care.

3. Building research capacity in the field has been an important challenge. It was essential that a research team with an overview of the field and the ability to keep up with developments nationally and internationally be centrally located within the Government. Mental health specialists in the US tended to be skeptical of this new research direction. Similarly, generating interest in primary care investigators in mental health has required comparable effort. However, as the importance of primary care research was demonstrated, an interest in the public health and clinical issues has extended into the larger academic research centers. Growth of the investigator-initiated grants program is evidence of such a shift toward a shared Government and academic role.

4. The use of many different approaches to further develop the field has been essential. These mechanisms vary from convening experts to facilitate national and international exchange to those which the Government can use to fund research. Contracts, grants and co-operative agreements involve different degrees of leadership on the part of the Government and can facilitate support of in-depth studies. For example, when multi-site

studies using a common protocol were needed, the co-operative agree-ment has been useful. Collaborative research with other Public Health Service agencies, in contrast, has made it possible to obtain a national picture of provider and patient behavior.

5. Continued growth of the primary care research program depends on its perceived usefulness. A research unit within the Government can serve two major functions: (1) it can provide the basic research expertise to evaluate Government health services policies; and (2) it can provide leadership for developing a public health research data base. Several examples of involvement in the policy arena include the health–mental health linkage program and the prospective payment approach of Diagnosis Related Groups (DRGs). Based on the program's evalu-ation of the Federal Linkage Initiative, a contribution was made to legislation, the short-lived 1980 Mental Health Service Systems Act, which called for mental health linkage workers in community health centers. Future policy-related research will most likely focus on reimbursement issues, as the controversy around diagnosis-related groups shifts to out-patient care. In the basic research areas of the program we expect that, with increased understanding of what takes place in primary care, approaches will be developed to improve the mental health care provided by health professionals and mental health specialists in primary care settings. Relevance of the findings will be determined by philosophers, policy makers, the health professionals and the patients themselves.

ATTACHMENT I

NIMH interests in primary care/mental health research

Epidemiological

1. Incidence and prevalence of mental disorders and psychosocial problems in primary care and the course of these disorders – duration, recurrence, and remission.
2. Relationships between co-occurring medical and psychiatric conditions.
3. Differences in presentation of mental disorders across the life span (e.g. is depression different in the elderly?)

Clinical practice

1. Relationships between the prevalence of mental disorders and the extent and adequacy of recognition, diagnosis and treatment (particularly use of psychotropic medications).
2. Barriers to providing mental health care – attitudes, training, time, medical decision-making, reimbursement, effect of medical role models.

3. Examination of approaches to improve clinical practice – usefulness of screening measures, physician and patient education, mental health consultation, availability of referral sources, value of computer assisted diagnosis, design of clinical protocols for management of mental disorder in primary care, special approaches for children, the elderly and low income populations.
4. Differences between the mental health role of health professionals and mental health professionals.

Service system

1. Effect of type of health organization (e.g. fee-for-service versus prepaid health plan) on the mental health care provided.
2. Effect of integrating mental health specialists into health organizations on the mental health care provided.
3. Effect of the gatekeeper role on referral to mental health specialists.
4. Effect of different reimbursement approaches on the use of mental health services, choice of setting, and the cost of care.

Methodological

1. Classification of mental disorder and psychosocial conditions in primary care with attention to identifying syndromes not previously classified.
2. Validation of screening measures for mental disorder.
3. The adequacy of outcome measures for diagnosis, functioning, disability, symptoms, social support, and stressors over repeated administrations.
4. Correspondence between patient and provider report of mental health conditions and treatment provided.
5. Classification of mental health treatments used in primary care.

REFERENCES

1. Cartwright, A. and Anderson, R. (1981) *General Practice Revisited*. London: Tavistock Publications.
2. Eisenberg, L. (1979) Interfaces Between Medicine and Psychiatry. *Comprehensive Psychiatry*, 20(1): 1–14.
3. Engel, G. (1977) The Need for a New Medical Model: A Challenge for Biomedicine. *Science* 196: 129–36.
4. Taube, C. A., Barrett, S. A. (eds) (1983) *Mental Health, United States, 1983*. DHSS Publ. No. (ADM) 83–1275. Rockville, MD: National Institute of Mental Health.
5. Joint Commission on Mental Illness and Health (1961) *Action for Mental Health*, Final Report. New York: Basic Books.
6. Rosen, B. M., Locke, B. Z., Goldberg, I. D., and Babigian, H. M. (1970) Identifying Emotional Disturbance in Persons Seen in Industrial Dispensaries. *Mental Hygiene* 54(2): 271–79. Reprinted in: R. L. Noland (ed.) (1973) *Industrial Mental Health Counseling*. New York: Behavioral Publications, pp. 55–68.

7. Rosen, B. M., Locke, B. Z., Goldberg, I. D., and Babigian, H. M. (1972) Identification of Emotional Disturbance in Patients Seen in General Medical Clinics. *Hospital and Community Psychiatry*, 23: 364–70.
8. Goldberg, I. D., Babigian, H. M., Locke, B. Z., and Rosen, B. M. (1978) Role of Non-psychiatrist Physicians in the Delivery of Mental Health Services: implications from three studies. *Public Health Reports* 93(3): 240–54.
9. Shepherd, M., Cooper, B., Brown, A. C., and Kalton, G. W. (1966) *Psychiatric Illness in General Practice* London: Oxford University Press.
10. Follette, W. and Cummings, N. A. (1967) Psychiatric Services and Medical Utilization in a Prepaid Health Plan Setting. *Medical Care* 5: 25.
11. Goldberg, I. D., Krantz, G., and Locke, B. Z. (1970) Effect of a Short-term Outpatient Psychiatric Therapy Benefit on the Utilization of Medical Services in a Prepaid Group Practice Medical Program. *Medical Care* 8(5).
12. Stockman, D. A. (1981) Premises for a Medical Marketplace: A Neoconservative's Vision of How to Transform the Health System. *Health Affairs* Winter, 1(1): 5–18.
13. Graduate Medical Education National Advisory Committee (1981) Final Report to the Secretary, United States Department of Health and Human Services, Vol. 1, Pub. No. HRA-81-651.
14. Regier, D. A., Goldberg, I. D., and Taube, C. A. (1978) The De Facto US Mental Health Services System *Archives of General Paychiatry*, 35: 685–93.
15. The President's Commission on Mental Health (1978) *Report to the President*, Vol. I. Washington, DC: US Government Printing Office.
16. Regier, D. A. and Rosenfeld, A. H. (1977) Report of the NIMH Workgroup on Mental Health Training of Primary Care Providers, Rockville, MD: National Institute of Mental Health.
17. American Academy of Pediatrics (1977) *The Future of Pediatric Education*. Report by the Task Force on Pediatric Education. Evanston, IL: American Academy of Pediatrics.
18. American Board of Internal Medicine (1979) Clinical Competence in Internal Medicine *Annals of Internal Medicine* 90: 402–11.
19. American Medical Association (1980) *Essential of Accredited Residencies*. Chicago: American Medical Association.
20. Goldberg, D. P., Steele, J. J., and Smith, C. (1980) Teaching Psychiatric Interview Techniques to Family Doctors. *Acta Psychiat. Scand.* Suppl. 285, 62: 41–7.
21. Burns, B. J., Scott, J. E., Burke, J. D., and Kessler, L. G. (1983) Mental Health Training of Primary Care Residents: A Review of Recent Literature (1974–1981). *General Hospital Psychiatry* 5: 157–69.
22. Hankin, J. R. and Oktay, J. S. (1979) *Mental Disorder and Primary Medical Care: An Analytical Review of the Literature*. National Institute of Mental Health, Series D, No. 5, DHWW Publ. No. (ADM) 78–661. Washington, DC: US Government Printing Office.
23. Parron, D. L. and Solomon, F. (eds) (1983) *Mental Health Services in Primary Care Settings: Report of a Conference*. National Institute of Mental Health, Series DN No. 2, DHSS Pub. No. (ADM) 83–995. Washington, DC: US Government Printing Office.
24. Robins, L. N., Helzer, J. E., Croughan, J., and Ratcliff, K. S. (1981) National Institute of Mental Health Diagnostic Interview Schedule. *Archives of General*

Psychiatry 38: 381–89.

25. Hoeper, E. W., Nycz, G. R., Cleary, P. D., Regier, D. A., and Goldberg, I. D. (1979) Estimated Prevalence of RDC Mental Disorder in Primary Medical Care. *International Journal of Mental Health* 8: 6–15.

26. Goldberg, I. D., Roghmann, K. J., McInerny, T. K., and Burke, J. D. (1984) Mental Health Problems Among Children Seen in Pediatric Practice: Prevalence and Management. *Pediatrics* 73(3): 278–93.

27. Hankin, J. R., Steinwachs, D. M., Regier, D. A., Burns, B. J., Goldberg, I. D., and Hoeper, E. W. (1982) Use of General Medical Care Services by Persons with Mental Disorders. *Archives of General Psychiatry* 39: 225–31.

28. Kessler, L., Tessler, R., and Nycz, G. R. (1983) The Co-occurrence of Psychiatric and Medical Morbidity in Primary Care. *Journal of Family Practice* 16(2): 319–24.

29. Mann, A. H. (1977) The Psychological Effect of a Screening Programme and Clinical Trial for Hypertension Upon the Participants. *Psychological Medicine* 7: 431.

30. Shepherd, M. (1983) *The Psychosocial Matrix of Psychiatry*. London: Tavistock Publications, p. 83.

31. Hoeper, E. W., Nycz, G. R., Kessler, L. G., Burke, J. D., and Pierce, E. W. (1984) The Usefulness of Screening for Mental Illness. *Lancet*, 7 January, 33–5.

32. Shapiro, S. (1983) Secondary Prevention with Adult Patients in Primary Care Settings. Final Report. Contract No. 278-81-0025(DB). National Institute of Mental Health.

33. Regier, D. A., Burke, J. D., Burnes, B. J., Clare, A., Gulbinat, W., Lipkin, M., Spitzer, R., Williams, J., and Wood, M. (1982) Proposed Classification of Social Problems and Psychological Symptoms for Inclusion in a Classification of Health Problems. In M. Lipkin and K. Kupka (eds) *Psychosocial Factors Affecting Health*, New York: Praeger Scientific, pp. 153–84.

34. Goldman, H. H., Burns, B. J., and Burke, J. D. (1980) Integrating Primary Health Care and Mental Health Services: A Preliminary Report. *Public Health Reports* 96(6): 535–39.

35. Burns, B. J., Burke, J. D. and Ozarin, L. D. (1983) Linking Health and Mental Health Services in Rural Areas. *International Journal of Mental Health* 12(1–2): 130–43.

36. Regier, D. A., Goldberg, I. D., Burns, B. J., Hankin, J. R., Hoeper, E. W., and Nycz, G. R. (1982) Specialist/Generalist Division of Responsibility for Patients with Mental Disorders. *Archives of General Psychiatry* 39: 219–24.

37. Coleman, J. V. and Patrick, D. L. (1976) Integrating Mental Health Services into Primary Medical Care. *Medical Care* 14: 8.

38. Marks, E. and Broskowski, A. (1981) Community Mental Health and Organized Care Linkages. In A. Broskowski, E. Marks, and S. Budman (eds) *Linking Health and Mental Health*. Beverly Hills, Calif.: SAGE Annual Reviews of Community Mental Health.

39. Corney, R. H. (1980) Factors Affecting the Operation and Success of Social Work Attachment Schemes to General Practice. *Journal of the Royal College of General Practitioners* 30: 149–58.

40. Jones, K. R. and Vischi, T. R. (1979) Impact of Alcohol, Drug Abuse and Mental Health Treatment on Medical Care Utilization: A Review of the Research Literature. *Medical Care* 17 (Suppl.): 12.

41. Hankin, J. R., Kessler, L. G., Goldberg, I. D., Steinwachs, D. M., and Starfield, B. H. (1983) A Longitudinal Study of Offset in Use of Non-psychiatric Services Following Specialized Mental Health Care. *Medical Care* 21(11): 1099–110.

42. Wells, K. B., Manning, W. G., Duan, J., Ware, J. E., and Newhouse, J. P. Cost Sharing and the Demand for Ambulatory Mental Health Services. Final Report. NIMH Contract No. 278-81-0045(DB), 182.

43. Schlesinger, H. J., Mumford, E., Glass, G. V., Patrick, C., and Sharfstein, S. (1983) Mental Health Treatment and Medical Care Utilization in a Fee-for-Service System: outpatient mental health treatment following the onset of a chronic disease. *American Journal of Public Health* 73(4): 422–29.

44. Manning, W. G., Leibowitz, A., Goldberg, G. A., Rogers, W. H., and Newhouse, J. P. (1984) A Controlled Trial of the Effect of a Prepaid Group Practice on Use of Services. *New England Journal of Medicine* 310(23); 1505–530.

45. US Department of Health and Human Services (1984) *The Hidden Mental Health Network – Provision of Mental Health Services by Non-psychiatrists.* ODAM Report No. 5–84. Washington, DC: DHHS.

46. World Health Organisation (1973) Report of Working Group, Copenhagen: World Health Organisation.

J. Orley and N. Sartorius

Mental illness in primary health care in developing countries

The main emphasis in this paper is on the situation in developing countries, although within this we are dealing with a very heterogeneous group of countries. There are the large countries with federal systems of government, such as China, India, Brazil and Nigeria; the small, more centrally organized countries, such as Mozambique or Thailand; the small island communities. some with populations less than 100,000 (comprising around thirty of the WHO's member states). Within the countries referred to as 'developing' there is a great variation in wealth and indeed a group of twenty-two have been identified as being the least developed. Development, however, is not just a matter of per capita income, since many of the oil rich countries are still considered as developing. There really is no clear definition of a developing country.

PRIMARY HEALTH CARE

Primary health care is a concept differing sharply from country to country and even from province to province within the same country. The definition stretches from seeing primary care as the totality of community efforts to improve health, to the restriction of primary care to only those actions done by official governmental personnel working under the orders of a central ministry of health. In some countries, such as India, there is only a limited number of general practitioners providing a first contact health service in many areas, whereas in many parts of Africa, general practitioners do not exist and nurses or physicians' assistants provide a first contact service. In yet others, any health worker within the *rural* area will be called a primary health care agent. The variations are endless and the definitions seem to change in response to professional interest, newly emergent sources of funding and changes of ministers.

The typical primary health care worker, now emerging in many of the developing countries comprising WHO's member states is a person selected from within a village or other community, with about six to ten years' schooling, who is given perhaps three months training following which he/she works (often part-time) and is paid by the community itself. Such workers concentrate on ensuring that a certain number of public health measures are carried through in the community. These include the provision of clean water and sanitation, simple malaria control (where appropriate), monitoring child growth and giving nutrition advice. Apart from carrying out very simple treatments, such workers would be expected to refer people for treatment to the next level of health care. This is often staffed by a health worker who has had ten to twelve years of schooling followed by two or three years health training. There are, however, member states where physicians provide this level of care. The attention to mental disorders at this level of care will depend largely on the training that such workers have received, the support they get from mental health teams, and the medications made available to them.

Although primary health care can refer to this level, the term should really refer to a system of care which emphasizes the role of such a level and re-orientates all levels of care to emphasize its role in support of such levels. Existing simple medical knowledge, if applied much more widely, would save many millions of lives each year and greatly improve health. This could be done by introducing appropriate technology for applying the knowledge at the community level, emphasizing the necessity for the community itself to participate actively in the process, and by promoting intersectoral collaboration using those people who do not always see themselves as health workers. Some measure of a country's progress towards achieving a system of primary health care is provided, for instance, by comparing how much of the nation's resources (e.g. its health budget) goes into supporting central hospitals situated in major cities with the amount that goes to institutions more closely involved in supporting the facilities at the periphery.

THE WHO MENTAL HEALTH PROGRAMME

Over the past ten years or more there has been increasing interest in developing countries in the treatment of mental illness and the promotion of mental health. In 1973, WHO convened a meeting on mental health services in developing countries and in the following year a WHO Expert Committee reported on this subject. Following an initiative by the World Health Assembly in 1975, that body passed a resolution calling for a special programme of technical co-operation in the field of mental health. This led to the formation of a group of African countries into the African Mental Health Action Group, which meets annually in Geneva and now includes nine countries among its members and two liberation movements. Its membership continues to grow.

The reports of experts brought together by WHO have emphasized the need for the decentralization of mental health services and the necessity for most mental health activity in developing countries to be carried out by those who would not be considered as mental health specialists. This approach was pursued by WHO in its collaborative study on Strategies for Extending Mental Health Care. Over this same period, WHO was formulating its policy for 'Health for All by the Year 2000', to be achieved through a system of primary health care. The Alma-Ata Conference recommended including the promotion of mental health as an essential element of primary health care, although this did not find its way into the Declaration resulting from that conference. Nevertheless several countries have added, since that time, the promotion of mental health to the essential elements in their own national plans. Such countries include Thailand and India. Already within the essential elements of primary health care in the Declaration of Alma-Ata, is the provision for the treatment of common diseases, and this has been thought by some to be sufficient to cover the provision of mental health care within a system of primary health care. There is no doubt that in all parts of the world affective disorders are extremely common, presenting to all levels of health worker, and under these circumstances the provision of mental health care should be given serious consideration when considering which common diseases deserve attention. The mental health services, however, have to take their place in the queue of those, such as the dental or ophthalmological services, who also consider that their own speciality demands particular attention within primary health care.

The argument that the promotion of mental health be included as a separate essential element in primary health care rests on the premise that for every single patient under the care of a health worker, attention should be given to that patient's psychological and social well-being. For whatever reason a person is brought into the health care system, he/she should be treated as a 'whole person' in a humane and caring way, taking account of the psychological and social, as well as the physical, problems presented. It is this broad approach to care which WHO has promoted through its mental health programme.

Even if we concentrate, however, on the prevention and treatment of mental disorders, we observe a serious lack of resources in the developing world. In many parts of the world there is only one psychiatrist for every million or so of the population, and these have little or no support from any system of family practice. Under these circumstances, most treatment, if it is to be done at all, has to be done by non-psychiatrists and in many cases by non-physicians. For this to be feasible, it is necessary for each country to identify a small number of priority conditions which it can expect these non-specialist health workers to be able to deal with, and the approach advocated by WHO is for this service to be embedded into a system of primary health care, with the general health workers at the health centre level carrying out these activities, supported where possible by specialist personnel working from a higher level of care. However, because sometimes there is a fear within general health services of dealing with mental patients, coupled with a reciprocal defensive position taken by those within mental health services, there may be an unfortunate tendency to develop 'vertical' mental health programmes based on mental hospitals providing an outreach programme through specialized mental health workers operating from mental health clinics.

STRATEGIES FOR MENTAL HEALTH CARE IN
PRIMARY HEALTH CARE

An analysis of the situation in many countries has provided elements of a strategy for the promotion of mental health within general health care. The needs of such a strategy include:

1. *A broad concept of the mental health programme.* As already noted this means that the programme should include attention to the psychosocial factors in all aspects of health care as well as attending to the prevention and treatment of mental disorders. This forms the basis of WHO's own mental health programme which also includes attention to the prevention and treatment of drug and alcohol abuse.

2. *A clear spelling out of the managerial strategy to achieve the promotion of mental health within general health care.* This would include the formation of the organizational structures to achieve this objective, the assurance of adequate training for health staff and the supply of appropriate medication to be used. Very often, countries have no clearly formulated mental health policy, let alone a plan by which the policy could be implemented, and very often mental health programmes have arisen as a response to social pressures for social control of certain deviants and to various crises which occur. If mental health is to be included as a component of primary health care in any national health plan, a fresh look needs to be taken by the government as to how its aims in this should be clearly formulated.

3. *In relation to mental disorders, the selection of priority conditions for care.* The criteria for the selection of these would include the frequency of the condition, community concern about the condition and above all the feasibility of providing effective treatment, particularly in the early stages of programmes when credibility is a key issue.

The national mental health programme for India has defined the following items as falling within the province of the multi-purpose worker who should be able to deal with them within his own community under the supervision and support of a medical officer:

(a) Management of psychiatric emergencies (e.g. acute excitement, crisis situations) through simple crisis management skills and appropriate utilization of specified medicines.

(b) Administration and supervision of maintenance treatment for chronic psychiatric conditions in accordance with guidelines by the supervisors.

(c) Recognition and management of *grand mal* epilepsy (particularly in children) through utilization of appropriate medicines under the guidance of a medical doctor.

(d) Liaison with the local school teacher and parents in matters concerning the management of children with mental retardation and behaviour problems.

(e) Counselling of problems related to alcohol or drug abuse.

Although in India, prescription of medication must be given by physicians, there are countries where perhaps non-physician health workers should be allowed to prescribe a limited range of medication. For instance where there is no physician easily available, isolated health workers who have had some training in mental health care and psychiatry should at least be able to start treatment with, say, a minor tranquillizer for states of acute excitement.

4. *Training for all health workers to include aspects of medical psychology as well as psychiatry.* Although the treatment of priority psychiatric conditions must form an essential core of the training, all health workers should be made aware of broad mental health issues relevant to their practice. They should be able to communicate effectively with their patients, taking account of their patients' health belief models. They should be able to break bad news to patients or relatives in a sympathetic way, deal with bereaved relatives and generally be able to take account of the affective needs of patients and their families.

5. *Mental health training*, at least in part, to be carried out in the situation in which the health workers will perform their activities once trained.

There is a growing recognition that the training of primary health workers to deal with mental disorders and promote mental health should not take place primarily in psychiatric hospitals but rather in settings more akin to those in which they will practice. There is a growing body of knowledge concerning this type of training and more efforts are needed to ensure that this information is more widely available. Training should be centred on the improvement of mental health skills, but unfortunately some tutors are unable or unwilling to take this approach, preferring to give conventional lectures or at best to lead discussion groups.

There is no doubt that, however trained, the primary health workers need supervision and further training from specialist mental health professionals. Indeed it could be argued that the prime function of such professionals in developing countries is not to see patients, although they must see some referrals, but to train and supervise other health workers. Unfortunately the remuneration provided to such professionals is sometimes dependent on the number of patients treated, so deterring them from these other functions.

6. *Training in teamwork to be provided*, such that multi-disciplinary activity really means a sharing of ideas and skills and not just a mechanism whereby physicians can mobilize those in other disciplines according to their own perceptions and needs.

7. *Mental health care at the primary level should be carried out by the general health workers at that level*, supervised directly or indirectly by mental health professionals. The service should not operate through a specialist outreach programme in which mental health specialists directly take care of psychiatric patients during regular visits to peripheral clinics (sometimes, however, this latter cannot be avoided).

8. *The encouragement of self-reliance by families and the teaching of patients and their families about living with disability*. The community based rehabilitation approach, fostered by WHO is of relevance in this respect, particularly when dealing with mental retardation.

9. *Simple evaluation techniques to be available and publicized*. In order that the workings of the mental health programme and the effectiveness of training can be monitored, the objectives of the mental health programme need to be very clearly formulated. Similarly, in any of the training programmes that are mounted to introduce mental health skills to health workers, the educational objectives should be formulated in such a way that there will be no problem in determining whether the training is successful.

CONCLUSION

If these strategies are followed, there is much that can be done for mental health within primary health care. One component of this most certainly concerns the prevention and treatment of mental disorders. The constraints that exist in developing countries force us to focus on certain priorities rather than attempt to cover too broad a field. Nevertheless, in this, there are lessons to be learnt that are applicable more universally.

J. E. Cooper

Discussant

The title of the session 'The View from Abroad' is somewhat ambiguous, in that it could be taken as an invitation to comment upon the British scene from the outside, or it could be taken to suggest the speakers would simply give the views and policies of the organizations or countries with which they are associated. All three speakers chose the latter interpretation and so have described activities, systems and policies outside the United Kingdom. I am, therefore, free to provide a brief comment upon what they might have said if they had adopted the first possibility – that is, how does the British system of primary care look to the outsider?

The answer must be that it looks very good indeed when compared to virtually all other countries. For all practical purposes, general practitioners in the UK provide all the primary and *medical* care (I emphasize medical for reasons which will become clear later). Virtually every person has a general practitioner and can consult him/her without financial penalty, and the proportion of privately financed (and therefore difficult to study) primary care is so small in most parts of the country that it can be ignored. Our system is therefore simple to describe, comprehensive, universally available, and comparatively easy to study. Our overseas friends may be forgiven if they wonder why, with all these virtues, our system is subjected to so little research.

The papers of Drs Sartorius, Orley and Henderson, coming from the World Health Organisation, necessarily reflect the policies and plans of that body.

Dr Henderson sets out the recommendations of several major World Health Organisation meetings, particularly the Alma-Ata (1978) declaration of 'Health For All by the Year 2000'. In the written form of Dr Henderson's papers this is now encoded as 'HFA/2000' like some new synthetic analgesic or hallucinogenic drug. He also comments upon meetings in Norway and Finland which further emphasize this important doctrine.

Dr Sartorius discusses some of the fundamental problems encountered when attempts are made to put these general plans and principles into practice; problems of definition, and problems generated by the finding that no two countries are alike in their needs and resources. This disparity is striking whether it is viewed from the outside, or viewed from within in terms of what a country regards as appropriate for itself. The Mental Health Division of the World Health Organisation in Geneva has a special responsibility towards the 'developing countries' to help them develop the mental health aspects of their primary care systems. However, Dr Sartorius has rightly pointed out that there are no easy and clear definitions of what is primary care, or what is mental health, or what is a developing country. We must all surely offer Dr Sartorius our sympathy, and be prepared to give all the help and encouragement we can in carrying out such a difficult task. Fortunately, there are some important common and recurring components of primary care in many settings which can be identified and fostered as the crucial elements; these are (1) that it is concerned with the first contact with medical services; (2) that the care provider has a commitment to take an overall view of the patient; and (3) to offer some continuity of care. Another important personal characteristic of the primary care worker, which is sometimes given insufficient emphasis, is that he/she should be a member of the local community in which he/she works.

Dr Barbara Burns gives us a most interesting and detailed historical account of the waxing and waning of mental health care activities in the USA, and provides an impressive list of existing and potential research work. It is perhaps paradoxical that an energetic research programme is being fostered in a country with a comparatively chaotic and poorly developed primary care system, where research must be difficult. This contrasts with the position in the United Kingdom, where there are fewer barriers to research, but where we seem to be less highly motivated. Perhaps we are too complacent, and simply do not realize how fortunate we are. Dr Burns' paper also reminds us of one basic difference that pervades the health care systems of the two countries; in the United Kingdom, the National Health Service was originally, and still is, organized for the benefit of the patients (initially against the resistance of the medical profession of that time). In the USA the health care system has developed for the convenience and for the advantage of the doctors.

An important difference between the contributions from the World Health Organisation and the National Institute of Mental Health needs to be emphasized. Drs Sartorius, Orley, and Henderson are dealing with the broad concepts of mental health care in primary health care systems but, in contrast, Dr Burns deals with the topic of this Conference: which is how best to deal with specified mental illness and mental disorders in primary medical care systems. The World Health Organisation necessarily has a wider and more difficult task but we here, like Dr Burns, can confine ourselves more comfortably to talking about how psychiatrists and general practitioners can best work together.

My final comment is a criticism of many of those who have spoken today for falling into the all too familiar trap of talking about 'mental disorders' or 'mental illness' as if these very broad overall categories have very much meaning. In the setting of a professional conference such as this, these categories are so broad as to be fairly meaningless, particularly to non-psychiatric listeners. Indeed, at times these terms can be positively misleading to administrators, laymen and politicians who know little or nothing about the wider variety of mental disorders. For instance, on hearing any one of many versions of the familiar statement that 'most cases of mental disorder are not dealt with by psychiatrists but are contained by general practitioners' some administrators and politicians can be heard to exclaim: 'Then what do psychiatrists do? Why do we need so many psychiatrists? Are they lazy or incompetent?' Of course, most people know that this generalization about general practitioners and mental disorders hides a crucial fact which psychiatrists know only too well. This is that virtually all the acute and serious cases of mental illness in this country (and most other developed countries) are referred straight away to psychiatrists and are rarely dealt with by general practitioners. The generalization only makes sense in relation to the patients presenting with the less severe and usually less acute conditions such as neuroses, personality disorders, and adjustment disorders (it is also worth noting that nobody knows how to cope constructively with a large proportion of these cases). I therefore make a plea for the abandonment of terms such as 'mental illness' or 'mental disorder' when discussing psychiatry in primary care, and suggest that we should indicate clearly which groups are being discussed. The obvious differentiations that need to be made are between (1) the small but very important group of severely and acutely mentally ill, (2) the chronically ill, and (3) the much more common, less severe and often transient conditions which have been, perhaps surprisingly, the focus of this meeting.

©1986 J. E. Cooper

H. Dilling

The view from abroad – West Germany

While the organization of health services in West Germany differs from the British pattern in several aspects there is broad agreement on therapeutic practices. The number of mentally ill people needing ambulatory care who are treated by general practitioners is smaller in Germany, where many practising neuropsychiatrists participate in this work. In 1983 there were 64,000 physicians in private practices in Germany; 13,500 of them were practising general medicine and about 10,500 internal medicine, whereas about 2,000 were working as neuropsychiatrists or psychiatrists in private practice and about the same number in psychiatric hospitals (Bundesärztekammer 1984). In England there are three times as many general practitioners for a smaller patient population.

The system of ambulatory clinics or polyclinics, however, is more restricted in our country; their tasks are more limited and more or less confined to teaching hospitals connected to universities. This development is enforced by the health care systems: in Germany the physicians are working as private entrepreneurs funded by a complicated system of health insurances, whereas most British physicians are working in the National Health Service and seem to have much less choice regarding how they work.

With the aim of assessing the rates of mentally ill patients in general practice we have carried out two epidemiological studies. The first was based on 1,274 interviews in 18 practices (Dilling, Weyerer, and Enders 1978). The second was conducted on the population of the small-town rural region of Traunstein/Bavaria. We then compared the opinions of the psychiatric interviewers with those of the family physicians who treated the same problems (Dilling and Weyerer 1984). In addition, we attempted to assess the amount of psychiatric treatment required for this population.

In the field study we evaluated 1,536 persons in three different communities. With 1,231 subjects we were able to compare the results of the psychiatric interviewers with the judgements of 31 family doctors, mostly general practitioners. Of all the subjects, 81.7 per cent had made at least one contact with their family physician during the previous year (*Figure 1*), during which time 24.1 per cent of the interviewed population had been treated for psychiatric symptoms. At the time of the interview 18.6 per cent suffered from symptoms meriting treatment. The family physicians indicated that in their opinion 17.8 per cent of the subjects had been treated for some kind of psychiatric symptom during the last year. In spite of the differences between the opinions of the interviewers and the family physicians, their judgements were broadly in agreement in respect of both case identification (61.6 per cent) and diagnosis. In only 11.9 per cent of cases was there marked disagreement. Often the general practitioners' profound knowledge about the patient and his family was very surprising; their personal understanding can rarely be attained by any medical specialist.

According to the family physicians, 9.5 per cent of the interviewed subjects needed treatment; the corresponding figure provided by the psychiatric interviewers was 12.2 per cent. The proportions of other diagnostic groups were comparatively smaller, for example, dementia at 1.6 per cent and alcoholism at 1.8 per cent according to the interviewers, and 2.4 per cent and 2.8 per cent respectively according to the family physicians.

In general, the more severe the disease, the higher the diagnostic agreement between family physician and interviewer. There was also a higher correspondence in respect of global categories than with diagnostic diagnoses.

The psychiatric interviewers recommended a psychiatric consultation in 12.2 per cent of cases, and suggested psychiatric treatment and psychotherapy for 3.8 per cent of the subjects. By contrast, family physicians referred patients for specialized help in 3.6 per cent of cases and advised treatment in only 1.3 per cent. This strongly supports the findings of other workers, namely that many family physicians tend to treat patients with emotional disturbances themselves, thus emphasizing the importance of a sound psychiatric training. On the other hand, in the last decade there has been a growing interest in psychotherapy, especially psychoanalytically-based therapy, among German family doctors.

It is not feasible for more than a small fraction of the population to be treated by psychiatric specialists. The figure of more than 10 per cent indicated by the interviewers appears to be utopian. So large a volume of patients

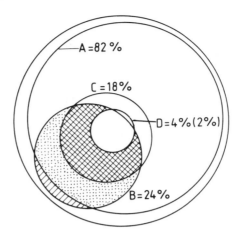

Figure 1   Results of the field study in the county of Traunstein, 1975–1979

Outer circle: all interviewed probands (*n* = 1536)
A   Percentage of probands with contact to their family physicians during the
                   last year
B   Percentage of probands with psychiatric disturbances during the last
                   year according to the psychiatric interviewers
C   Percentage of probands with psychiatric disturbances during the last
                   year according to the family physicians
D   Need for psychiatric specialist treatment according to the family
                   physicians (actual utilization during the last year)

Source: Modified diagram according to Goldberg and Huxley (1980)

can be treated only by primary care physicians, most of them general
practitioners. For the patient, furthermore, this less costly service enables
them to avoid the adoption of a 'psychiatric career'.

To accomplish this task the family doctor has to learn how to recognize and
handle psychiatric patients, and how to use the knowledge about transference
and counter-transference in the patient–doctor relationship. Nowadays,
more attention is paid to these practical questions in medical school than in
the past. This approach enables the patient's therapeutic needs to be assessed
by means of the technique adopted by Balint (1957). In addition, the family
physician should be able to employ formal diagnostic categories, for example,
those of the International Classification of Diseases.

Several workers have pointed to the deficiencies in current diagnostic
psychiatric schemata when applied to the illnesses encountered in general
practice. Most current systems of psychiatric diagnoses are constructed by
hospital physicians who rarely appreciate the problems posed by mental

ill-health in extra-mural settings. Research workers, too, must confront the difficulties created by an inadequate nosology.

In practice, clinicians who restrict themselves to 'target' symptoms such as 'anxiety' and 'depressive mood', tend to employ drugs on an empirical basis. In most cases it is necessary to know more about the patient, so that a plan of treatment can take account of psychological as well as pharmacological considerations. In Germany, at present there is much discussion about the use and abuse of benzodiazepines, with special reference to the potential dangers of dependence. Only recently has the importance of the low-dose dependence been appreciated and we are now detecting more cases. The family doctor, it appears, should prescribe such medication only if specially indicated, for example, during an acute personal crisis or for the sedation of a suicidal person with a severe agitated depression. The result of such restricted prescription will be a reduced use of minor tranquillizers.

In sum, our studies show that an important task in Germany is to advance the training of general practitioners in the identification and management of patients with psychiatric disturbances. With the help of their psychiatric colleagues they will assuredly play a more important part in the treatment of mental illness.

REFERENCES

Balint, M. (1957) *The Doctor, His Patient and the Illness*. Pitman: London.
Bundesärztekammer (1984) Ergebnisse der Ärztestatistik aus dem Tätigkeitsbericht '84 der Bundesärztekammer. In: *Deutsches Ärzteblatt 81*. 1425–432.
Dilling, H., Weyerer, S., and Enders, I. (1978) Patienten mit psychischen Störungen in der Allgemeinpraxis und ihre psychiatrische Überweisunasbedürftigkeit. In: Häfner, H. (ed.) *Psychiatrische Epidemiologie*. Springer: Berlin, 135–60.
Dilling, H. and Weyerer, S. (1984) Prevalence of mental disorders in the small-town rural region of Traunstein (Upper Bavaria). *Acta Psychiatrica Scandinavica* 69: 60–79.
Dilling, H., Weyerer, S., and Castell, R. (1984) *Psychische Erkrankungen in der Bevölkerung*. Enke: Stuttgart.

J. L. Vazquez-Barquero and J. F. Diez Manrique

The view from abroad – Spain

THE STARTING POINT FOR THE DEVELOPMENT OF PRIMARY HEALTH CARE

The present situation of social, administrative and political change in Spain is affecting the health service structure of the country. This structure, which was historically conceived as a 'hospital-centred', 'medically-orientated' system of care, still carries the additional drawback of dependence on multiple administration.

This inadequate situation has been progressively transformed in recent years through a series of legislative reforms culminating in a 'General Law of Health' which the Spanish Ministry of Health is preparing and which will be geared to the creation of a 'National Health Service'. The consequence of this reform will be the development of a decentralized, unified and integrated health system capable of satisfying the needs of individuals close to the communities where they live. For this, the system would be ultimately directed to a 'health' rather than to a 'medical' concept of care.

In this new community-orientated health structure the primary care services are planned as a central component. The activities of these services will be orientated towards the implementation of the principal thrusts for action designated in the World Health Organisation (WHO) global strategy for 'Health for All by the Year 2000' (HFA/2000), namely: promotion of more healthy life styles; intensification of efforts to reduce preventable conditions; and provision of adequate health care accessible to all.

A starting point for this process of change was made by the promulgation in 1979 of a law (Real Decreto No. 3303/78 1979) establishing a postgraduate residential training on Primary Health Care and designating this activity as a medical speciality, with the title 'Family and Community Medicine'. This new development was complemented three years later by the decision to establish Pilot Primary Health Centres (Real Decreto No. 2392/82 1982). From these pilot experiences we are now moving towards developing a comprehensive network of primary health care centres.

The implementation of this primary care structure has been accompanied by a series of legislative policies regulating the responsibilities, functions, and structure of the Primary Health Centres (Real Decreto No. 137/84 1984). These have incorporated the principles stated in the Alma-Ata Declaration (1978) for primary health services, and further specified in the Global Strategy of HFA/2000, in May 1981. Their principal aims are therefore:

1. to integrate all primary care resources into a co-ordinated and comprehensive care structure;
2. to supply to all individuals, in their own community, a decentralized comprehensive, permanent and continuous primary health care. This care should be capable of satisfying not only physical but also mental needs;
3. to assume that primary care should be the initial component of a continuing health care process and the basic element of the future 'National Health Service';
4. to promote the need to extend the primary 'medical care' concept into a much broader concept of primary 'health care';
5. to stimulate the acceptance that a desirable primary health care activity should be based on the recognition of each individual as a bio-psychosocial unit.

EVALUATING THE PRESENT STATE OF HEALTH SERVICES FOR THE MENTALLY ILL

The mental health system suffers from a series of deficiencies which reproduce, at a higher level, those of the general medical services and which have been historically aggravated by long-standing policies. We are, therefore, still confronted with a service structure which maintains a multi-form administrative dependency, which remains isolated from the general health system, and which is based almost exclusively in old mental hospitals where patients are segregated from their own community. In this 'bed-centred' system the emphasis is put on a 'medical' rather than on a 'health' system of care. It is thus possible to detect a paucity of policies directed to the promotion of mental health, the prevention of mental illness, and the social rehabilitation of patients.

Against this background many mental health professionals have attempted local reforms of the services for the mentally ill in the past decade. These efforts, which in the majority of cases sprang from the old mental hospitals of the local authorities, were finally abandoned. The general failure of these experiences shows that the up-dating of the Spanish traditional mental health system could only be feasible if planned in combination with actions directed towards (1) promotion of adequate mental health activities in the general health system, and specially at the primary care level; (2) development of community and social services capable of satisfying the needs of mental patients in the community; and (3) development of programmes directed to promoting mental health and preventing mental illness.

The implementation of these far-reaching policies demands that the psychiatric reform be integrated in a general health and social services national reform. This point of view has been well understood by the Spanish Ministry of Health, which, in its 'Law for the Sanitary Reform', currently being elaborated, incorporates a series of articles on mental health (Ministerio de Sanidad y Consumo 1984c). The principles underlying these articles have been extensivly elaborated in the 'Document for a Mental Health Policy' which the Ministry has recently passed to the 'Committee for Psychiatric Reform' (Ministerio de Sanidad y Consumo 1984b). In this document it is explicitly stated that the general objectives of the future psychiatric reform will be (1) the integration of mental health care in the general frame of the future national health system, and (2) the suppression of the remaining traces of the segregation of mentally ill patients.

This broad objective will therefore affect not only the specialized mental health structure, but also the social welfare and general health services. The immediate implications of these policies on the specialized mental health services will be fourfold:

1. to move the focus of their attention from the mental hospital to the community;
2. to transfer the old mental hospital inpatient units for alternative services on to the community and the district general hospital;
3. to collaborate fully with the primary health services in the role as first line of medical care; and
4. to establish continuous liaison with the social welfare and general health services.

From the point of view of the general health services the consequences of these policies will be to promote an holistic view of illness and health on medical settings. For this purpose active liaison work with specialized mental health services will be essential. It will also be assumed that mental health care is one of the main responsibilities of the primary care services.

MENTAL HEALTH IN PRIMARY CARE: AN AIM FOR
THE FUTURE

The importance of the role of the general practitioner in mental health care
was clearly recognized in the report of the WHO working group meeting on
'Psychiatry in General Practice' (World Health Organisation 1973) and
endorsed by the Alma-Ata Declaration (World Health Organisation 1978)
and a later report of a working group on 'First Contact Mental Health Care'
(World Health Organisation 1984).

In accord with this outlook the different health reforms, legislated by the
Spanish administration have emphasized the need to establish mental health
care as one of the priorities of the primary care team (Real Decreto No.
3303/78 1979; Real Decreto No. 2392/82 1982; Real Decreto No. 173/84
1984). Thus in the 'Guide for the Functioning of Primary Health Team',
recently published by the Spanish Ministry of Health (Ministerio de Sanidad y
Consumo 1984a), it is explicitly stated that the aims of primary care services in
the field of mental health should include an active contribution to the dimuni-
tion of psychiatric morbidity through interventions directed at common
disturbances of mental health; the decrease of socio-cultural factors which
affect mental health adversely; the protection of the mental health of high risk
groups; the reduction of needs for specialized mental health care, especially
inpatient care; the early social rehabilitation of patients with mental illness;
the promotion of attitudes and life patterns which could facilitate mental
health; the encouragement of active participation of community members in
actions directed towards the promotion of mental health; the increase of the
psychotherapeutic abilities of members of the team; the mental health epidemiological surveillance.

This general objective will generate a wide variety of concrete actions on
acute and long-term mental health care which the primary health team should
be ready to assume. For this it is critical that the team be capable, first, of
identifying the different types of emotional disturbances and, second, of
discerning the sort of intervention needed for each disorder and the level
required.

To assume these responsibilities it is important that the primary health
system works in close liaison with the social welfare and specialized mental
health services. In this respect the legislative reforms specify that the role of
the specialized mental health professionals should be to provide not only
education, but also support and consultation for the primary health care
givers.

To enable primary care professionals to cover these demands it is essential
that they have access to the training programmes which traditionally were
dedicated to mental health specialists. This notion has in fact been assumed in
the Real Decreto No. 3303/78 (1979), in which it is specified that the training
scheme for 'Family and Community Medicine' should include a rotational

period for social psychiatry and specialized mental health services. This should be complemented, after the residential period, by permanent contracts at primary care settings, with specialized mental health professionals. Such training schemes should also be extended to the whole of the primary care team. The educational objectives of these programmes will be geared not only to the acquisition of technical knowledge on mental illness, but also towards shaping an holistic view of illness and health (Ministerio de Sanidad y Consumo 1984a).

The philosophy of these assistential reforms rests on the multiple assumptions. First, mental health care should be provided at a primary health level for as many people as possible, and only when this level is technically insufficient the contribution of the specialized mental health services should be requested. Second, unnecessary psychiatrization should be prevented and an effort should be made, at each level of mental health care, to supply the minimum degree of health care required for the patient. Third, the promotion of active mental health care at the primary level means an enlargement of the concept of mental illness to a much wider concept of mental health.

It is apparent that this extension of responsibilities which the developing Spanish primary care system is assuming is very much in accord with the WHO global strategy for 'Health for All by the Year 2000'. What is challenging about these new developments is the fact that for the first time many professionals will not only need to abandon the secure redoubt of their hospitals and move into the community to collaborate with primary care teams, but will also need to start thinking about illness and health as 'biopsychosocial' entities.

REFERENCES

Ministerio de Sanidad y Consumo (1984a) 'Guia de Funcionamiento del Equipo de Atencion Primaria'. *Coleccion Atencion Primaria No. 1 Servicio de Publicaciones*. Madrid: Ministerio de Sanidad y Consumo, September.

Ministerio de Sanidad y Consumo (1984b) Documento de Politica Psiquiatrica. *Comision Ministerial para la Reforma Psiquiatrica*. Madrid: Ministerio de Sanidad y Consumo.

Ministerio de Sanidad y Consumo (1984c) Capitulo de La Salud Mental. *Borrador de la Ley General de Sanidad*. In Documento de Politica Sanitaria 2a parte. *Comision Ministerial para la Reforma Psiquiatrica*. Madrid: Ministerio de Sanidad y Consumo, October.

Real Decreto No. 3303/78 (1979) De Regulacion de la Medicina de Familia y Comunitaria como Especialidad de la profesion Medica. Madrid: Ministerio de Sanidad y Seguridad Social, *BOE No. 29* 2 February.

Real Decreto No. 2392/82 (1982) Sobre creacion de Unidades Piloto de Medicina de Familia. Ministerio de Sanidad y Seguridad Social. *BOE No. 230* 25 September.

Real Decreto No. 137/84 (1984) Ordenacion de los Servicios Sanitarios. Estructuras Basicas de Salud. Ministerio de Sanidad y Consumo. *BOE No. 27* 1 February.

World Health Organisation (1973) The Development of comprehensive mental health services in the community. Report on a conference (Euro 54141). Copenhagen: World Health Organisation.

—— (1978) 'Psychiatry and Primary Medical Care'. Report on a working group (ICP/MNHO1911). Copenhagen: World Health Organisation.

—— (1978) 'Alma-Ata 1978: Primary Health Care'. Health for All Series No. 1. Geneva: World Health Organisation.

—— (1978) 'Global Strategy for Health for All by the Year 2000'. Health for All Series No. 3. Geneva: World Health Organisation.

—— (1984) *First-contact Mental Health Care*. Euro report 92. Copenhagen: World Health Organisation.

M. Tansella and C. Bellantuono

The view from abroad – Italy

THE NATIONAL HEALTH SERVICE AND THE PSYCHIATRIC REFORM IN ITALY

Law No. 833 of December 1978 (Istituzione del Servizio Sanitario Nazionale) brought about a major development in the delivery of health care in Italy and introduced the National Health Service (NHS).

The basis for the NHS is the promotion of health, prevention of sickness, care and rehabilitation, as well as the improvement of the personal and general environment. The three levels controlling the service are the state, the regions and the municipalities. The twenty Italian regions are divided in 670 local social health units (Unita Locale Socio-Sanitaria or ULSS). Each ULSS provides services for a population of from 50,000 to 200,000 and is sub-divided into social health districts which provide all basic services for a population of about 10,000. The services, both hospital and community-based, are integrated and co-ordinated within the ULSS. The regions and the state co-ordinate these aspects of health activities which are appropriate for regional and for national or international level, respectively.

Since 1 January 1979, health care has been delivered to all residents free of charge, but a fee has to be paid by patients for certain drugs and diagnostic tests. Psychiatric care and psychotropic drugs (apart from benzodiazepines) are completely free. Health insurance is compulsory for all citizens and has been dealt with through one organization since January 1980. New psychiatric legislation (Law No. 180, May 1978) was later incorporated in Law No. 833 and is therefore now part of the Health Reform.

The main features of the Italian Psychiatric Reform have been extensively described elsewhere (Tranchina, Archi, and Ferrara 1981; Tansella, Siciliani, and Meneghelli 1982; Zimmermann-Tansella *et al.* 1984). Most of them are in line with major trends in European psychiatry (World Health Organisation 1973a, b, 1978, 1980a, b). Some relevant aspects of the reform are as follows:

1. according to the psychiatric Law, policy for the prevention, care and rehabilitation of mental illnesses should normally be based on community facilities, i.e. the choice therapeutic setting has moved outside the hospital;
2. hospital evaluation and treatment take place in general hospital fifteen-bed psychiatric units, which *must* be integrated in a comprehensive psychiatric service, community-based and serving a well-defined catchment area;
3. for a defined population the same multi-disciplinary team should be responsible for both extramural and intramural care.

Some other innovative elements of Italian reform not present in psychiatric policy in other European countries so far, are mainly connected with the procedures for involuntary admissions (which may *only* occur in the general hospital psychiatric units), and with the cessation of admissions to mental hospitals of *new* patients (from May 1978) and of *all* patients since then, in order to achieve a gradual dismantling of these institutions.

PRIMARY CARE AND PSYCHIATRIC SERVICES.
A CLOSE LIAISON TO BE ESTABLISHED

In Italy, in spite of the high rate of doctors (1:265 inhabitants), the prescribed rate of one general practitioner per 1,000 inhabitants has not yet been achieved. For instance, in the Veneto Region, which is considered to have one of the most advanced health care systems in Italy, this rate was 0.75 and 0.94:1,000 inhabitants aged thirteen years and above, in 1981 and 1982 respectively. Some characteristics of the Italian primary care system are:

1. GPs do not receive specific training. Many of them have a postgraduate education in internal medicine or other specialties. In the last few years, however, an increasing number of junior physicians are working as GPs;
2. the majority of GPs are in practice by themselves, while a minority work in partnership with one or more other doctors, generally all without the support of other health care professionals (health visitors, social workers, district nurses);

3. it is necessary for patients to see the GP before seeing the specialist or attending hospital or community departments. Patients with psychiatric symptoms, however, may be referred directly to the psychiatric services;
4. epidemiological data on mental disorders in primary care settings are scanty, and therefore planning and service organization have so far been based mainly on empirical and 'political' decisions.

The need for a close liaison between psychiatrists and primary health services (World Health Organisation 1973b) has been repeatedly stressed in this country. Unfortunately, this goal has not yet been fully achieved. After the approval of the health reform, however, the psychiatrists working in the Community Psychiatric Service and the GPs operating in the same area have now a good chance of establishing a close collaboration.

DATA FROM THE SOUTH VERONA COMMUNITY
PSYCHIATRIC SERVICE (CPS)

The South Verona Community Psychiatric Service (CPS), set up in 1978 and run by the Istituto di Psichiatria, Universita di Verona, comprises a number of well-integrated services and provides comprehensive care for an approximately 75,000 inhabitants. More than 76 per cent of the residents contacting psychiatric services in the year are treated by the CPS (Zimmermann-Tansella *et al.* 1984). In order to describe some aspects of the links between the CPS and the GPs, pooled 1982 and 1983 data from the South Verona Psychiatric Case Register were used. GPs referred to the CPS only 12 per cent of the 522 first ever CPS patients and 4 per cent of those patients ($N = 300$)

Table 1   *First-ever contacts with the South Verona CPS. Pooled 1982 and 1983 data, by diagnosis and referral source.*

	referral source	
	GP (N = 62) %	other sources (N = 460) %
diagnosis		
functional psychosis	1.6	8.9
organic psychosis	4.8	2.6
neurosis	62.9	49.1
alcoholism and drug addiction	8.1	9.1
personality disorder	1.6	6.7
other diagnosis, not known and no abnormalities	21.0	23.6

already known to the CPS who re-contacted the services after a break of 90 days or more. On the other hand, patients referring themselves were 42 per cent and 50 per cent respectively. First-ever CPS contacts, by diagnosis and referral source, are reported in *Table 1* (Tansella 1984). The most common diagnosis for patients referred by GPs is 'neurosis', followed by 'alcoholism and drug addiction' and 'organic psychosis'.

A pilot study in a GP practice in this area showed a high (47.5 per cent) psychiatric morbidity (Fontanesi *et al.* 1985). A possible explanation of the low rate of GPs' referral to the psychiatric services may be that the GPs are themselves treating the majority of patients with minor psychiatric disturbances who attend their practices, or are referring them to private psychiatrists. Further studies are in progress, using larger and more representative samples of general practices, in order to fully assess community psychiatry and primary care links in our area.

CONCLUDING COMMENTS

One important aspect of the Italian psychiatric reform is the overcoming of the dichotomy between hospital and community psychiatry. In the United States this split led to the development of Community Mental Health Centers separately staffed and not integrated with the existing inpatient services, including the state mental hospitals. In Italy, on the contrary, in the ULSS where the Reform has been fully implemented, the Community Psychiatric Service (CPS) covers all aspects of care, ensuring longitudinal intervention and continuity of case management. The CPS, in other words, is functioning as a comprehensive, well-integrated district service, generally situated close to the patients' homes and easily accessible. As stressed before, this approach to psychiatric care has also the advantage of facilitating professional links between the psychiatric team and the GPs, according to the 'liaison-attachment' model founded on the pioneer work by Shepherd *et al.* (1966), which seems for the Italian situation the most rational model to improve the quality of care for patients with minor psychiatric disturbances. The crucial point now is which action to take to obtain a fruitful collaboration between psychiatrists and GPs. In our opinion the basic steps are, on the one hand, to extend psychiatrists' training into the community and to change their attitudes to mental health care traditionally based on hospital practice, and on the other, to improve GPs' ability to identify and manage psychiatric and emotional problems.

ACKNOWLEDGEMENTS

This study has been supported by the Consiglio Nazionale delle Ricerche (CNR, Roma), progetto Finalizzato Medicina Preventiva e Riabilitativa 1982–1987, Contracts No. 83.02851.56 and No. 84.02543.56, and by the Ministero della Pubblica Istruzione (MPI, Roma).

REFERENCES

Fontanesi, F., Gobetti, C., Zimmermann-Tansella, Ch., and Tansella, M. (1985) Validation of the Italian version of the GHQ in a general practice setting. *Psychological Medicine* 15: 411–16.

Shepherd, M., Cooper, B., Brown, A. C., and Kalton, G. (1966) *Psychiatric Illness in General Practice*. London: Oxford University Press.

Tansella, M. (1984) Unpublished data from the South-Verona Psychiatric Case Register.

Tansella, M., Siciliani, O., and Meneghelli, G. (1982) Implementing a community psychiatric service in South-Verona under the new Italian Mental Health Act. A two-year analysis. *Psychiatry and Social Science* 2: 105–14.

Tranchina, P., Archi, G., and Ferrara, M. (1981) The new legislation in Italian psychiatry. An advanced Law originating from alternative practice. *International Journal of Law and Psychiatry* 4: 181–90.

World Health Organisation (1973a) *The Development of Comprehensive Mental Health Services in the Community*. Copenhagen: World Health Organisation Regional Office for Europe.

—— (1973b) *Psychiatry and Primary Medical Care*. Copenhagen: World Health Organisation Regional Office for Europe.

—— (1978) *The Future of Mental Hospitals*. Copenhagen: World Health Organisation Regional Office for Europe.

—— (1980a) *Constraints in Mental Health Care*. Copenhagen: World Health Organisation Regional Office for Europe.

—— (1980b) *Changing Patterns in Mental Health Care*. Copenhagen: World Health Organisation Regional Office for Europe.

Zimmermann-Tansella, Ch., Burti, L., Faccincani, C., Garzotto, N., Siciliani, O., and Tansella, M. (1984) Bringing into action the psychiatric reform in South-Verona. A five-year experience. In C. Perris and D. Kemali (eds) *Focus on the Italian Psychiatric Reform Law. Acta Psychiatrica Scandinavica* 71, supplement 316: 71–86.

K. Zaimov

The view from abroad – Bulgaria

I am a representative of a communist country. It is well known that there are differences in the forms of health care organization in such countries and others. The psychiatric morbidity, however, is the same; the patients suffer in the same way and their needs are largely the same. In consequence, there is no doubt that by mutual understanding and through exchange of experience we can do much for the health of our patients.

In Bulgaria the specialized psychiatric assistance is delivered by psychiatric hospitals and by psychiatric dispensaries. The dispensaries exist in all districts and they function mainly as ambulatory services. Most of them also have a small number of beds for 'minor' psychiatric disorders.

The primary care settings – the 'front line' in our health service – consist of multi-profile polyclinics in the towns (in which the physicians are of all medical specialities) and of medical services in the villages with one physician, helped by a nurse, a maternity nurse and other para-medical assistants. In practice, the village doctors function as general practitioners, but until now this speciality has not been officially represented in our health system. There is a scheme for its introduction in the near future.

The provision of mental health care in primary care settings of our health system therefore depends on finding ways to 'equip' the physicians in our polyclinics and the village doctors with the necessary psychiatric knowledge and practical skill. I would like to say briefly what has been done in this respect so far, and what needs to be achieved in the future.

In 1976 the Council of Ministers decreed a 'Programme for Prophylaxis and Promotion of the Mental Health of the Bulgarian People'. This programme has conceptual, directive and operative parts. It is supra-departmental, and all departments and institutions are under an obligation to co-operate in its implementation. Psychiatric university clinics and the psychiatric dispensaries are charged with the responsibility of the programme. The programme aroused the interest of all Bulgarian physicians in mental health problems, including physicians working in the primary care settings.

Another feature of our system is that, in accordance with the decisions of the President of the Medical Academy[1] all medical specialists with academic rank regularly visit the district towns of our country in order to assist and improve the diagnostic and therapeutic process in the local medical services. Within this framework psychiatrists with academic rank also visit the district towns. During their visits they not only consult patients but also give lectures to all physicians on relevant topics. This work is also important for transferring psychiatric knowledge into the 'first line' of medical care.

In recent years psychiatric consulting rooms for neuroses and other 'minor' disorders have been set up at the polyclinics. This step will undoubtedly contribute to the better care of all patients with mental health problems.

Finally, I would like to point out that in November 1984 a Mental Health Research and Teaching Centre for collaboration with the World Health Organisation was inaugurated in Sofia. One area of research is the effectiveness of psychosocial interventions in primary care settings, led by Professor Iv. Temkov, Dr. T. Tomov, and others. The work will begin with a course of postgraduate study in psychiatry for specialists in internal medicine of six polyclinics selected from the three towns of Sofia, Pleven, and Russe. After the course in the polyclinics experimental and control groups of patients will be selected for study. All patients in the experimental groups will be screened by the participants in the course for mental health problems, and all 'positive' respondents will be examined by psychiatrists, who will also examine 10 per cent of the 'negative' respondents. The control groups will consist of the same number of patients with similar diagnoses, treated by physicians untrained in psychiatry. The outcome of the groups' research will be compared six months later. The study will be carried out with standardized instruments, and the findings will be of importance in the planning of psychiatric services in the structure of the polyclinics in our country.

NOTE

1. The Medical Academy was founded in Bulgaria in 1972. It integrates all institutions for medical teaching and for medical scientific research. Its activities are directed by the President in Sofia.

Biswajit Sen

The view from abroad – India

The concept of mental illness in primary care is of fairly recent development in the health scene in India. The attention of health planners, and indeed, that of the majority of the psychiatric community has been tardy in focusing on this aspect of health care. Reliable data about the extent and nature of mental illness seen in primary care settings are hard to come by. Harding *et al.* (1980), using 'stringent criteria to establish the presence of psychiatric morbidity' found that 17.7 per cent of patients attending a primary care facility in north India were suffering from mental disorder. Roychowdhury (1975, personal communication), using data from his general practice case register in Calcutta, expressed the view that about one in five of his patients had recognizable psychiatric problems. These are the cases who seek help. There is also some evidence to suggest that there are at least an equal proportion of cases in the community who do not seek help but whose illness is of a degree to warrant treatment (Nandi *et al.* 1976).

Currently, there are just over 1,000 qualified psychiatrists in India, which has a population in excess of 750 million. With a doctor–patient ratio of 1:8,000 in the rural areas where three-quarters of the population live, the country can hardly hope to emulate the models of primary care achieved in Europe. It is necessary, here, to specify what is meant by primary care, who is to provide it, and what kind of disorders qualify for such care.

If by primary care we mean care provided by a person who is responsible for the overall medical needs of the patient and is in a position to provide continuity of care, then it is obviously not the doctor, but the health auxiliary who is the appropriate person to provide such services. A health auxiliary (or health worker, as he/she is known in India) is a member of a health team led by a health professional (a doctor or a public health nurse) who is trained to assist the professional worker in certain well-defined tasks. Preferably, he/she should also be a member of the community he/she serves. The mental disorders which come under the purview of the health auxiliary are acute psychosis, chronic psychosis, depressive illness, and epilepsy (Wig, Murthy, and Harding 1981).

It is apparent that a training programme tailored to the needs of health auxiliaries will be required for this purpose. It will have to be based on a problem-oriented approach focusing on specific tasks the health auxiliaries can perform and integrate in their routine work. Such a training programme has been prepared by Wig and Murthy at Chandigarh. There is growing evidence that the health auxiliaries can acquire the skills and confidence to care for mentally ill persons. It has also been demonstrated that there is satisfactory acceptance by the community of these para-professionals in the capacity of mental health care providers. In addition, it has been shown that a limited range of drugs in their hands is sufficient to deal with the majority of the mental disorders mentioned above (Wig and Murthy 1980).

What is now needed is for such programmes of training in mental health care for health auxiliaries to be taken up at a national level. While the Government of India has recognized this need explicitly in its National Health Policy (1983), it will be some time before such a national programme is put into effect. This is understandable in view of the fact that India is still faced with massive problems such as malnutrition, high rates of infant and child mortality, and pressing needs for the provision of drinking water, sanitation, and immunization. In such circumstances, it is the voluntary agencies which must come forward to pioneer programmes which can help to deliver mental health care 'to the doorstep of the people'.

Such an effort is expected to take shape in the form of a mental health centre which will be situated in Calcutta, the most populous city of India (over 10 million). Apart from having the traditional inpatient/outpatient services, the centre will act as a referral source for mental health out-posts in the neighbouring slums and the surrounding villages. These out-posts will be staffed by trained auxiliaries. They will also serve as training centres for health auxiliaries from governmental or voluntary sources. An integral part of the project will be an ongoing research programme on various aspects of mental health in the primary care setting.

REFERENCES

Harding, T. W., De Arango, M. V., Ballazar, J., Climent, C. E., Ibrahim, H. H. A., Ladrigo-Ignacio, L., Srinivasa Murthy, R., and Wig, N. N. (1980) Mental Disorders in Primary Health Care: A Study of Their Frequency and Diagnosis in Four Developing Countries. *Psychological Medicine* 10: 231–41.

Nandi, D. N., Ajmani, S., Ganguli, H., Banerjee, G., Boral, G. C., Ghosh, A., and Sarkar, S. (1976) A Clinical Evaluation of Depressives Found in a Rural Survey in India. *British Journal of Psychiatry* 128: 523–27.

Wig, N. N. and Srinivasa Murthy, R. (1980) *Manual of Mental Disorders for Peripheral Health Personnel*. Chandigarh: Dept. of Psychiatry, PGIMER.

Wig, N. N., Srinivasa Murthy, R., and Harding, T. W. (1981) A Model for Rural Psychiatric Services – Raipur Rani Experience. *Indian Journal of Psychiatry* 23(4): 275–80.

T. A. Cheng

The view from abroad – Taiwan

Although there has been no general practice research of mental illness hitherto in Taiwan, the frequency of psychiatric cases among the primary care attenders is by no means low. Many of the general practitioners or medical specialists make a clinical diagnosis of 'psychoneurosis' for those of their patients who have somatic symptoms without a demonstrable organic basis. A pilot study of mental disorders carried out recently (Cheng 1985) showed that the rate of help-seeking in the group of 'cases' was significantly higher than that of the 'non-case' group (42.1 per cent and 18.5 per cent respectively over one week). It was more surprising to find that none of the 'cases' was receiving psychiatric help. Those who had sought help had all consulted their general practitioner or medical specialist. The rate of psychiatric 'cases' among all the medical attenders in the previous week was 44.4 per cent, 38 out of a total sample of 150. The decision to seek help was significantly correlated with the presence of somatic symptoms, somatic concern, and anxiety state. Most of the 'cases' found in this pilot survey were categorized as minor mental disorders with a combination of anxiety, depression, and somatic symptoms as the presenting phenomena.

The task of establishing a new taxonomy is important not only for the needs of family doctors but also for epidemiological research. Such research might well include cross-cultural comparative studies. An internationally accept-able diagnostic system of minor mental disorders, if this is possible to achieve, would greatly facilitate the completion of the clinical picture of mental disorders.

Although in Taiwan there has been no research into the screening for mental illness in primary care settings, the screening of general populations has been undertaken in recent years. A newly designed and developed questionnaire (Cheng and Williams 1985) has been used in both urban and rural communities (Cheng 1985), and the results are now being analysed.

It is too early to discuss the policy of the care of mental illness in primary care settings in Taiwan, but the high prevalence of minor mental disorders (26 per cent in the author's pilot survey) indicated that most of the patients with these will have to be taken care of by general practitioners. In view of the shortage of psychiatric staff and of psychiatric teaching in undergraduate courses of every medical college, the health authority has recently proposed a five-year programme to improve mental health care. It is hoped that research into mental illness, especially its minor forms, will receive increasing attention in future. The programme includes a training course in clinical psychiatry for medical specialists working in public general hospitals. If the effects of this programme turn out to be favourable, then a further training course for the general practitioner might well follow.

REFERENCES

Cheng, T. A. (1985) A pilot study of mental disorders in Taiwan. *Psychological Medicine* 15.

Cheng, T. A. and Williams, P. (in press) The design and development of a screening questionnaire (CHQ) for use in community study of mental disorders in Taiwan. *Psychological Medicine*.

H. Katschnig, G. Eichberger,
M. Schimek, and L. Seidi

The role of the general practitioner
in the care of discharged
psychiatric patients – a pilot study
in a rural area in Austria

The following empirical contribution to 'The view from abroad' illustrates one important and little studied aspect of the practical, clinical, and research significance of current developments in mental health practices in primary care settings (eds).

INTRODUCTION

While more and more psychiatric patients are being discharged from mental hospitals, the provision of community psychiatric services for the more severely mentally disturbed is still lagging behind. This is especially so in rural areas, where large distances render the provision of community care more difficult, and it is understandable that models of community psychiatric services have typically first been set up in urban areas. What *is* available and rather easily accessible in most rural areas, is primary health care. The purpose of this paper is to explore the possible role of the general practitioner in providing care for the more severely disturbed psychiatric patients in a rural area of Austria, leaving aside the general practitioner's known role in the management of minor mental disorders (Shepherd *et al.* 1966). In the framework of the project 'Mental health services in pilot study areas' carried out under the auspices of the Regional Office for Europe of the World Health Organisation between 1977 and 1984 (World Health Organisation, in press), in 1977 a special survey was undertaken in the Austrian pilot study area, the county of Mistelbach, in order to provide some data on the possible role of the general practitioner in the aftercare of psychiatric inpatients discharged from a mental hospital. For that purpose, a cohort of patients discharged from the psychiatric hospital serving the county of Mistelbach was followed up for two years in order to find out whether they contacted the general practitioners of the area.

THE ROLE OF THE GENERAL PRACTITIONER IN THE AUSTRIAN HEALTH CARE SYSTEM

In 1977, 5,524 general practitioners were working in Austria (population 7.5 million), each serving on average 1,361 inhabitants. More than 98 per cent of the Austrian population is covered by national health insurance schemes, giving access to medical inpatient and outpatient care practically free of charge. General practitioners usually work in solo practices (as do the specialist consultants) and have contracts with social security. In some senses, the general practitioner is the gatekeeper for medical care, since in many instances specialist care can only be acquired after referral by a general practitioner.

THE AUSTRIAN PILOT STUDY AREA

The county of Mistelbach (a predominantly rural area) was deliberately chosen for the Austrian pilot study area in the World Health Organisation project, since a substantial proportion of the Austrian population live in rural areas. The county is situated north of Vienna, in the northeastern part of the province of Lower Austria. With a population of 75,000, it comprises just 1 per cent of the total population of Austria. Its population density is low (58 inhabitants per square kilometre). Of the labour force, 40 per cent is employed in agriculture, and the degree of industrialization is low.

Psychiatric inpatient treatment for the population of Mistelbach is available at the Klosterneuburg psychiatric hospital just outside the city borders of Vienna. The capital town of the county, also called Mistelbach, is approximately 60 km away from the psychiatric hospital. In 1977, an independent psychiatrist was working in the town of Mistelbach and there was also a psychosocial service ('Psychsozialer Dienst'), consisting of a psychiatrist from the psychiatric hospital in Klosterneuburg and a social worker. Mistelbach was the first psychiatric sector of nine such sectors in the catchment area of Klosterneuburg psychiatric hospital. The task of the psychosocial service is mainly outpatient treatment and home visits for discharged patients from the psychiatric hospital. Mistelbach also has a general hospital. In 1977, 14 specialist doctors and 42 general practitioners were working in the district. Each general practitioner served the medical needs of about 1,703 inhabitants.

THE COHORT

For the purpose of the study reported here, the first 200 consecutive admissions to the Klosterneuburg psychiatric hospital originating from the county of Mistelbach were defined as a cohort to be followed up. One patient later turned out not to be a resident of the county of Mistelbach and was excluded. Therefore, 199 patients entered the study. *Table 1* shows the diagnoses of these patients according to ICD–8. Organic psychoses and addiction make up nearly 60 per cent of all patients (reflecting the high prevalence of alcoholism in this wine-growing area). The next largest diagnostic group is schizophrenia/paranoid states with 18.1 per cent. There is a preponderance of male patients (57.3 per cent). Of all the patients, 15.6 per cent were under 30 years of age and 28.8 per cent were 60 years of age or older.

In the two years after admission, 25 patients had died and 3 were still in the hospital (*Table 2*). Therefore, 171 (85.9 per cent of the original cohort) were

Table 1   *Diagnostic distribution of a cohort of 199 psychiatric patients from the county of Mistelbach admitted to the Klosterneuburg psychiatric hospital after 1 May 1977 and discharged within two years (ICD–8 numbers in brackets)*

	admission	*discharged within two years*
organic psychoses (290–94)	67 (33.7%)	50 (29.2%)
schizophrenia/paranoid states (295, 294)	36 (18.1%)	35 (20.5%)
affective psychosis (296)	11 (5.5%)	11 (6.4%)
neurosis, personality disorders (300–02)	10 (5.0%)	10 (5.8%)
addiction (303, 304)	51 (25.6%)	47 (27.5%)
mental retardation (310–15)	8 (4.0%)	7 (4.1%)
other	16 (8.0%)	11 (6.5%)
total	199	171

Table 2   *Cohort of 199 psychiatric inpatients admitted to the Klosterneuburg psychiatric hospital from the pilot study area of Mistelbach*

2-year follow-up after admission	
not discharged	3 (1.5%)
deceased in hospital	25 (12.6%)
discharged	171 (85.9%)
total	199 (100.00%)

discharged back into the community. These 171 patients constitute the cohort which was followed up for contacts with general practitioners in the two years after discharge. The diagnoses of these patients is also given in *Table 1*. Since most deaths occurred in the diagnostic groups of organic psychosis and addiction, the other diagnostic groups have relatively higher percentages in the discharge group than in the admission population.

RESULTS

Since it was not possible to search the files of *all* 42 general practitioners of the county of Mistelbach for *all* discharged patients, an economic strategy had to be chosen. In the first analysis of the case notes of the discharged patients, it turned out that a large proportion of these patients had had a contact with a general practitioner in the period before being admitted to the psychiatric hospital. In fact, 130 of the 171 discharged patients had had such a general practitioner contact before admission (*Table 3*).

Our research strategy consisted of contacting those general practitioners who were mentioned in the hospital case notes to find our whether *their* patients had turned up again within two years of discharge. This, of course, provides only a minimum estimate of general practitioner contacts of discharged psychiatric patients. The 41 patients who had not had a general practitioner contact before admission were not checked for such general practitioner contacts after discharge. It was not possible to check whether those patients who had had a general practitioner contact turned up at other

Table 3   *Diagnostic distribution of a cohort of 171 patients from the county of Mistelbach discharged from the Klosterneuburg psychiatric hospital according to whether they had a GP contact before admission or not (ICD–8 diagnoses in brackets)*

	GP contacts before admission (followed up)	no GP contacts before admission (not followed up)
organic psychoses (290–94)	38 (29.2%)	12 (29.3%)
schizophrenia/paranoid states (295, 297)	27 (20.8%)	8 (19.5%)
affective disorders (296)	8 (6.2%)	3 (7.3%)
neurosis, personality disorders (300–02)	9 (6.9%)	1 (2.4%)
addiction (303, 304)	37 (28.5%)	10 (24.4%)
mental retardation (310–15)	4 (3.1%)	4 (7.3%)
other	7 (5.4%)	4 (9.8%)
total	130	41

general practitioners during follow-up; nor did we check for possible general practitioner contacts outside the county of Mistelbach.

In *Table 3* it is shown that the diagnoses of those patients who had had a general practitioner contact (and who were followed up) and those who had not had a general practitioner contact before admission (and were not followed up) were roughly comparable.

The main finding was surprising. Only 10.8 per cent of those patients checked for general practitioner contacts had no contact with 'their' general practitioner during the two years after discharge (*Table 4*). Therefore, nearly 9 out of 10 discharged patients who had had a general practitioner contact before admission turned up at their general practitioner at least once in the two year follow-up period. It was also surprising to note that 46.2 per cent of these patients had a high frequency of such contacts: namely, more than one contact per month.

Table 4   *Cohort of 130 psychiatric inpatients discharged from the Klosterneuburg psychiatric hospital back to the pilot study area of Mistelbach*

2-year follow-up after discharge checked for GP contacts	
more than one GPcontact per month	60 (46.2%)
less than one GP contact per month	56 (43.1%)
no GP contacts	14 (10.8%)
total	130 (100.00%)

Table 5   *Diagnostic distribution of a cohort of 130 patients from the county of Mistelbach discharged from the Klosterneuburg psychiatric hospital according to whether they had or did not have at least one contact with their GP in the two years after discharge (ICD–8 diagnoses in brackets)*

	GP contacts in 2 years after discharge	no GP contacts in 2 years after discharge
organic psychoses (290–94)	29 (25.0%)	9 (64.2%)
schizophrenia/paranoid states (295, 297)	27 (23.3%)	
affective psychosis (296)	8 (6.9%)	—
neurosis, personality disorders (300–02)	9 (7.8%)	—
addiction (303, 304)	34 (29.3%)	3 (21.5%)
mental retardation (310–15)	3 (2.6%)	1 (7.1%)
other	6 (5.2%)	1 (7.1%)
total	116	14

It was not possible in this study to evaluate the impact of the general practitioner contacts. But the simple fact that more than two-thirds of discharged patients had at least one (and most had many more) general practitioner contact within two years of discharge is noteworthy. Since this is a very conservative estimate, the results point to the fact that general practitioners could be an important source of help for discharged psychiatric patients. As is shown in *Table 5*, in some diagnostic groups – the functional psychoses and neuroses – *all* patients had at least one contact with their general practitioner after discharge.

CONCLUSION

We can conclude that primary health care physicians in rural areas have contacts with most discharged psychiatric patients. Thus, general practitioners in rural areas do not only deal with a large amount of 'minor psychiatric disorders' (Strotzka 1969) but obviously also carry the burden of seeing, if not caring for, the more severely disturbed psychiatric patients. We could not evaluate how well the general practitioners did this work, but given the dangers of social isolation for severely disturbed mental patients, the fact that general practitioners had contacts with these patients may have been valuable in itself.

General practitioners have limited possibilities for providing help to these patients partly due to their limited psychiatric training and partly because of the time pressure under which they have to work. But, together with a specialist service, such as the psychosocial service for the county of Mistelbach, they can serve as a catalyst between the psychiatric patient, his family and the specialist service, even carrying out some of the therapeutic tasks with the family of the mental patient themselves.

Data collection for this study was carried out by the psychosocial team (G.E. and L.S.). This process led to the psychiatrist and social worker having contacts with the general practitioners, and it turned out that most of them were pleased to become acquainted with their sector specialist team. The model of one or two specialists for such a population (here, 75,000 inhabitants) working together with primary health care physicians, constitutes a general model for community psychiatry in rural areas. The specialist team could have an education effect, through repeated contacts with the primary health care physicians. It may be that such a model is not only useful for the less densely populated rural areas of industrialized countries but also for developing countries.

REFERENCES

Shepherd, M., Cooper, B., Brown, A. C., and Kalton, G. (1966) *Psychiatric Illness in General Practice*. Oxford University Press: Oxford (2nd edn, 1981).

Strotzka, H. (1959) *Kleinburg – eine sozialpsychiatrische Feldstudie.* Österreichischer Bundesverlag: Wien.
World Health Organisation (in press) *Mental Health Services in Pilot Study Area.* Copenhagen: World Health Organisation.

Shamai Davidson

The view from abroad – Israel

In order to appreciate the role of psychiatry in the primary health care setting in Israel it is necessary to understand the nature and problems of the burgeoning new society which came into being in the years following the establishment of the State in 1948.

Before the Second World War and during the British mandatory period there was, in general, an avoidance of psychiatric disturbance by the society and psychiatric services were rudimentary. Traditional beliefs of a messianic nature in the 'therapeutic powers' of the historic Holy Land of Israel combined with the pioneering values of the collective settlement (kibbutz) movement to create an expectation of solution or transcendence of personal psychological problems by the mere virtue of settlement in the country and participation in its social and spiritual aims.[1]

Psychiatric illness was dealt with mainly by neurologists trained in the neuro-psychiatric schools of central Europe as well as a number of refugee psycho-analysts from Germany and Austria who established a psycho-analytic institute in Jerusalem in the 1930s which had a particular influence in some of the collective settlements. After the establishment of the State in 1948 there was an influx of psychiatrists including some trained in Britain and the USA and a network of improvised mental hospitals was quickly established which were immediately involved together with the general medical services in dealing with the problems of major illness resulting from the mass immigration. Awareness of transcultural and environmental factors grew rapidly in the face of the large numbers of immigrants from Middle Eastern countries whose ethnic health and illness behaviour patterns were unfamiliar and for whom European and American psychiatric and psychotherapeutic techniques were often unsuitable. A further large section of the immigrant population was comprised of massively traumatized survivors of the concentration camps and other situations of the Nazi persecution and genocide of the Jews of Europe. Their experiences of extreme stress and loss and the sequelae were by and large avoided by psychiatrists and physicians in the general belief in the rehabilitative and socio-therapeutic powers of the new country. The survivors themselves usually willingly participated in the general pattern of avoidance of the painful events of the past through active engagement in the challenges of building and defending the new State. Only in recent years has there been growing recognition of the special psychological needs of this population.

The recurrent wars, security crises and terrorist attacks resulted in the development of high quality casualty and surgical services. The need for an extensive army psychiatric service with special training in the treatment of battle reactions, and so on, took a long time to be fully recognized. There is now a well-established military service manned mainly by psychiatrists on reserve duty. The large number of bereaved families and the other results of severe stress deriving from Israel's specific problems dealt with for so long by stoic denial are at last receiving increasing attention by society and the mental health services.

For many years after the establishment of the State the creation of an adequate basic psychiatric service was the main concern. A network of mental hospitals was developed using improvised buildings in which psychosis and severe mental disturbances could be adequately dealt with by biological treatments within a therapeutic milieu by psychiatrists whose training often included psychodynamic psychotherapy. A network of psychiatric outpatient clinics was developed, some of which were independent of mental hospitals situated in the community in the proximity of primary health care clinics.

Social psychiatric concepts were always understood to be important and plans were drawn up[2] for the development of the psychiatric services in the community but little psychiatric staffing and motivation was available for this purpose. With the division of the country during the past five years into catchment areas served by the main mental hospitals, psychiatric services in the community have been developing.

The primary health care services in Israel are well developed with general practitioner and pediatric teams of physicians and nurses working together in health centres situated in every district throughout the country. Most of the physicians are immigrants from central and eastern Europe. Graduates from Israel's high quality medical school preferred hospital specialization although a reversal of this trend is beginning with the development of postgraduate departments for specialist training in family medicine in the medical schools.

Community surveys which studied general practices found that up to 45 per cent of the patients have psychiatric symptoms in Israel[3] as in Britain[4], the vast majority of whom are not referred for psychiatric help. Unfortunately, most of the general practitioners have not had sufficient knowledge and skills to deal with the common emotional disturbances. They were often aware that emotional disturbance was involved in the presenting somatic complaints but did not know how to relate it, and felt frustrated and helpless. The avoidance of psychological disturbances (apart from major psychiatric illness) prevailing in the clinical departments of the medical school was thus continually re-inforced over the years.

The approach to this large mass of disturbance has been mainly in somatic terms with a vast amount of unnecessary and repeated physical investigations and the large-scale prescription of vitamins, tranquillizers and to some extent anti-depressives (usually in inadequate dosage).

Attempts to understand the emotional origins of somatic complaints or to listen to the patients problems and stresses have been negligible. The district health centres belong to the Trade Union Health Service which provides comprehensive health insurance for 90 per cent of the population. The running of the district clinics has been dominated by an administrative bureaucracy concerned mainly with numbers of visits to the clinic.

The teaching of psychiatry in the medical schools for medical students has been mainly carried out in the framework of clinical clerkships in the teaching mental hospitals or psychiatric departments of general hospitals with little or no systematic teaching in the general practice clinic or in the general medical and other departments of the general hospital. The clinical knowledge acquired by medical students is thus mainly centred on hospitalized psychiatric patients with the teaching of skills in the diagnosis and treatment of acute psychosis and serious psychiatric disturbance. The acquisition of knowledge and therapeutic skills in relation to the common emotional disturbances and their handling is limited. Children are treated in the district health centres by paediatricians with little understanding of emotional development and behavioural problems in childhood or of family dynamics. The teaching of child psychiatry is included in the clinical clerkship in the mental hospital but as with adult psychiatry has little effect on the acquisition of relevant knowledge and skills for paediatric general practice.

It has become increasingly obvious in recent years that the psychiatric instruction of undergraduates in the medical schools as well as the post-graduate refresher courses have had insufficient impact on the knowledge and handling of psychiatric illness in general practice.

There have been ongoing attempts throughout the years by many psychiatrists usually based in psychiatric outpatient clinics to establish liaison services in general practice clinics[5].

These services have mainly consisted of group case-consultation discussions with a psychiatrist who visits the primary health care team in the district clinic usually only once or twice a month. In addition, group work using Balint principles has also been carried out for small numbers of specially motivated physicians but these have served mainly to develop psychodynamic knowledge of application only to a small number of selected patients. Sporadic lectures and short postgraduate courses related to the handling of the acute severely disturbed patient or the use of anti-depressive and tranquillizer drugs has also been a feature for many years. However, little was achieved by these methods in terms of really developing the understanding and skills of the family doctor in relation to the large numbers of patients suffering from the common emotional disturbances.

In order to change this situation it is obvious that a new approach has to be devised. Major efforts need to be invested in order to change the deeply entrenched avoidance of emotional disturbance by the primary health care physicians. What is required is the 'unlearning' of patterns of practice based on neutralization of the physician's personality and avoidance of emotional involvement together with the learning of new patterns in the handling of patients based on awareness of the central importance of the doctor's personality in his therapeutic interaction with the patient.

Highly motivated psychiatrists were selected for a pilot project involving the creation of a new model of liaison psychiatry in the catchment area (250,000 population) of the Shalvata Psychiatric Centre in the Sharon region of Israel. This involved the placement of a suitable psychiatrist in the health centre as a regular presence in the team of GPs and nurses.

The psychiatrist is available for individual consultation on any problem any member of the team deems necessary. Contact is informal and unstructured and can be based on a brief on-the-spot consultation in the course of a routine visit to the family doctor. If it is decided that the psychiatrist should see the patient when this may be carried out immediately or an appointment arranged when more time would be allocated for a psychiatric evaluation. Where possible the GP is present during the psychiatric interviews.

From one-half to an entire working day a week is spent in each of the clinics according to the number of GPs with the psychiatrist being maximally available for immediate individual approaches from the team members during this time.

Over the months of regular face-to-face informal contact between the GP and the psychiatrist within the setting of the district clinics the attitude of the GPs towards psychiatric problems gradually changes. They learn to listen and how to conduct an interview through observing the psychiatrist who becomes a familiar colleague instead of a remote specialist. This essentially apprenticeship model enables an ongoing dialogue between the psychiatrist and the physicians in the primary care team. In this open communication process the psychiatrist soon learns that psychiatric jargon is not understood and he/she is thus required to develop a language of formulation meaningful to the GP.

Not all psychiatrists are able to function in this way, which emphasizes the importance of the correct selection of suitable psychiatrists with special motivation and a flexibility of approach as well as a mobile adaptability and availablity for a large number of doctors in the different clinics served. The openness of communication which develops enables a gradual reduction of anxiety and defensiveness in the presence of the psychiatrist with a developing readiness for self-exposure in relation to revealing feelings about the patient's emotional disturbances as well as their own problems. The readiness of the psychiatrist to leave the hospital or specialist clinic and be available on-the-spot in the GP's place of work without the pressure of time and other duties changes the image of the anxiety-provoking psychiatrist to that of a human being ready to be exposed to colleagues with different attitudes.

The development of awareness and self-confidence by GPs in relation to the emotional problems of their patients implies a readiness to become involved emotionally in a controlled way and the ability to discuss freely their relationships with their patients. The process of 'getting to know' each other which is the prerequisite for the growth of understanding between the psychiatrist and the GP takes time which both parties to the dialogue must be prepared to invest. There can be no definite guide-lines for this model of liaison-attachment. The psychiatrist is often required to go through a stage of giving information direct guidance and theoretical explanation before getting to a free discussion with the family doctor of the patient's problems and his/her feelings and thoughts within the doctor–patient relationship.

We have been developing this model over the past few years within our catchment area steadily increasing the psychiatric staffing allocated for this service from a beginning part-time psychiatrist to the present two full-time psychiatrists (a general psychiatrist and a child psychiatrist). Ten family doctor health centres are now covered by this service involving about thirty GPs and general paediatricians. The initial results which are now being evaluated in terms of the benefits for the general practitioners and their patients are most encouraging with the removal of stigma and early detection and treatment of psychiatric disturbance. There is greatly increased patient satisfaction and a significant reduction in the number of routine and special investigation and in the prescription of drugs.

The effect on the outpatient psychiatric services both adult and child is more complex and more difficult to evaluate but we believe that the whole pattern of referral to the psychiatric clinic will be significantly altered with the continued development of the liaison-attachment model of psychiatrist-family doctor co-operation.

REFERENCES

1. Palgi, P. (1963) Immigrants, Psychiatrists and Culture, *Israel Annals of Psychiatry and Related Disciplines* 1: 43–58.

2. Miller, L., Pollak, H., and Bertram, H. (eds) (1979) *Contributions to Community Psychiatry in Israel*. Jerusalem: Jerusalem Academic Press.
3. Aviram, U. and Levav, I. (eds) (1981) *Community Mental Health in Israel*. Tel-Aviv: Cherikover.
4. Shepherd, M., Cooper, B., Brown, A. C., and Kalban, G. W. (1966) *Psychiatric Illness in General Practice*. London: Oxford University Press.
5. Bar-el, I., Bester, R., and Klein, H. (1982) Experience in Community Mental Health Consulation. *Israel Journal of Psychiatry and Related Sciences* 19: 173–80.

PART 7

FUTURE TRENDS IN
RESEARCH AND POLICY

Sir Desmond Pond

Future trends in research and policy

For some years now the research input into the Department of Health and Social Security's policy making and deliberations has been mainly through the committees known as Research Liaison Groups. A number of such groups were set up following the Rothschild reorganization of government science. Those that are relevant to the topics under discussion are concerned with mental illness, mental handicap, child care, the elderly and the homeless, and addictions. In addition, a separate type of committee was set up last year to look at primary health care research generally. Each of these groups has produced documents on research strategy and priorities, some of them being updated every few years. These documents help us in the Office of the Chief Scientist to decide which projects to try and finance in the coming years. These committees and their reports are not of course the only channel of communication between the policy makers, the researchers and those who provide service in the National Health Service (NHS). There are also many other formal and informal contacts.

The Department of Health and Social Security (DHSS) support of research in the health services is exclusively indirect, that is to say we have no in-house research units save one small one on social security. Contracts are placed in university departments. Many of these are of the well known three year project type, but we also support a number of longer-term research groups closely similar to the research units supported by the Medical Research Council. The

DHSS is, of course, not the only funding body concerned with mental illness and primary care, though I think it is only fair to remind this audience that it is the DHSS which has provided the most consistent and generous support for what are still regarded as Cinderella subjects of research, and were even more so ten or more years ago.

I would stress that the views expressed in this paper are entirely my own, and should not be taken as expressing any official Department views, though of course I have drawn heavily upon the ideas of many of my colleagues here.

In looking at the various documents on research strategy and priorities, I am impressed by certain common themes appearing in most of them, and my paper will be largely confined to a discussion of these general themes rather than any detailed commentary on particular proposals put forward in any one document. The following is a list of the general topics I wish to discuss:

1. prevention
2. detection and screening
3. multi-disciplinary aspects
4. training
5. impact of information technology
6. special problems relating to age
7. development or implementation of research results

PREVENTION

The first – prevention – is the one least well covered in all these documents. In fact, one can say that it is only in the field of mental handicap that primary prevention plays a large and significant role. This is, of course, mainly as a result of the exciting biomedical developments in the detection of genetic anomalies, which could lead to a significant reduction in the number of children born with serious defects. Biomedical research has not come up with anything as exciting and fundamental as this work as regards the rest of mental illness. Little can be said about primary prevention in the psychosocial field, though there is something to be said for the phrase 'anticipatory guidance before the event' from the Royal College of General Practitioners/Royal College of Psychiatrists report (1981) on the Prevention of Psychiatric Disorders in General Practice.

DETECTION

As regards detection, I should like to mention the importance of the early detection of the medical, psychological and social effects of alcohol misuse. The use of routine biochemical tests and psychosocial inquiries should be extended to the primary care sector as well as for hospital inpatients and outpatients. The fact that such screening and detection techniques may turn up more patients than the present services can actually treat, constitutes no excuse for not developing them.

MULTI-DISCIPLINARY ASPECTS

Multi-disciplinary aspects of management have also been the subject of several sessions already, but I would like to stress that in all the research strategy and priorities documents, the importance of research and development in this area takes a very high priority. There is no doubt that a large number of innovations in the delivery of health care are taking place all over the country. Many of them are scarcely reported or even described; fewer still have any effective evaluation of their work built into the planning. In the planning and evaluation of the community care of the mentally ill, the community physicians have so far played little part. The transition from hospital to the community has been largely planned (if at all) by the providers of mental health service themselves, extending outwards with little if any interaction with parallel medical developments which usually lag well behind the psychiatric developments.

Partly as a reflection of the present government's concerns, the Department is very interested in health economics and cost effectiveness. Many more attempts should be made to look at the economics of primary care than are at present undertaken. The DHSS largely supports at least three units that are relevant to work in this field – the Health Economics Unit at York (shared with the Economic and Social Research Council), the Social Policy Research Unit also at York, and the Personal Social Services Research Unit at the University of Kent at Canterbury. The last two units have comparatively little health input, but the Social Security aspects of health care in the community are assuming increasing importance. I suspect that the Social Security costs of supporting those with chronic mental illness are much greater than the money spent in the health services on their detection and treatment. Paykel *et al.*'s study of the role of the community psychiatric nurse shows clearly that health costs for both hospital and general practitioners are minor for patients in receipt of social security benefit and support from the local authority social services (Paykel *et al.* 1984). More studies of this kind are urgently needed, even though the resulting evidence will probably show that, contrary to the view of early enthusiasts, community care costs more than institutional care.

In addition to the multi-disciplinary aspects of research and development I should also point out that there are inter-departmental aspects which require co-ordination for services purposes at the local level, and for policy and research purposes largely at the national level. I am thinking, for example, of the interest of the Home Office and the Department of Education and Science in child care, of the Department of the Environment's interest, through housing policy, in the care of the elderly, not to mention the multitude of government bodies who have a hand in alcohol use and abuse. I have the impression that in some local areas the co-ordination between departments is patchy; likewise there are fairly effective Whitehall inter-departmental committees but the twain rarely meet to induce interactions between the central committees and local research and development.

TRAINING

As regards training, I have in mind not only the various professional groups but also the growing army of volunteer helpers who, with guidance and support but with comparatively little, if any, formal training, can achieve so much. The Office of the Chief Scientist is not involved in the organization and financing of training, except in a very limited way, but these constitute the concern of other parts of the DHSS and the NHS and numerous professional bodies, such as the Royal College of Psychiatrists and the Royal College of General Practitioners. However, so far as I know, only community psychiatric nurses have a training specifically directed to the care of the mentally ill in the community. The Joint Committee on Higher Psychiatric Training states that trainees should have experience in community work and domiciliary visiting. Community care is essentially multi-disciplinary and interesting questions arise on the efficiency and efficacy of so-called role-blurring and role-sharing, in the detection and the management of mental illness. Duplication or demarcation disputes are particularly liable to occur in the case of minor mental illness and the psychosocial aspects of medical disorders, both of which consume an inordinate amount of service time and personnel.

The evaluation of most training schemes is conspicuously lacking. A few do try to evaluate the effectiveness of training schemes with regard to students achieving the goals of the schemes of training, but fewer still look at the effectiveness of the trainee as regards changing the relevant clients' behaviour or attitudes. The problem is complicated by the fact that we have no satisfactory measures of the quality of life. Efforts to try to promote research on the effectiveness of psychotherapy confront major methodological problems, though much the same applies to work on the economic aspects or cost effectiveness of primary care. Where the money goes can be worked out without too much difficulty; changes in the quality of life consequent on the expenditure are another matter.

The settings for training and research into primary care in the broadest sense have not been properly considered. There is no doubt that the curious amalgam of different interests and abilities, has been for at least 150 years by far the most important setting for the major advances in biomedical knowledge. With the changes in the ways of managing patients by increasing home care, and with the even greater changes that will come about as a result of information technology, the definition of a hospital becomes increasingly difficult to define. However, I am of the opinion that, by whatever definition, a hospital is not the best base for research into primary care. Nor can the DHSS alone provide the necessary intellectual base for such research which needs at least the collaboration of the Family Practitioner Services, the Royal College of General Practitioners and the university departments of general practice. The creation of these research bases should be one of the urgent priorities in primary health care research.

Further, not even a better base for primary health care research will provide all that is necessary for work on the community care of the mentally ill whose long-term management also involves local departments of social services and the departments of social security, not forgetting the voluntary organizations and, increasingly, private care. A surprising number of local authority social service departments have small research facilities mainly interested in statistics and service evaluation, but much of the work needs more fundamental thinking. As well as research into social organization there are also the uses, by psychiatrists as well as psychologists, of psychological techniques of training and treatment which have little intellectual or practical connection with health care in the narrow sense of medicine. Some years ago I put forward the view that we urgently needed the psychosocial equivalent of the teaching hospital, which could draw together the psychological and social techniques that have theoretical and practical aspects in common, whether they are applied to the occupational, forensic, educational or health fields. Without some such co-ordinated action the academic quality of teaching and research in the social services generally will inevitably be low.

IMPACT OF INFORMATION TECHNOLOGY

I should refer briefly to what is currently referred as information technology, as the Department of Trade and Industry has recently put a number of computers into general practices to evaluate their effectiveness, though sadly without any very previously well thought out planning, with the honourable exception of Professor Peter Warr's work based on the Sheffield Applied Psychology Unit. Computerized information which could well be needed to study mental illness by a variety of professions, raises a host of problems of confidentiality, which will undoubtedly limit its use for some time to come. Furthermore, as far as I know, few psychiatric hospitals have yet computerized any part of their records so that the important primary care/hospital interaction, which could be greatly facilitated by direct computer links, will not be functioning for a long time. Research on the computerized diagnosis of mental illness similar to that which has been done by De Dombal in Leeds would certainly be welcome. Research on the computerized psychiatric interview is another field which I think deserves encouragement. Neither of these latter advances needs be confined to hospital use.

SPECIAL PROBLEMS RELATING TO AGE

Now I wish to refer briefly to some of the special problems of particular groups, especially age groups. In the narrow sense, mental illness in childhood is relatively rare, but a significant part of the GP's time is taken up with minor ailments of childhood, which are often related to family stresses. The natural history of these conditions deserves further study. Most other childhood psychiatric disturbances, for example child abuse, delinquency, behaviour disorders generally, are as closely connected with the interests and resources of the educational system and the social services as with the medical profession, and the child psychiatrist often sits, or falls, uneasily in the middle. The inter-departmental problems to which I have already referred loom particularly large in the children's field. However, the major changes in the care and development of children result from changes in social attitudes and behaviour that are occurring in society generally, and are influenced scarcely at all by official policies, let alone the results of research. The biological nuclear family is no longer an ideal or even a statistical norm in some quarters. The separation of sexual activity and reproduction facilitates many variations in the pattern of the adult care of children. There is also the opposite influence of strong, even closed-in, cultural groups, mainly of different ethnic origins, often tinged with religious differences. These may operate very successfully as family groups producing stable children so long as the children are not exposed to intolerable strains of cross-cultural differences, which might be met at school but which will certainly occur when the children move out of school into the world at large. Social science research workers can do little more than observe and comment on what is going on, and the primary care setting is probably as good a base as any for such work.

As regards the prevention of childhood disorders, we are all familiar with the large amount of research that has been done in the past, much of it stimulated by ideas such as the cycle of deprivation. Sadly, the effects of intervention, whether in homes, school or elsewhere are still equivocal. The wider applications of intervention, even if considered worthwhile, are constrained not only by the aforementioned social forces but also by economic factors that are almost equally uncontrollable. Though chastened by these factors, we should nevertheless not abandon research in these fields, for if workers in the health and social services do not document the ill effects of some social and psychological practices no one else will do so. It is in the community that the early signs of stress will appear and we should not wait till they appear in the institutional statistics.

In the senium, mental illness is more deeply involved with the biological changes of ageing so that thus geriatric and psychogeriatric services are more or less inseparable. Major research concerns at the present time are the different forms of community care, especially their cost differences. The Department, the Medical Research Council and the Social Sciences Research

Council are currently thinking about the value of a longitudinal cohort study of the elderly as a means of trying to answer some of the many questions related to the development of the increasing dependency that can result from both the physical and the mental changes associated with ageing. This is almost the only epidemiological study which the Department is currently considering.

Between the young and the old there are most of the rest of us, and I personally do not think that we have so far had our fair share of research interest! There are such matters as the management of neurotic illness with the newer psychological techniques, pioneered mainly on outpatients but applicable in the community. There is much chronic disabling disease of medical origin – arthritis, heart disease, progressive neurological disorders, asthma, diabetes, epilepsy – which forms the core of so-called maintenance medicine. Many of these conditions carry psychological and social problems and, in particular, may lead to depression. There are a number of special interest patient groups concerned with particular conditions in this field, but the economical and efficient management of chronic illness within the primary care setting needs further elucidation.

DEVELOPMENT OR IMPLEMENTATION OF RESEARCH RESULTS

Finally, I should like to make a plea for more involvement of researchers in the development of the results of their findings. In the biomedical field there are usually doctors (and often patients too) only too ready and eager to try the new treatment, while it is still working, according to some cynics. This pressure comes from the emotional involvement of both doctor and patient in the relief of pain and the postponement of death, especially in spheres where good effects are usually more or less immediately obvious. No such tension is generated by the need for these institutional or behavioural changes which often carry only long-term effects. Researchers often lose heart and they feel, sometimes with justification, that the results of their labours disappear onto dusty shelves. Likewise the DHSS, which does not direct the NHS, also often feels frustrated by the failure of the health and social services to apply the results of research. However, Patten et al. show that the more personal involvement of researcher and policy maker tends to result in new ideas and practices receiving more attention. Accordingly, I would finish with a plea for more interest and concern on the part of researchers in the problems of development.

© 1986 Sir Desmond Pond

Donald Irvine

Future trends in research and policy

In Great Britain, general practice is the main provider of primary and continuing medical and nursing care for people living at home whose behaviour is disturbed because they are mentally ill, or because they have a physical illness with significant psychological and social components, or because they present an episode of turbulence in their lives as a medical complaint. Professor Shepherd and his colleagues have shown through their studies in the Institute of Psychiatry that patients with these illnesses comprise a very substantial part of the clinical work of most general practitioners.

The Conference has been shrewdly timed for it coincides with a major policy review which has now begun in general practice. My purpose is to say briefly where we are now, in general terms, in our development as a system of care and as a discipline and, looking forward, to note the main influences on our future direction.

GENERAL PRACTICE TODAY

I regard the formation of the Royal College of General Practitioners in 1952 as the starting point of modern general practice in this country for it indicated, albeit diffusely, that general practice was a discipline as well as a system of care. In the thirty years that have elapsed since then there have been significant changes: general practice has been largely rehoused and re-equipped;

the practice team has been established; and the main skeletal elements of the discipline are now well formed as a result of studies into patterns of morbidity, of classification, on the content and nature of consultations, and on the structure and processes of care.

Consequently, entry standards have been established through vocational training, educational methods and graduate organizations have been formed and shaped to meet the needs of established general practitioners, and a start has been made on the development of methods for assessing performance and outcome of care. University departments of general practice have been widely established where previously there were none. And morale and confidence among general practitioners has altered dramatically for the better since the nadir of the 1960s, so ensuring that some of our most able medical graduates select general practice as their first career choice.

Of course problems remain with every aspect I have described and they reflect our persistently outstanding problem, namely, the unexpectedly wide variations in the quality of care given by individual doctors. These variations have been shown by studies which have examined the problem from several angles to be due to fundamental differences in attitudes to, and an understanding of, the complaints which patients bring to their doctors. This is especially so in the field of mental illness.

Hence the substantial differences in, for example, the range of services available, in patterns of prescribing, consulting, team work, referral or almost any other activity you care to mention. Hence the observation that general practitioners at one end of this broad spectrum still see general practice as the sum of a number of specialities practised in isolation at a superficial level, whereas a growing number of general practitioners at the other end of the spectrum see it as a discipline with all the individual and corporate obligations and commitments to patients and other professional colleagues that such a concept holds. And hence, therefore, the fact that the community at large finds good general practice highly desirable but is prepared increasingly to think that poor general practice is replaceable.

POLICIES FOR PROMOTING QUALITY

This is where we are at the moment. Where to now? Within the Royal College of General Practitioners a broad policy thrust aimed at improving the quality of patient care in general practice has begun, recognizing fully and frankly that society has other options for care if and where we do not succeed. While much detail remains to be considered in the coming year, during which the Government should be publishing its own Green Paper, the main elements are taking shape. These are:

1. The development of a framework and of methods for establishing a dynamic standard-setting system in general practice which would embrace

all members of the practice team. We want to create a climate in which a self-critical attitude and an inquiring mind is seen as an asset and a sign of strength, and a life-long habit for every member of the practice team. This is a massive undertaking. It will involve us in, for example rebuilding our College so that its professional influence on education and standards of practice is local, requiring commitment from every member. Teaching practices should set the pace. I think that it is mainly through shared standard-setting activities that practice team roles will be clarified, modern methods of practice management will be adopted, and the relationships between the practice team and other caring professions will be clarified. The development of a professionally based standard-setting system is at the heart of our College's Quality Initiative.

2. We want to foster an active and constructive contribution from people who are registered with us as patients or clients and, through this, to describe more clearly the range and quality of services which people can expect from any general practice at any point in time. Well informed patients, co-ordinated as the consumer influence, are bound to affect our standards of care in future by promoting competition. They may also cause us to reconsider current etiquette on advertising, open access and referral.

3. A reappraisal and major overhaul of the academic foundations of general practice is now overdue. Today, university departments are responsible for our contributions to basic medical education while responsibility for vocational training and continuing education rest with the regional post-graduate organizations. Research in general practice is underdeveloped because it is not seen by most general practitioners as an essential function of their subject. Research in general practice is carried out mainly by university departments, the College and special units, such as the General Practice Research Unit.

   The Royal College of General Practitioners, recognizing that we are at the beginning of the end of the first phase of our academic development, is bringing the university departments and regional postgraduate organizations together with the object of developing a coherent academic strategy for the next decade. There are very many difficult professional problems to be tackled. However, high on our list of priorities is the need to provide more opportunities than there are at present for young doctors to acquire the basic skills of research method. Another priority is to develop effective mechanisms for working out policy issues involving research and development with bodies such as the Department of Health and Social Services and the Medical Research Council and with our sister Colleges.

4. We recognize that developments within practice itself and of our academic fabric are unlikely to succeed in the common objective of promoting quality unless accompanied by a revision of the practitioner's contract so that it becomes more performance sensitive. The basis exists in the trainer's contract. The built in competitive incentive needs to be adapted

so that it extends to all general practitioners. I have been very heartened to see that people are now beginning to suggest how this might be done.

5. The last element in our pursuit of quality concerns our administration of family practitioner services. We expect Government to make the new family Practitioner Committees more effective than they are at present at administering the contract so that bad practice is actively discouraged. The new committees should also become active in planning services locally, in promoting better links with the hospital and the social services and in helping the local community to have an active say in their general practice. To achieve their task these committees will require a higher quality of administration backed by modern computer-based data systems. Government will have to put its hand in its pocket.

GENERAL PRACTICE AND MENTAL ILLNESS

In Sir Desmond Pond's paper, and in the other papers delivered, we learn about the main areas in the field of mental illness in primary care which people think are ripe for research and development. I have no wish to add to these now for, in general, they seem sound. In explaining our policies for the development of general practice as a whole I hope that you will be able to see the contributions to this Conference in context. Most important of all, I hope that I have conveyed to you our sense of urgency, our new realization and acceptance of my profession's responsibilities and our determination as an important discipline in British medicine to get to grips decisively with our outstanding problem of quality control.

General Discussion

CHAIRMAN: PROFESSOR M. SHEPHERD

Dr Pamela Mason: We are getting towards the end of what has been a fascinating day-and-a-half, and I felt as a member of the Mental Health Policy Division in the Department of Health and Social Security, that I should like to take the opportunity to give back to you some of the things which have been going through my mind. This meeting has been most timely, and I think that is the key phrase of our response.

As Professor Shepherd said in opening, this was an opportunity for practitioners of a variety of professions, researchers, research managers and policy makers within the Department to share thoughts. We have been able to listen to a continuing debate and developments, particularly about classifications, and one of the things which seemed to come out so clearly is that the complexities of classification in the psychiatric setting are as nothing as to the complexities in the general practice setting. As Dr Irvine said, I think much more work has to be done actually in the context of a general practice setting. We have listened to a debate about screening and early case-finding, and ethics (both political and economic) and perhaps the thing that we will take away with us is the comment from Professor Goldberg: Can we afford not to? I feel that this was meant both in cost-effective terms and cost-benefit terms, and in terms of the patient concerned.

We have heard of the complexity of the use of the phrases 'primary care', 'mental health', and 'mental illness' and I shall not go into that, except to say that primary care is something, as Dr Sartorius pointed out, that we take in each country to formulate for ourselves, and that is something that we shall continue to do. Of course, primary care is primarily something which considers the needs of the population and individual patients. We keep coming back to individual needs. We must see community and patient participation and collaboration between professionals, agencies and lay members. Primary care is not isolated but should be an integrated and comprehensive part of the whole system. We have been concerned with the balance between primary care and specialist care in the context of debates about cure or prevention, about the management of disease and about the development of self-help and personal responsibility for health.

What of policy making? It seems perhaps unnecessary to remind you, but in a sense policy making in a central government department, in the Mental Health Division for instance, obviously must be firmly based on scientific information; hence our welcome for this meeting, the work of the General Practice Research Unit and others throughout the country, and much of the work which we have heard during these two days. Of course, we have to take note of political and professional developments, media developments, what the ordinary person is saying, and general consumer development. Basically, we are asking ourselves, and we shall be asking ourselves again, what is the problem? What is the nature and extent of turbulence in general practice, the distress of the patient? What is the spectrum of disorder that we should be concerned about? In seeking ways of meeting new needs, are we meeting old needs more effectively or are we meeting a wider spectrum of needs? I think this is worthy of much debate when one thinks about allocation of resources. But in defining needs and analysing ways of meeting these needs, we have to ask ourselves: What kinds of treatment, by what sorts of staff, in what sorts of settings, what sorts of teams – noting very much the pain and pleasure, and the discussion about teams and collaboration, and the benefits and drawbacks? What kind of collaboration? What sort of organization is needed? What sort of management skills and other structures are required? Finally, and basically perhaps, what kind of training is needed in the various professions? I will not respond to all the research findings; Sir Desmond has very ably covered that this morning.

I think what we need to do in this session is to think about the question: What can we do to develop further? I think it was Dr Evans who said that the main elements are in place. As we look around, there are events outside us that policy-makers must take note of and seek to use more clearly the Green Paper on the work of primary care, and also the Select Committee deliberations on community care. I believe both these should be closely considered. In doing so, we have to take stock and see this as a moment in which a number of developments have been brought together, and to think about the levels on which activity could take place; about what it is that government should be doing; what it is that other governments might be doing; what the professions should be doing; what the Royal Colleges should be doing; what sort of training should be given; and what the public should be doing.

Professor J. Knowelden: I note Sir Desmond's point that community physicians have cared to be absent here, and regret this, particularly since reorganization of services and collaboration between a number of different groups have been discussed. I do not think that services or projects are ever too young for evaluation. I have been involved too many times in being asked to help evaluate a scheme which is already well developed. Unless we plan right from the beginning how to structure the development of the service, there is really no opportunity at the end to evaluate it. Evaluation should come in right at the beginning.

Dr J. E. C. Tower: I should like to focus on the question of multi-axial classification for diagnostic purposes. A couple of months ago there was a paper in the *British Medical Journal* concerning urinary frequency and dysuria in non-pregnant women. All these women (about 90) had frequency and dysuria. All of them sent off midstream urine (MSU) to the laboratory, but before they got the results the GPs were asked to prescribe either an appropriate antibiotic, if they thought the MSU was going to be positive, or a simple urinary antiseptic if they thought not. Two interesting things emerged. One was, to the GPs' surprise, that they were 80 per cent accurate in forecasting which of the mid-stream urines were going to be normal. The other, surprise was that the group who had no bacteriuria in their urine had had a much greater proportion of emotional disturbance over the previous twelve months. Serum negative arthritis is another thing which every GP will frequently come across, but we do not really have a language in which to be able to tell people about it. Dr Dunn complained yesterday that GP diagnoses were so variable that really, putting it politely, they are not worth the paper they were written on.

I think it is possible that GPs have quite a shrewd idea of what is going on most of the time, but they just do not have a language in which to communicate this, and therefore statistical results from general practice make statisticians' hair stand on end.

Dr Orley: One issue which has arisen over the course of this meeting and which has not been developed at all, has been the question of psychiatric disorders other than emotional disturbances, and I wondered what the Department of Health and Social Security (DHSS) policy in this direction would be. I am thinking of the more severe psychoses, for example, schizophrenia; chronic mental patients being discharged back into the community, what is the role of the practice unit in this; alcohol problems; and I am thinking particularly of the mental handicapped and other handicapped and disabled people within the community. The general practice unit team has obviously got an important role to play in the support for disabled people within the community, and I see this as a mental health activity. I do not know to what extent it falls under the ambit of mental illness, but I think it should fall within it.

Dr P. Freeling: I think one theme not emphasized enough although inherent in a lot of what has been said, is the relative lack of training in research method and research experience for general practitioners. Even in vocational training, general practitioners are not given the opportunity to gain skills and perceptions which enable them to share in research rather than be studied. I think it is a pity – although we are very grateful to them – that we have had to rely on the enterprise of charitable organizations such as the Mental Health Foundation to get anything off the ground in the way of training programmes for general practitioners, particularly in psychiatric research. We are grateful for the Mental Health Foundation, but perhaps the DHSS and the universities might see this an an appropriate move for them to follow.

Dr Irvine: One of the main reasons for the college's concern – which is well shared by our colleagues in academic departments – about where we go from here in research, is that we have not actually got a coherent research strategy worked out. We are, though, much clearer now that we are past the stage of organizing and implementing vocational training, that this is the next major area which has to be examined. My feeling is that in looking for research scholarships; in creating protected time for young principals to be attached to departments of general practice to do the kind of fellowships that David Morrell has pioneered around St Thomas's; in seeking attachments to multi-disciplinary health care research units, and to other units in other disciplines; we are at the stage where we need to be in order to take every research opportunity we can get to increase the number and nucleus of practitioners in the subject who have these skills. The starting point has to come from us, and other people have to react rather than take the initiative themselves.

Professor Jefferys: We need much more research on outcomes from the patient's point of view. The kinds of measures of outcome that are simply changes in the GPs workload, more or less consultation with patients, are not in themselves adequate; we have to tackle functional measures which concentrate on patients and different forms of treatment. It is only when we really begin to establish the kinds of measures at that level, that it seems to me that we shall be able to see whether or not the shifts and changes in workload apply. In this connection, people should not talk about general practitioners bearing the whole burden of mental illness in this community. It is the patients and the patients' relatives who bear the burden; general practitioners, like hospital consultants, can escape. A lot of other people cannot.

Dr I. Falloon: It seems that we are talking about a mental illness service rather than a mental health service. A great many of the problems we see in psychiatry can be seen as mental illness. However, a number of the problems seen in general practice and other primary care settings (and we have not mentioned other agencies such as the churches and the police, which provide much primary care in the community) are really mental health problems, where somebody comes with some kind of dysphoria which might reach case proportions on research instruments but in fact would not be identified as a mental illness or as a nervous breakdown. We do not have large numbers of people who see themselves as having a mental health problem; they are dysphoric, unhappy with their lives, or have problems with living. These problems are probably not technically within the illness framework of the National Health Service, but they are certainly within the mental health remit. We have not taken much interest in classifying and developing these problems in the framework of an educative health promotion service. I wonder whether the DHSS has really taken this into consideration.

Professor I. Marks: I should like to put together the theme we discussed earlier this morning about one in five psychiatrists now working in primary care and the comments made by Dr Irvine about the attempts being built into general practice to have quality control and assurance. Perhaps this is the time also for the DHSS and the Royal College of Psychiatrists to give thought to how quality control and assurance is going to be built into the practice of psychiatrists in primary care.

Michael Shepherd

Chairman's closing remarks

In opening the conference the Chief Medical Officer took an historical perspective. He went back only three years in attempting to indicate the interest of the Department of Health and Social Security in this field, but made no mention of the tripartite meeting involving the Royal College of Psychiatrists, the Royal College of General Practitioners and the Association of Directors of Social Services held nine years ago under the auspices of the Department. The Chief Medical Officer of the day was reported as saying that he was undertaking to invite representatives of the DHSS to discuss the subject, including the possible role of the community physician. In his view, furthermore, the joint meeting had been highly successful and he was sure this was one of the ways in which people improved their understanding and by which progress in the community mental illness services might be inspired. He felt that the time had come to re-examine the traditional way in which services were provided.

All that was nine years ago. Since then there has been a deafening silence from the DHSS. During this period, however, there has been one major shift of opinion concerning policy. In the 1970s, as Henkel and Kogan have pointed out:

'It was assumed that policy makers and scientists belonged to quite different knowledge systems and institutions, and carry their respective roles best when care divisions of expertise and task are maintained. The policy makers are well able to formulate their research needs and there is a strong, independent scientific community with the research capacity and the experience to meet those needs under contract.'

That view has since been modified and it is interesting that at the end of their report, Henkel and Kogan put forward alternative models, one of which seems, perhaps unwittingly, to have dominated this meeting. This is that in health and personal and social services research there can be multiple authorities and multiple knowledge systems and that a key issue in the promotion of policy should link research with a better understanding of the policy process and the relationship between different forms of knowledge and action.

That is about as far as one is able to go in delineating the activities of the policy-makers and their possible policy initiatives, because most of us are not privy to their discussions and can merely try to indicate the directions in which we would like to see things moving. What about the professional community which has, understandably, taken up much of the discussion? In organizing the programme for the meeting we have tried to put on a window display simply to illustrate the spectrum of available activities, and participants will doubtless emphasize different aspects of the work, according to their own interests.

On the evidence presented, my own view would be first, that in practically every area there is a great deal to be done. We can define the field, I think, a little more clearly than we could ten or fifteen years ago, but the amount of research that has been carried out turns out to be small. Of all the topics which have been covered, I agree that definition and classification are fundamental. The case for a glossary of terms is a strong one when so many concepts are ill defined. Not only 'community' but 'hospital' and 'mental health' are still vague entities and Dr Horder has defined a general practitioner as 'mortar between the bricks as well as one of the bricks'.

In view of Dr Ryle's comments, furthermore, I feel I should single out for very brief mention that most ambiguous term 'psychotherapy'. His use of selected misquotations deflects attention from the central issue concerning psychotherapy in the context of this meeting. This, I think, is the conclusion reached by Jerome Frank who cannot be accused of bias against psychotherapy and whose book, *Persuasion and Healing*, is a major landmark in research in this field. Elsewhere, Frank writes:

'With most patients the placebo may be as effective as psychotherapy because the placebo condition contains the necessary and possibly the sufficient ingredient for much of the beneficial effect for all forms of psycho-therapy. This is a helping person who listens to the patients' complaints and offers a procedure to relieve them thereby inspiring the patients' hopes and combating demoralisation.'

(Frank 1983)

What Frank and many other sympathetic observers, including myself, are suggesting, is that serious attention should be focused on the non-specific placebo effect which tends so often to be discarded but is in fact the key factor in this sphere. Perhaps I should remind Dr Ryle of his father's comment that psychology is more than half the practice of medicine. With alternative medicine sprouting up all around us I would further suggest to the DHSS that placebology could prove to be a cost-effective sphere of enquiry.

This meeting has made it clear that most of the research so far has been carried out by either psychiatrists or social scientists in a particular field in the mental health problems. Dr Irvine's point, which is one that I and some of my colleagues have been urging for some time, is that if this field is to move forward, something has to be done to bring in general practitioners on a more active basis. The whole question of how that should be done is, I think, a policy matter, but it may be worth recalling what Lord Platt wrote on this subject when he discussed the issue of research in general practice thirty years ago:

'The conventional picture of the research worker is that of a rather austere man in a white coat with a background of complicated glassware. My idea of a research worker, on the other hand, is a man who brushes his teeth on the left side of his mouth only so as to use the other side as a control and to see if toothbrushing has any effect on the incidence of caries. If he has been badly educated in elementary principles, he might clean only his top teeth and not the bottom ones, but that would admit a possible error of selection for the top and bottom sets being morphologically different, may differ inherently in their resistance to disease. If he is a really good worker, on the other hand, he will urge his brother, preferably an identical twin, to clean only the right side and compare results. The cultivation of this approach becomes crucial because the spectrum of disease presented to the general practitioner is quite different from that encountered in hospital and constitutes a special area of inquiry in its own right.'

In the field of mental health, as well as of physical health, there is a great deal of research which general practitioners could undertake by themselves or in collaboration with others. In the long run their contribution should prove indispensable to further progress.

REFERENCES

Henkel, M. and Kogan, M. (1981) *The DHSS Funded Research Units: the process of review*. London: Brunel University, Department of Government.

Frank, J. D. (1973) *Persuasion and Healing: A Comparative Study of Psychotherapy*. Baltimore: Johns Hopkins Press.

—— (1983) The placebo is psychotherapy. *The Behavioral and Brain Sciences* 6: 291–92.

Platt, R. (1953) Opportunities for research in general practice. *British Medical Journal* i: 377–80.

PART 8

PRIORITIES AND IDEAS FOR RESEARCH ON MENTAL HEALTH IN PRIMARY CARE SETTINGS

Greg Wilkinson and Paul Williams

Priorities and ideas for research on mental health in primary care settings

INTRODUCTION

In this study, we took the opportunity to investigate a group of experts' (clinicians, research workers, and policy makers) priorities and ideas for research on mental health in primary care settings. This was done in conjunction with their participation, by invitation, at the Conference. A more detailed account of this work is given elsewhere (Wilkinson and Williams 1985).

Our strategy involved using the Delphi questionnaire method of studying group opinion (Dalkey 1969). This technique was originally developed in a business context for eliciting opinion on questions for which there were no definitive answers and which could not be 'evaluated in the classical sense' (Pill 1971). The main features of the method are anonymity, feedback, and iteration. Participants in a Delphi study are given information and their anonymous judgements on specific questions are obtained; summaries of the respondents' judgements are prepared and returned to them; and, their judgements are solicited again. This process may be continued, depending on the reason for the Delphi study, until the change in group opinion between successive judgements is negligible.

The Delphi method has been used in a variety of medical settings (Milholland, Wheeler, and Heieck 1973; Romm and Hulka 1979; Koplan and

Farer 1980; Lyons 1981), including the design of a health policy research and development system (Gustafson *et al.* 1975), for forecasting trends in health care organizations (Starkweather, Gelwicks, and Newcomer *et al.* 1975), and to determine health priorities (Kumaran *et al.* 1976; Moscovice *et al.* 1977). Two recent British applications are particularly illustrative for our purposes. First, Charlton *et al.* (1981) have described a Delphi study of the National Health Service (NHS) spending priorities of professional and lay policy-makers in the Kent health area; and second, Bond and Bond (1982) have conducted a Delphi survey of clinical nursing research priorities with a sample of nurses working in the north of England.

Our aim was to obtain information from experts in the field about their priorities and ideas for research on mental health in primary care settings: (1) by asking them to allocate hypothetical annual research budgets; and (2) by inviting them to respond to open-ended questions. In keeping with the importance of economic appraisal, the focus of all our questions was on research which was likely to maximize the benefits for service developments.

METHOD

Subjects

All participants at the conference on mental illness in primary care settings were considered eligible to take part in the study, except for staff of the Department of Health and Social Security (DHSS) and members of the DHSS Mental Illness Research Liaison Group (MIRLG). The sample was randomly divided into two sub-groups (I and II).

Design

The study was conducted as a Delphi survey in two rounds. In round one, four weeks before the conference took place, all eligible participants were sent (1) a postal questionnaire (questionnaire A) and (2) the MIRLG annotated list of 'subjects needing further investigation in the primary care field' (Department of Health and Social Security 1980). Each participant was asked to return the completed form within two weeks. In round two, sub-group I were sent another postal questionnaire (questionnaire B) two weeks before the Conference began and were requested to return it before the Conference started. Immediately after the Conference, sub-group II were sent questionnaire B.

Questionnaires

These were developed on the basis of the MIRLG strategy statement, 'Research into Prevention of Mental Illness and Services for the Mentally Ill'

– including its Appendix A – 'subjects needing further investigation in the primary care field' (Department of Health and Social Security 1980). Participants were told to answer all questions from their own point of view, that there were no 'right' or 'wrong' answers, and they were assured of confidentiality.

Questionnaire A (round one): Questionnaire A asked participants for personal background details, and then consisted of two main sections.

The first section invited participants to allocate hypothetical annual research budgets for research on mental illness in primary care settings, in order to maximize the likely benefits for service developments. They were asked to write sums of money in boxes, in response to the following:

1. Distribute a £10 million research budget among six 'priority areas . . . in which research needs to be promoted' (Department of Health and Social Security 1980) (i.e., chronically disabling mental illness, children and adolescents, emergency and compulsory admission to hospital, primary care, neuroses and associated disorders of personality, and the elderly mentally ill).
2. Distribute a £1 million research budget among seven 'subjects needing further investigation in the primary care field' (Department of Health and Social Security 1980) (i.e., problems of mental health presenting to primary care services, psychiatric screening in general practice, effectiveness of treatment measures, training requirements for family doctors in psychiatric skills, role and training requirements for social workers, professional role definitions, and medical patterns of work).
3. Distribute a £100,000 annual research budget *cut* among the seven subjects for investigation in the primary care field.
4. Distribute a £100,000 annual research budget *increase* among the seven subjects for investigation in the primary care field.

The second section invited the participants to write answers to open-ended questions about their ideas for research on mental illness in primary care settings. They were asked to consider research from the point of view of service developments, and to respond to the following:

5. State what you think are likely to be the most productive topics for research in each of the seven subjects in the primary care field.
6. Suggest additional main subjects for investigations in the primary care field which may have come to your attention since the MIRLG strategy was made known (Department of Health and Social Security 1980).

Questionnaire B (round two): Questionnaire B contained identical questions to those in 1 to 4 in Questionnaire A above, but, in addition, provided results of the median allocations made in round one by the individual respondent and by all respondents taken together.

Content analysis

Respondents' ideas about further research were collated and examined by content analysis, a 'method of reducing unstructured records, either written or verbal into a quantifiable form . . . one studies not only what is said, but also the form of the material and the grammatical presentation. . . . Omissions are also noted' (Patten and Press 1975).

RESULTS

Description of sample

One hundred and eleven conference participants were eligible to take part in the study. Ninety-four (85 per cent) (72 men and 22 women; mean age 44 years; age range 25–68 years) returned questionnaires that contained usable information. There were 44 psychiatrists, 18 general practitioners, 20 from social science disciplines (psychology, sociology, and social work), and 12 from a variety of other professions, e.g. statisticians. Forty gave their main occupation as research work, 34 indicated that it was clinical work, 5 that it was administration, 4 that it was policy making, 9 that it was a combination of the above, and in 2 cases the respondent was retired.

Priorities

Detailed findings regarding the respondents' priorities are reported elsewhere (Wilkinson and Williams 1985).

The results obtained from sub-groups I and II were very similar to each other, and they are not, therefore, reported separately. The median allocations made by the professional and occupational groups were analysed.

1. *Distribution of £10 million for research into six priority areas*. There was almost perfect agreement between the groups in their rankings of the hypothetical annual research budget distributions of £10 million among the six priority areas. The three top-ranked priority areas were, in descending order: (1) *primary care*; (2) *the elderly mentally ill*; and (3) *chronically disabling mental illness*.

2. *Distribution of £1 million for research into the seven subjects in the primary care priority area*. As before, there were high levels of agreement in the respondents' rankings of hypothetical annual research budget distributions of £1 million amongst the seven subjects in the primary care priority area. The three top-ranked subjects for investigation were: (1) *effectiveness of treatment measures*; (2) *problems of mental health presenting to primary care services*; and (3) *training requirements for family doctors in psychiatric skills*.

3. *Distribution of hypothetical research budget cut of £100,000 among the*

seven subjects in the primary care priority area. There was again a generally high level of agreement in the rankings of the hypothetical annual research budget distributions of a *cut* in allocation of £100,000 for research into the seven subjects in the primary care priority area. The three lowest ranked subjects (i.e., those subjects which received the least *cut* in budget allocation) were: (1) *effectiveness of treatment measures* (ranked seven); (2) *training requirements for family doctors*; and (3) *problems of mental health presenting to primary care services.*

4. *Distribution of hypothetical research budget increase of £100,000 among the seven subjects in the primary care priority area.* Again, there were generally high levels of agreement in the rankings of the hypothetical annual research budget distribution of an increase of £100,000 for research into the seven subjects in the primary care priority area. The three highest ranked subjects were, in decreasing order: (1) *effectiveness of treatment measures*; (2) *problems of mental health presenting to primary care services*; and (3) *training requirements for family doctors in psychiatric skills.*

Ideas

Respondents were invited to write answers to open-ended questions about their ideas for research on mental illness in primary care settings. There was some overlap of ideas among the various categories.

A. *Problems of mental health presenting to primary care services*

topic	ideas	examples
classification	19	'development of an acceptable system of classification – almost certainly this will require to be multiaxial'
specific mental disorders	16	'those affecting the chronically mentally ill, and substance abuse'
clinical outcome	9	'studies of the natural history of mental disorders in primary care settings, and their association with physical illness and social circumstances'
all	73	respondents seldom acknowleged the existence of previous related research or the problems involved in carrying out such investigations

B. *Psychiatric screening in general practice*

topic	ideas	examples
specific mental disorders	18	'the elderly, families, and those who abuse alchohol'
clinical outcome of screening	13	'does screening prevent misdiagnosis? If so, does it make any difference in the end, i.e. are there enough treatment resources?'
screening instruments	8	'develop and assess screening instruments suitable for use in general practice'
economic outcome of screening	7	'evaluate the cost effectiveness of psychiatric screening in general practice'
all	66	only three of the ideas appeared to draw attention to the general practitioner's role in screening, e.g. 'concentrate on case detection and definition *in the surgery* as part of a normal interview'. One respondent answered as follows: 'the only research I would consider is on its feasibility'

C. *Effectiveness of treatment measures*

topic	ideas	examples
clinical outcome	15	'outcome research using adequately complex models of intervention, and individual as well as group targets for intervention, with controls'
comparison of psychotropic drugs with other treatments	14	'controlled trials of effectiveness of drugs v. support/counselling v. behaviour therapy in the treatment of anxiety/depression'
particular services or personnel	12	'comparative evaluation of formal (social services) and informal social support'
most effective use of psychotropic drugs	10	'particularly in long-term use'
measurement of clinical outcome	5	'develop measures of effectiveness' and 'effectiveness for what? Providing patient satisfaction? Reducing intensity of symptoms? Producing behaviour change? Long-term life change?'
behaviour therapy	4	'applicability of behaviour modification and anxiety management interventions'

topic	ideas	examples
counselling psychotherapy	3	'the appropriate role of counselling/ psychotherapy in primary care'
all	79	only two ideas concerned economic aspects of the effectiveness of treatment measures and treatment compliance

D. *Training requirements for family doctors in psychiatric skills*

topic	ideas	examples
skills in non-pharmacological treatment techniques	15	'We need to heighten GPs' interviewing skills and communication. GPs need much more awareness and understanding of the significance of patients' communications about emotional problems'
clinical management and outcome	14	'studies of effects of training on clinical management' and 'case control studies of GPs trained in psychiatric listening skills versus those not so trained, in relation to clinical outcome'
recognition of mental disorder	9	'the crucial area is that involving factors which affect the practitioner's initial decision to consider the possibility of psychiatric disorder'
aspects of psychiatric management in general practice	8	'devise experiments which test the efficacy of different psychiatric management strategies: treatment choices and treatment methods'
training schemes	4	'make available adequate postgraduate facilities for training'
all	61	other ideas concerned diagnostic skills, interview styles, and behaviour therapy skills. There were few ideas of an experimental nature, and one respondent considered that this research should be undertaken 'only if based as well-tested methods – preferably tested by double-blind methods'

E. *Role and training requirements for social workers*

topic	ideas	examples
teamwork	13	'examine relationships between social and medical services' and 'evaluate patterns of working with GPs on a professional contractual basis, i.e. written understanding'
clinical outcome	8	'evaluate different intervention strategies and their effects on patient well-being (overall, and in a given practice)'
counselling	5	'increase the emphasis on time-limited goal-specific intervention with individuals and families'
models of social work intervention	4	'assess the value of consultation/education versus direct patient care/treatment'
all	53	other ideas concerned specialist/generic social work training, preventive work, the organization of social work, and the Mental Health Act. There were ten vague comments on this topic, and one respondent stated that this subject was of 'marginal' importance. Only two ideas contained the notion that an empirical approach to this subject might be of value

F. *Professional role definitions*

topic	ideas	examples
teamwork	15	'methods of working in teams (with mixed compositions) and evaluations of these in relation to client outcome'
specific professional roles	14	'study the value of giving surgery receptionist and nurses some training in acquiring understanding and skills relevant to mental health'
role structure (clear/ blurred)	9	'investigate the nature and roots of intra- and inter-disciplinary conflict in relation to a sample of patients of similar age and diagnosis'

topic	ideas	examples
all	59	there were five personal statements on this topic, and five negative comments, e.g. 'I doubt if this is researchable in any useful way'. Three respondents mentioned economic appraisal as part of their research idea; two respondents considered the role of volunteers; and only one discussed research methodology

G. Medical patterns of work

topic	ideas	examples
psychiatric team in the community	27	'a cost-effectiveness study of a) the psychiatric team confined to the traditional hospital setting, b) the psychiatric team based in general practice surgeries, c) the psychiatric team (including psychology and social work) providing a comprehensive community-based service'
specific activities	10	'examine the effectiveness of time spent on psychotherapy in relation to subsequent patient demands'
specific personnel	6	'the work of community psychiatric nurses in general practice'
delegation	4	'delegation of identification of relapses to relatives and other voluntary carers (after training)'
inter-practice variation	4	'comparison of work patterns between groups/ individual GPs, in relation to: referral rates; prescribing patterns and rates; the outcome of care; the "natural history" of disorders'
all	64	one idea (each) concerned crisis intervention, referrals to specialist care, and the use of computers in this area of work. There were 13 vague comments or personal statements. Four respondents mentioned the cost-benefit approach to this subject, and two mentioned the need to 'identify the frequency of ineffective, repetitive interventions'

Additional main subjects for investigation in the primary care field

Subjects that were predicted to have a high priority for investigation within the next ten years were the treatment of patients with chronic mental illness in general practice, the management of alcoholism in primary care settings; the evaluation of the role of self-help and voluntary organizations in mental health care; and the use of 'expert systems' and information technology in the care of the mentally ill in general practice.

DISCUSSION

Respondents' priorities for research which maximized benefits for service developments were found to be generally alike regardless of professional or occupational grouping, as was shown by their similar round one and round two budget distributions. Sub-groups I and II produced results which were indistinguishable from each other, and from those of the other respondents taken together. This suggests that the respondents' research priorities were securely based and were not appreciably influenced by feedback or attendance at the Conference, which is perhaps not surprising, in view of their expert knowledge and experience of the field.

The four questions in the priorities sections of the questionnaire were based upon the MIRLG strategy statement (Department of Health and Social Security 1980). The first two, the distribution of £10 million among six priority areas and the distribution of £1 million among seven subjects for investigation, were designed to simulate the health economic practice of programme (or, in this case, sub-programme) budgeting. Because this is intended to

> 'provide data relevant to "broad-brush" planning it is not necessary to present precise details on the budgets. . . . Programme planning is a planning framework which can influence the decision-makers not only to take an overview of the . . . services generally, but to take an overview which relates to broad health care goals.'   (Mooney *et al.* 1980)

The criticism that the MIRLG categories for research were not mutually exclusive is acknowledged in this approach.

The respondents' *top-ranked priority area* was *primary care* (again, not surprisingly, in view of the nature of the study sample), and this was followed by the elderly mentally ill and chronically disabling mental illness priority areas. Their *top-ranked subject for investigation* in the primary care area was *effectiveness of treatment measures*, and this was followed by problems of mental health presenting to primary care services, and training requirements for family doctors in psychiatric skills. Respondents were apparently willing to 'spend' roughly two-thirds of their budgets on the three priority areas, and about half their budgets on the three subjects for investigation. It is worth noting that these rankings were made on a cardinal scale, that is, since the respondents allocated their budgets out to different areas, it is possible to state that, for example, a £2 million allocation to one field is twice a £1 million allocation to another.

The distributions of either a *cut*, or an *increase*, of £100,000 in a hypothetical annual research budget for research into the seven subjects designated by the MIRLG as needing investigation in the primary care priority area, were included to simulate the economic practice of marginal analysis. Economic choices in health services research are not normally couched in terms of whether or not to devote scarce resources to a given priority area or subject for investigation, but, rather, they are framed in terms of the following. Given the current mix of provision, should more or fewer resources be provided to maximize the likely benefits? In such circumstances, incremental or marginal costs and benefits of expansion or contraction of research programmes are more relevant than the total costs and benefits of the existing programmes (Mooney *et al.* 1980).

It then becomes apparent that the appropriate questions here are:

1. if a given amount of resources are available to fund a research programme, could these resources be redistributed within the programme to result in an increased total benefit, for service developments, from the programme?;
2. if resources for the programme were cut, how best could this cut be distributed to ensure the minimum loss in benefit from the programme?; and
3. if additional resources were made available for the programme, how best could these be distributed to ensure the maximum increase in benefit from the programme?

The results for the distribution of either a cut, or an increase, of hypothetical annual research budget showed that the respondents' top-ranked subject for investigation, from the point of view of maximizing the benefit for service developments, was effectiveness of treatment measures. The second- and third-ranked subjects were problems of mental health presenting to primary care services and training requirements for family doctors in psychiatric skills.

Respondents were found to be highly consistent in their priorities for subjects needing investigation (Wilkinson and Williams 1985). The ranking of their distributions of a hypothetical annual research budget of £1 million and a budget increase of £100,000 was identical, and there was a very strong inverse relationship between these rankings and the rankings obtained for the distribution of a hypothetical annual research budget cut of £100,000.

Content analysis of respondents' ideas for productive research, from the point of view of service developments, in each of the seven subjects in the primary care field, showed that their main priorities were for, respectively, studies of the classification, management and outcome of the whole range of mental disorders, affecting patients of all ages, in primary care settings; the evaluation of screening for mental disorders in general practice in relation to the clinical outcome for patients; the need for studies of the effectiveness of treatment for patients with mental disorders in general practice, particularly psychotropic drug treatment; the training of family doctors in non-pharmacological techniques of psychiatric interventions in general practice, in relation to the clinical management and outcome for patients with mental disorders; team work, and the roles of specific personnel, in relation to the clinical outcome for patients with mental disorders in primary care settings; and, lastly, the evaluation of the impact of the psychiatric team in general practice. We were intrigued, in particular, to note that there were infrequent references to developments in information technology and the economics of health care in the respondents' statements about research into mental health in primary care settings.

It has to be stressed that content analysis is of uncertain reliability and validity. The ideas put forward by respondents were at times subject to our interpretation, since they were not always precisely stated. In addition, no account was taken of the existence of previous work or of methodological problems in the assessment of respondents' ideas. On the other hand, content analysis is one of the few techniques available for analysing unstructured material, which might be of great potential value and might otherwise be lost to any form of empirical assessment.

These results may be taken to be indicative of experts' current subjective priorities for research into mental illness in primary care settings. We would emphasize, however, that the experts' priorities were obtained using only one of several possible methodologies, albeit one which has the merit of requiring participants to give explicit responses. The findings could usefully be combined with data from other sources to inform policymakers' decisions about future research in this area. In relation to this, one respondent added the rider: 'administrative needs for information and research priorities should not in my view be equated. Allocation of research funding should, I think, be very dependent on a question being researchable and on researchers having imaginative and practical proposals.' This view gives rise to the suggestion that there is also a need for further enquiries into the relationship between research and policy in this area. Efforts to improve resource allocation for research into mental health in primary care settings appear to be necessary. Initially, they might best be centred on the achievement of greater precision and quantification in the definition of research and policy objectives.

ACKNOWLEDGEMENTS

This study was carried out as part of a research programme planned by the General Practice Research Unit at the Institute of Psychiatry, under the direction of Professor Michael Shepherd and with the support of the

Department of Health and Social Security. We would like to thank Professor Gavin Mooney, Health Economics Research Unit, University of Aberdeen, and Dr J. A. Roberts, London School of Hygiene and Tropical Medicine, for their helpful advice on the design of the questionnaires. Mr John Elvidge, Scottish Office, commented helpfully on a draft of this report.

The views expressed are those of the authors and do not necessarily reflect those of the Department of Health and Social Security.

REFERENCES

Bond, S. and Bond, J. (1982) A Delphi survey of clinical nursing research priorities. *Journal of Advanced Nursing* 7: 565–75.

Charlton, J. R. H., Patrick, D. L., Matthews, G., and West, P. A. (1981) Spending priorities in Kent: A Delphi study. *Journal of Epidemiology and Community Health* 35: 288–92.

Dalkey, N. C. (1969) *The Delphi Method. An Experimental Study of Group Opinion.* Santa Monica: The Rand Corporation.

Department of Health and Social Security (1980) *Research into prevention of mental illness and services for the mentally ill.* London: Department of Health and Social Security.

Gustafson, D. H., Delbecq, A. L., Hansen, M., and Myers, R. G. (1975) Design of a health policy research and development system for Wisconsin. *Inquiry* 12: 3.

Koplan, J. P. and Farer, L. S. (1980) Choice of preventive treatment for isoniazid-resistant tuberculous infection. *Journal of the American Medical Association* 244: 2736–740.

Kumaran, K., Hansen, R. C., and Rowe, M. (1976) The Delphi technique in a psychiatric hospital. *Dimensions in Health Service* 53: 32–4.

Lyons, H. (1981) Solution by consensus. *Health and Social Services Journal* 91: 1515–516.

Milholland, A. V., Wheeler, S. G., and Heieck, J. J. (1973) Medical assessment by a Delphi group opinion technic. *New England Journal of Medicine* 288: 1272–275.

Mooney, G. H., Russell, E. M., and Weir, R. D. (1980) *Choices for Health Care.* London: Macmillan.

Moscovice, I., Armstrong, P., Shortell, S., and Barnett, R. (1977) Health services research for decision-making: the use of the Delphi technique to determine health priorities. *Health, Politics, Policy, and Law* 2(3): 288–410.

Patten, M. P. and Press, J. (1975) Sociological methods in psychiatric research. In P. Sainsbury and N. Kreitman (eds) *Methods of Psychiatric Research.* London: Oxford University Press.

Pill, J. (1971) The Delphi method: Substance, context, a critique and an annotated bibliography. *Socioeconomic Planning Sciences* 5: 57–71.

Romm, F. J. and Hulka, B. S. (1979) Developing criteria for quality of care assessment: Effect of the Delphi technique. *Health Services Research* 14: 309–412.

Starkweather, D. B., Gelwicks, L., and Newcomer, R. (1975) Delphi forecasting of health care organisations. *Inquiry* 12: 4.

Wilkinson, G. and Williams, P. (1985) Priorities for research on mental health in primary care settings. *Psychological Medicine* 15, 707–15.

Conference on Mental Illness in Primary Care Settings, Institute of Psychiatry, London: 17–18 July 1984: participants and observers

LIST OF PARTICIPANTS

Dr M. E. Abrams,
Department of Health and Social Security,
14 Russell Square,
London WC1B 5EP

Dr E. D. Acheson,
Chief Medical Officer,
Department of Health and Social Security,
Alexander Fleming House,
Elephant and Castle,
London SE1 6BY

Mr A. C. Adams,
Social Work Services Group,
43 Jeffrey Street,
Edinburgh EH1 1DN

Prof. A. M. Adelstein,
Department of Medical Statistics and
  Epidemiology,
London School of Hygiene and Tropical
  Medicine,
Keppel Street (Gower Street),
London WC1E 7HT

Prof. G. W. Ashcroft,
Department of Mental Health,
Clinical Research Centre,
Royal Cornhill Hospital, Cornhill Road,
Aberdeen AB9 2ZH

Dr Lia Bandera,
Istituto di Ricerche Farmacologiche 'Mario
  Negri',
Via Eritrea 62,
20157 Milano,
Italy

Mr P. Beard,
Director of Nursing Services (Mental
  Health),
Mental Health Unit,
309 Grays's Inn Road,
London WC1X 8QF

Dr P. Bebbington,
MRC Social Psychiatry Unit,
Institute of Psychiatry,
De Crespigny Park,
Denmark Hill,
London SE5 8AF

Dr K. Bergmann,
Consultant Psychiatrist,
The Bethlem Royal Hospital and The
    Maudsley Hospital,
Denmark Hill,
London SE5 8AZ

Dr T. H. Bewley,
Consultant Psychiatrist,
Tooting Bec Hospital,
Tooting Bec Road,
London SW17 8BL

Sir Douglas A. K. Black,
1 Park Square West,
London NW1 4LJ

Dr R. Blacker,
Honorary Senior Registrar,
Department of Psychological Medicine,
St. Bartholomew's Hospital,
West Smithfield,
London EC1A 7BE

Dr M. Bloor,
MRC Medical Sociology Unit,
Institute of Medical Sociology,
Westburn Road,
Aberdeen AB9 2ZE

Dr Paola Bollini,
Istituto di Ricerche Farmacologiche 'Mario
    Negri',
Via Eritrea 62,
20157 Milano,
Italy

Dr K. Bridges,
Clinical Research Fellow,
Department of Psychiatry,
University of South Manchester,
Stopford Building,
Oxford Road,
Manchester M13 9PT

Dr Monica Briscoe,
General Practice Research Unit,
Institute of Psychiatry,
De Crespigny Park,
Denmark Hill,
London SE5 8AF

Dr A. Brook,
The Tavistock Clinic,
Tavistock Centre,
120 Belsize Lane,
London NW3 5BA

Dr D. I. Brough,
Consultant Psychiatrist,
Lewisham Hospital,
Lewisham High Street,
London SE13 6LH

Dr A. C. Brown,
Consultant Senior Lecturer in Mental
    Health,
Department of Mental Health,
University of Bristol,
39/41 St Michael's Hill,
Bristol BS2 8DZ

Dr B. J. Burns, Acting Chief,
Applied Biometrics Research Branch,
Division of Biometry and Epidemiology,
Alcohol, Drug Abuse and Mental Health
    Administration,
5600 Fishers Lane, Rockville,
Maryland 20857,
USA

Dr M. V. Burton,
Clinical Psychologist,
Walsgrave Hospital,
Clifford Bridge Road,
Walsgrave,
Coventry CV2 2DX

Dr J. R. Butler,
Acting Director,
Health Services Research Unit,
Cornwallis Building,
The University,
Canterbury,
Kent CT2 7NF

Ms Elizabeth A. Campbell,
Department of Psychiatry,
Warneford Hospital,
Oxford OX3 7JX

Dr A. Cartwright,
Institute for Social Studies in Medical Care,
14 South Hill Park,
Hampstead,
London NW3 2SB

Ms Cherie Chadwick,
General Practice Research Unit,
Institute of Psychiatry,
De Crespigny Park,
Denmark Hill,
London SE5 8AF

Mrs M. J. Charlesworth,
Director of Nursing Services,
Towers Hospital,
Gipsy Lane,
Humberstone,
Leicester LE5 0TD

Dr A. Cheng,
Taiwan Provincial Kaohsiung Mental
  Hospital,
2 Fu Cheng Street,
Ling Ya District,
Kaohsiung,
Taiwan,
Republic of China

Prof. A. W. Clare,
Department of Psychological Medicine,
St. Bartholomew's Hospital Medical
  College,
West Smithfield,
London EC1A 7BE

Dr I. R. Clout, OBE,
Chairman,
The Bethlem Royal Hospital and The
  Maudsley Hospital Special Health
  Authority,
Denmark Hill,
London SE5 8AZ

Prof. B. Cooper,
Abteilung Epidemiologische Psychiatrie,
Zentralinstitut fur Seelische Gesundheit,
6800 Mannheim 1 J5,
Postfach 5970
West Germany

Prof. J. E. Cooper,
A Floor,
South Block,
University Hospital,
Queen's Medical Centre,
Nottingham NG7 2RD

Prof. J. R. M. Copeland,
University Department of Psychiatry,
Royal Liverpool Hospital,
PO Box 147,
Liverpool L69 3BX

Dr R. H. Corney,
General Practice Research Unit,
Institute of Psychiatry,
De Crespigny Park,
Denmark Hill,
London SE5 8AF

Dr C. M. Corser,
Consultant Psychiatrist,
Bangour Village Hospital,
Broxburn,
West Lothian EH52 6LW

Dr J. Crammer,
Reader,
Institute of Psychiatry,
De Crespigny Park,
Denmark Hill,
London SE5 8AF

Dr D. L. Crombie,
Director,
Birmingham Research Unit,
The Royal College of Practitioners,
Lordswood House,
54 Lordswood Road,
Harborne, Birmingham B17 9DB

Dr M. B. Dastgir,
Medical Officer,
Department of Health & Social Security,
Room B611, Alexander Fleming House,
Elephant and Castle,
London SE1 6BY

Dr M. B. Davies,
Medical Research Council,
20 Park Crescent,
London W1N 4AL

Prof. R. Harvard Davis,
Department of General Practice,
Welsh National School of Medicine,
Health Centre,
Maelfa,
Llanedeyrn
Cardiff CF3 7PN

Prof. Dr. med. H. Dilling,
Medizinische Hochschule Lubeck,
Klinik fur Psychiatrie,
Ratzeburger Allee 160,
D-2400 Lubeck 1,
West Germany

Dr B. Essex,
Sydenham Green Health Centre,
London

Dr Ian Falloon,
Buckingham Hospital,
Buckingham MK18 1NU

Dr P. Freeling,
St. George's Hospital Medical School,
Jenner Wing,
Level O,
Cranmer Terrace,
London SW17 0RE

Dr H. L. Freeman,
Consultant Psychiatrist,
Hope Hospital,
Eccles Old Road,
Salford,
Lancs M6 8HD

Dr J. Fry,
138 Croydon Road,
Beckenham,
Kent
BR3 4DG

Mrs J. M. Firth,
Under-Secretary,
Department of Health and Social Security,
Room B214, Alexander Fleming House,
Elephant and Castle,
London SE1 6BY

Mr J. Gabe,
General Practice Research Unit,
Institute of Psychiatry,
De Crespigny Park,
Denmark Hill,
London SE5 8AF

Prof. D. P. Goldberg,
Department of Psychiatry,
The University Hospital of South
    Manchester,
West Didsbury,
Manchester M20 8LR

Dr E. M. Goldberg,
Berkhamsted,
Hertfordshire

Mr G. A. Golding,
Department of Health and Social Security,
Room C420, Alexander Fleming House,
Elephant & Castle,
London SE1 6BY

Mr H. N. Grindrod,
Director of Social Services,
London Borough of Croydon,
Taberner House,
Park Lane,
Croydon CR9 2BA

Prof. B. Gurland,
Center for Geriatrics and Gerontology,
Faculty of Medicine,
Columbia University,
100 Haven Avenue,
Apt 29F,
New York, NY10032
USA

Dr D. R. Hannay,
Woodside Health Centre,
Barr Street,
Glasgow G20 7LR

Mr W. B. Harbert,
Director of Social Services,
County of Avon,
PO Box No 30, Avon House North,
St. James Barton,
Bristol BS99 7NB

Dr Marita Harper,
Senior Medical Officer,
Department of Health and Social Security,
Eileen House,
80–94 Newington Causeway,
London SE1 5EF

Dr C. M. Harris,
Department of General Practice,
St. Mary's Hospital Medical School,
Lisson Grove Health Centre,
Gateforth Street,
London NW8 8EG

Dr P. A. Harris,
PO Box 8,
Welwyn Garden City,
Hertfordshire AL7 3AY

Dr Ursula Haug,
Clinical Psychologist,
Department of General Practice,
St. Mary's Hospital Medical School,
Lisson Grove Health Centre,
Gateforth Street,
London NW8 8EG

Dr J. H. Henderson,
Regional Officer for Mental Health,
WHO Regional Office for Europe,
8 Scherfigsvej,
DK-2100,
Copenhagen 0
Denmark

Dr J. D. Hendry,
Lecturer in Mental Health,
Clinical Research Centre,
Royal Cornhill Hospital,
Cornhill Road,
Aberdeen AB9 2ZH

Prof. P. M. Higgins,
Department of General Practice,
Guy's Hospital Medical School,
St Thomas Street,
London SE1 9RT

Dr R. H. Higgs,
Director,
Department of General Practice Studies,
King's College Hospital Medical School,
Denmark Hill,
London SE5 8RX

Dr J. E. Holmes,
Consultant Psychiatrist,
Department of Psychological Medicine,
University College Hospital,
Gower Street,
London WC1

Dr J. Horder,
98 Regent's Park Road,
London NW1

Dr G. Horobin,
Deputy Director,
MRC Medical Sociology Unit,
Institute of Medical Sociology,
Westburn Road,
Aberdeen AB9 2ZE

Dr B. J. Hunt,
Community Physician (Research and
    Planning),
Brighton Health Authority,
Brighton General Hospital,
Elm Grove,
Brighton BN2 3EW

Dr P. Huxley,
Lecturer in Psychiatric Social Work,
Department of Psychiatry,
University of Manchester,
Stopford Building,
Oxford Road,
Manchester M13 9PT

Dr J. G. Ingham,
MRC Unit for Epidemiological Studies in
  Psychiatry,
University Department of Psychiatry,
Royal Edinburgh Hospital,
Morningside Park,
Edinburgh E10 5HF

Dr D. H. Irvine, OBE,
Redesdale,
Wansbeck Road,
Ashington,
Northumberland
NE63 8JE

Prof. M. Jefferys,
32 Bisham Gardens,
London N6 6DD

Dr R. Jenkins,
General Practice Research Unit,
Institute of Psychiatry,
De Crespigny Park,
Denmark Hill,
London SE5 8AF

Dr D. B. Kamerow, Epidemiology Fellow,
Primary Care Research Section, Room
  18C-14,
Division of Biometry and Epidemiology,
Alcohol, Drug Abuse and Mental Health
  Administration,
Rockville,
Maryland 20857
USA

Mr B. Kat,
District Psychologist,
Durham Health Authority,
County Hall,
Durham DH1 5UN

Univ. Doz. Dr H. Katschnig,
Psychiatrische Universitatsklinik,
Allgemeines Krankenhaus der Stadt Wien,
Wahringer Gurtel 74–76,
1090 Wien
Austria

Dr M. King,
General Practice Research Unit,
Institute of Psychiatry,
De Crespigny Park,
Denmark Hill,
London SE5 8AF

Prof. J. Knowelden,
Department of Community Medicine,
Medical School,
Beech Hill Road,
Sheffield S10 2RX

Prof. I. Kolvin,
Child Psychiatry Unit,
Hospital for Sick Children (Fleming
  Memorial),
Great North Road,
Newcastle-upon-Tyne NE2 3AZ

Mr C. Lake,
Nursing Officer,
Department of Health and Social Security,
Room C519, Alexander Fleming House,
Elephant and Castle,
London SE1 6BY

Dr Jennifer Lloyd,
Medical Officer,
Welsh Office,
Cathays Park,
Cardiff CF1 3NQ

The Hon Mr R. Loder,
Chairman,
The Mental Health Foundation,
8 Hallam Street,
London W1N 6DH

Dr G. Low-Beer,
Consultant Psychiatrist,
Horton Hospital,
Epsom,
Surrey

Dr A. Macdonald,
General Practice Research Unit,
Institute of Psychiatry,
De Crespigny Park,
Denmark Hill,
London SE5 8AF

Dr E. M. McLean,
Consultant Psychiatrist,
Springfield Hospital,
61 Glenburnie Road,
London SW17 7DJ

Mr P. V. Mancini,
Department of Health and Social Security,
Room 718, Friars House,
157–168 Blackfriars Road,
London SE1 8EU

Dr A. H. Mann,
Reader,
Academic Department of Psychiatry,
Royal Free Hospital School of Medicine,
Pond Street,
London NW3 2QG

Dr J. Mari,
General Practice Research Unit,
Institute of Psychiatry,
De Crespigny Park,
Denmark Hill,
London SE5 8AF

Prof. I. Marks,
Institute of Psychiatry,
De Crespigny Park,
Denmark Hill,
London SE5 8AF

Dr A. C. Markus,
The Health Centre,
East Street,
Thame,
Oxon OX9 3JZ

Dr S. T. Marzano,
Como,
Cia Mentana 30,
Italy

Dr P. G. W. Mason,
Senior Principal Medical Officer,
Department of Health and Social Security,
Alexander Fleming House,
Elephant and Castle,
London SE1 6BY

Dr Ingeborg Meller,
Nervenklinik der Universitat Munchen,
Psychiatrische Klinik und Poliklinik,
Nussbaumstrasse 7,
8000 München 2,
West Germany

Mrs Inge Midforth,
Principal Social Work Service Officer,
Department of Health and Social Security,
Room B415, Alexander Fleming House,
Elephant and Castle,
London SE1 6BY

Dr E. Miller,
District Psychologist,
Cambridge Health Authority,
Department of Psychiatry (Addenbrooke's
    Hospital),
2, Benett Place,
Lensfield Road,
Cambridge CB2 1EL

Dr A. R. K. Mitchell,
Consultant Psychiatrist,
Fulbourn Hospital,
Cambridge CB1 5EF

Prof. H. G. Morgan,
Department of Mental Health,
University of Bristol,
39/41 St. Michael's Hill,
Bristol BS2 8DZ

Prof. D. C. Morrell,
Department of General Practice,
St. Thomas' Hospital Medical School,
80 Kennington Road,
London SE11 6SP

Ms Joanna Murray,
General Practice Research Unit,
Institute of Psychiatry,
De Crespigny Park,
Denmark Hill,
London SE5 8AF

Ms June Neill,
National Institute for Social Work,
Mary Ward House,
5–7 Tavistock Place,
London WC1H 9SS

Dr P. J. Noble,
Chairman of the Medical Executive
   Committee,
The Bethlem Royal Hospital and The
   Maudsley Hospital,
Denmark Hill,
London SE5 8AZ

Dr J. Orley,
Senior Medical Officer,
WHO Division of Mental Health,
1211 Geneva 27,
Switzerland

Prof. E. S. Paykel,
Department of Psychiatry,
St. George's Hospital Medical School,
Jenner Wing,
Cranmer Terrace,
Tooting, London SW17 0RE

Dr J. E. Pedley,
Specialist in Community Medicine,
Aylesbury Vale Health Authority,
Peverel Court, Portway Road,
Stone, Aylesbury,
Bucks HP17 8RP

Sir Desmond Pond,
Chief Scientist,
Department of Health and Social Security,
Alexander Fleming House,
Elephant and Castle,
London SE1 6BY

Dr Ruth Porter,
Deputy Director,
The Ciba Foundation,
41 Portland Place,
London W1N 4BN

Dr Barbara Rashbass,
Medical Research Council,
20 Park Crescent,
London W1N 4AL

Dr R. Ratcliff,
Principal Medical Officer,
Scottish Home and Health Department,
St Andrews House,
Edinburgh EH1 3DE

Dr L. Ratoff,
363 Park Road,
Liverpool L8 9RD

Dr D. P. Richards,
Community Physician,
Community Health Services,
Croydon Health Authority,
Taberner House,
Park Lane,
Croydon, Surrey CR9 3BT

Dr J. A. Roberts,
Senior Lecturer in Health Economics,
Department of Community Health,
London School of Hygiene and Tropical
   Medicine,
Keppel Street (Gower Street),
London WC1E 7HT

Dr E. K. Rodrigo,
General Practice Research Unit,
Institute of Psychiatry,
De Crespigny Park,
Denmark Hill,
London SE5 8AF

Dr D. Rothman,
Senior Medical Officer,
Department of Health and Social Security,
Room B614, Alexander Fleming House,
Elephant and Castle,
London SE1 6BY

Dr A. Ryle,
Consultant Psychotherapist,
St. Thomas' Hospital Medical School,
80 Kennington Road,
London SE11 6SP

Dr R. Sadoun,
Unite de Recherches sur L'Epidemiologie
    des Troubles Mentaux,
U.110, 2ter Rue D'Alesia,
75014 Paris,
France

Dr N. Sartorius,
Director,
WHO Division of Mental Health,
1211 Geneva 27,
Switzerland

Mrs M. B. Sealey,
Director of Nursing Services (Community),
Croydon Health Authority,
Community Health Services,
Taberner House,
Park Lane,
Croydon, Surrey CR9 3BT

Dr D. Sharpe,
Department of General Practice,
St. Thomas' Hospital Medical School,
80 Kennington Road,
London SE11 6SP

Miss Daphne M. Shepherd,
Department of Social Work Studies,
The University of Southampton,
Southampton
SO9 5NH

Prof. Michael Shepherd,
Director,
General Practice Research Unit,
Institute of Psychiatry,
De Crespigny Park,
Denmark Hill,
London SE5 8AF

Dr A. Sippert,
Principal Medical Officer,
Department of Health and Social Security,
Room B306, Alexander Fleming House,
Elephant and Castle,
London SE1 6BY

Mr N. Smeeton,
General Practice Research Unit,
Institute of Psychiatry,
De Crespigny Park,
Denmark Hill,
London SE5 8AF

Dr S. Stansfeld,
General Practice Research Unit,
Institute of Psychiatry,
De Crespigny Park,
Denmark Hill,
London SE5 8AF

Dr R. E. Steel,
St Johns House,
28 Bromyard Road,
Worcester WR2 5BU

Dr G. Strathdee,
General Practice Research Unit,
Institute of Psychiatry,
De Crespigny Park,
Denmark Hill,
London SE5 8AF

Mr H. D. Swales,
The Sir Jules Thorn Charitable Trust,
24 Manchester Square,
London W1M 5AP

Mr J. Tait,
Principal Nursing Officer (Mental Health
    Division),
Department of Health and Social Security,
Room D305, Alexander Fleming House,
Elephant and Castle,
London SE1 6BY

Prof. M. Tansella,
Istituto di Psichiatria,
Policlinico,
37134 Verona
Italy

Dr D. Taylor,
Office of Health Economics.
12 Whitehall,
London SW1A 2DY

Prof. G. Teeling-Smith,
Office of Health Economics,
12 Whitehall,
London SW1A 2DY

Dr H. Tegner,
1 Forest Hill Road,
Honor Oak,
London SE22

Mr D. A. Tombs,
Director of Social Services,
The County Council of Hereford and
    Worcester,
County Hall,
Spetchley Road,
Worcester WR5 2NP

Dr J. E. C. Tower,
The Surgery,
Clerk's Field,
Headcorn,
Kent TN27 9QL

Dr P. J. Tyrer,
Consultant Psychiatrist,
Mapperley Hospital,
Porchester Road,
Nottingham NG3 6AA

Prof. J. L. Vazquez-Barquero,
Servicio de Psiquiatria y Psicologia Medica,
Centro Medico Nacional 'Marques de
    Valdecilla',
Facultad de Medicina,
Santander,
Spain

Dr D. C. Watt,
Consultant Psychiatrist,
St. John's Hospital,
Stone,
Aylesbury,
Bucks HP17 8PP

Dr S. Weyerer,
Nervenklinik der Universitat München,
Psychiatrische Klinik und Poliklinik,
Nussbaumstrasse 7,
8000 München 2,
West Germany

Dr D. Wilkin,
Senior Research Fellow,
The Department of General Practice,
DHSS Research Unit, University of
    Manchester,
Rusholme Health Centre,
Walmer Street,
Manchester M14 5NP

Dr Greg Wilkinson,
General Practice Research Unit,
Institute of Psychiatry,
De Crespigny Park,
Denmark Hill,
London SE5 8AF

Dr Paul Williams,
Deputy Director,
General Practice Research Unit,
Institute of Psychiatry,
De Crespigny Park,
Denmark Hill,
London SE5 8AF

Mrs P. M. Williamson,
Assistant Secretary,
Department of Health and Social Security,
Mental Health Division,
Room C422, Alexander Fleming House,
Elephant and Castle,
London SE1 6BY

Dr J. M. G. Wilson,
Musselburgh,
Midlothian EH21 7RP

Prof. J. K. Wing,
Director, MRC Social Psychiatry Unit,
Institute of Psychiatry,
De Crespigny Park,
Denmark Hill,
London SE5 8AF

Prof. K. Zaimov,
Head, Department of Neurology,
    Psychiatry and Neurosurgery,
Medical Academy,
Boul. Georgi Sofijski No. 1,
1431 Sofia,
Bulgaria

OBSERVERS

Dr A. Boardman,
Research Fellow,
Lewisham Multiprofessional Psychiatric
 Research Unit,
19 Handen Road,
London SE12 8NP

Dr N. Bouras,
The Department of Psychiatry,
Guy's Hospital Medical School,
London Bridge,
London SE1 9RT

Prof. S. Davidson,
Department of Psychiatry,
Warneford Hospital,
Oxford

Dr Ruth Fleminger,
Consultant Psychiatrist,
Ealing Hospital,
St. Bernard's Wing,
Uxbridge Road,
Southall,
Middlesex UB1 3EU

Dr Hema Ghadiali,
St Crispin Hospital,
Duston,
Northampton NN5 6UN

Dr M. T. Gledhill,
528 Finchley Road,
London NW11 8DD

Dr W. Kinston,
Health Services Organisation Research
 Unit,
Brunel Institute of Organisation and Social
 Studies,
Brunel University,
Uxbridge, Middlesex

Dr V. Pillai,
Consultant in Child Psychiatry,
Department of Child and Family
 Psychiatry,
2 Brookside,
Cambridge,
CB2 1JE

Dr D. Stephens,
50 Half Moon Lane,
London SE24 9HU

Name index

Weinstein, M. C. 64
Weinstein, N. 19
Weissman, M. 8–9, 11, 17–18, 133
Weyerer, S. 204–05
Wheeler, S. G. 263
Widlocher, D. 19
Widmer, R. 12–13
Wiens, A. W. 125
Wig, N. N. 222
Wilkin, D. 167
Wilkinson, G. 126, 263–75
Williams, C. D. 11, 14
Williams, P. 17, 57–65, 72–5, 79–82, 105,
    141–54, 225, 263–75

Williams, T. A. 7–8
Wilson, J. M. G. 58–9, 62, 68, 78–9
Wing, J. K. 7, 11, 14, 17, 58, 60, 132, 153
Wing, L. 7
Winokur, G. 16
Wright, J. H. 9

Yager, H. 9
Young, J. 18

Zaimov, K. 219–20
Zimmermann-Tansella, Ch. 215–16
Zung, W. W. K. 9

Subject index